Pneumatic Hermeneutics
The Role of the Holy Spirit in the Theological
Interpretation of Scripture

PNEUMATIC HERMENEUTICS

THE ROLE OF THE HOLY SPIRIT IN THE THEOLOGICAL INTERPRETATION OF SCRIPTURE

LEULSEGED PHILEMON

CPT Press
Cleveland, Tennessee

Pneumatic Hermeneutics
The Role of the Holy Spirit in the Theological Interpretation of Scripture

Published by CPT Press
900 Walker ST NE
Cleveland, TN 37311
USA

email: cptpress@pentecostaltheology.org
website: www.cptpress.com

ISBN-13: 978-1-935931-82-9

To Fikir, my wife
and
To Naod, Aaron, and Abel, my sons

Contents

FOREWORD

I remember early on in my introductory New Testament courses how, term after term, almost like clockwork, a student would raise the question, 'Okay, but what about the Holy Spirit?' I had presented a range of questions – and taught my students to pursue them all: What is the genre of this book? What is the literary form of this passage? What about this text's sociocultural background? Does this text draw on Israel's Scriptures? And so on. All of this is well and good, my students seemed to say, but what about the role of the Holy Spirit in the work of interpreting Scripture?

It is true: like other New Testament scholars, I had been trained to listen carefully to the text, to hear its voices. We were taught to recover the voice of the historical Jesus or, perhaps, the real Moses. We learned how to hear the voices of the early communities who collected, shaped, and passed on to others their earliest traditions. We were schooled in listening to the voice of the text's editors (or redactors) as they sculpted those traditions into the texts we read today. We were instructed in hearing the voices of those communities that gave these texts their final form. But our tools and methods extended only so far, never really accounting for the task of attuning our ears, our hearts, our lives to hear well the voice of the Holy Spirit in our interpretive work. We attended to all sorts of human voices but not so much to God's voice.

My students, then, were right to raise their question. They recognized, however intuitively, a gulf between what our major Christian traditions profess about the Old and New Testament Scriptures and the interpretive practices that have guided readings of those biblical texts in the modern era. If we acknowledge that God stands behind the Bible, that God reveals himself through the Scriptures, that the Scriptures are in some significant sense God's word, that the Holy Spirit was involved in the formation of these writings and in the church's recognition of them as the canon of Scripture, should we not expect that the Holy Spirit would be integrally involved in Christian interpretation of Scripture, now and always? And, if we respond affirmatively to these questions, how then do we account for the Holy Spirit's contribution?

As Leulseged Philemon documents, and documents well, in this important book, the disconnect between profession and practice my first-year students instinctively identified is widespread. It has even characterized much of the last two or three decades of work among theological interpreters of Scripture, in spite of the self-consciously ecclesial location and commitments typical of this movement. With surprisingly few exceptions, the plain question of the Spirit's guidance in scriptural interpretation has hardly been recognized, much less explored theologically.

In some ways, this desideratum would be puzzling to a Christian theologian and reader of Scripture like Leulseged Philemon. On the one hand, this is because he hails from Ethiopia, where the influence of modern biblical scholarship generally has not constrained overmuch what interpretive practices may or may not occupy the church. On the other hand, this is because he belongs to the global Pentecostal movement, which has been slow to exchange its distinguishing emphasis on the Holy Spirit's work for the routines and protocols of modernist biblical scholarship – slow, that is, to exchange human-centered interpretive postures and procedures for pneumatic hermeneutics.

Accordingly, Philemon first locates himself within the movement concerned with theological interpretation of Scripture in order to document its theological inadequacies concerning the hermeneutical role of the Holy Spirit. He then accounts for the centrality of the Holy Spirit in our primary theological traditions, thus setting up what is now the transparent necessity of a robust understanding of the hermeneutical role of the Holy Spirit. For assistance in addressing this need, he turns to the Pentecostal tradition, since theologians working within this tradition are distinguished by their setting aside any pretense of coming to Scripture neutrally (as the accredited standards of biblical studies in the modern era expects of its practitioners), then by their seeking how best to identify how they are influenced and how they ought to be influenced by their theological and ecclesial commitments to the priority of the Holy Spirit's work in their reading of Scripture. Finally, Philemon points the way forward by exploring the roles of the Holy Spirit in the Acts of the Apostles, focusing in the end on the Holy Spirit's hermeneutical role in three pivotal texts: Peter's Pentecost address, Philip's encounter with the Ethiopian eunuch, and the Jerusalem Council. In this way, he moves us from recognizing the chasm separating profession and practice concerning the relationship between Christian Scripture and Holy Spirit engagement and toward practices that more fully embody our professions.

Still more work needs to be done in providing a theological account of pneumatic hermeneutics; but, with this theological, historical, and biblical project, Leulseged Philemon has set us on the right path.

Joel B. Green
Fuller Theological Seminary

ACKNOWLEDGMENTS

I would first like to thank God for all his provisions and the strength he gave me throughout this process. This book may have never come to completion without his presence and continued guidance.

It is also a pleasure to express my indebtedness to several individuals and organizations for their support, in many ways, as I work through this project. I am so grateful to Dr Joel B. Green, my teacher and mentor who relentlessly, but kindly, guided me through the program and the writing of this monograph. I consider him as one of the significant blessings in my journey of doctoral studies. I would also want to thank Dr. Kenneth J. Archer who has been my second mentor for this writing.

This work would not have been possible without the financial support of Langham Partnership, Scholar Leaders International, Central Peninsula Church, and Menlo Park Presbyterian Church. I am thankful for the encouragement, support, and prayer of my colleagues at the Ethiopian Graduate School of Theology and my Christian communities in Addis Ababa, Ethiopia and Los Angeles, California.

Finally, special thanks go to my best friend and wife Fikir who has been with me all the way through with her consistent love, emotional support and encouragement. My sons Naod, Aaron, and Abel have been the source of my joy and vigor that motivated me to work hard towards the fruition of this book.

ABBREVIATIONS

Anvil	*Anvil: Journal of Theology and Mission*
ATF	*Australian Theological Forum*
ATR	*Anglican Theological Review*
BA	*Biblical Archaeologist*
BSac	*Bibliotheca Sacra*
CBQ	*Catholic Biblical Quarterly*
CPT	Center for Pentecostal Theology
CurrBiblicRes	*Currents in Biblical Research*
ERT	*Evangelical Review of Theology*
ExAud	*ExAuditu*
GOTR	*Greek Orthodox Theological Review*
IJST	*International Journal of Systematic Theology*
IVP	InterVarsity Press
JEPTA	*Journal of the European Pentecostal Theological Association*
JETS	*Journal of the Evangelical Theological Society*
JPT	*Journal of Pentecostal Theology*
JPTSup	Journal of Pentecostal Theology Supplement
JR	*Journal of Religion*
JTI	*Journal of Theological Interpretation*
JTISup	*Journal of Theological Interpretation Supplements*
JTVI	*Journal of the Transactions of the Victoria Institute*
MH	*Methodist History*
NICNT	New International Commentary on the New Testament
Paraclete	*Paraclete: A Journal Concerning the Person and Work of the Holy Spirit*
Pneuma	*Pneuma: The Journal of the Society for Pentecostal Studies*
SJT	*Scottish Journal of Theology*
SVSP	St. Vladimir's Seminary Press
SVTQ	*St. Vladimir's Theological Quarterly*
Theol	*Theology*
ThTo	*Theology Today*

TS	*Theological Studies*
WesTJ	*Wesleyan Theological Journal*
WJKP	Westminister John Knox Press
WW	*Word and World*
WTJ	*Westminister Theological Journal*

1

INTRODUCTION

The Holy Spirit, Theology, and Biblical Interpretation

The contemporary sensibility to read biblical texts theologically entails several thought-provoking concerns in biblical interpretation and theological method. One of these concerns is *pneumatic hermeneutics* – that is, the role of the Holy Spirit in the practice of theological interpretation of Scripture. Of course, Christian theology has always given a significant position to the Holy Spirit in relation to Christian Scripture. As part of his role in revelation, redemption, and Christian life, the Holy Spirit is widely regarded as having been involved in the generation, preservation, transmission, and interpretation of Scripture. However, despite the central position attributed to the Holy Spirit vis-à-vis Christian Scripture, more needs to be done, especially concerning the role of the Spirit in reading Scripture theologically. What the Holy Spirit does in theological interpretation and how this role is explained in a constructive way are significant questions that demand thorough and careful attention.

Despite the prevalent view among biblical scholars and many Christian theologians that emphasizes the anthropological character of Scripture, there is a discernible awareness within contemporary Christian theology that Scripture is given to disclose the Triune God and his purposes for his creatures. John Webster, for instance, describes Scripture as 'an element in the drama of God's redeeming and

communicative self-giving'.[1] This involves the role that Scripture
plays in God's activity in presenting him as 'Lord and Savior'.[2] More
precisely, in his most recent work, Webster portrays Scripture as 'the
sign and instrument of God's loving address of intelligent creatures'.[3]
This is similar to the way Kevin J. Vanhoozer construes Scripture as
'part of God's broader plan to give us access to himself through Jesus
Christ'.[4] Voices like these in the contemporary conversation about
theological interpretation represent the traditional view that affirms
the divine origin of Scripture. Based on this assessment, there is a
relatively common perception in present-day Christian theology that
Scripture has a divine origin – that is, it is inspired by God.

Although different groups understand biblical inspiration in diverse ways, belief in inspiration has long been considered an important affirmation of the Church. Generally taken for granted since
the early Church, until it became controversial during the Reformation as a corollary to the principle of *sola Scriptura*, the notion of
divine inspiration has not demanded vigorous articulation and clarification. New Testament writers, for example, simply claimed that the
Scriptures are inspired by the Spirit of God, without any attempt to
validate their view.[5] Even for the early Church fathers divine inspiration was not a primary point of argument per se in the same sense
as, for example, the doctrine of the Trinity or the twofold nature of
Christ.[6] It was simply taken for granted as a self-evident assertion that
Scripture was divinely inspired.[7] We find little evidence of any effort

---

[1] John Webster, *Holy Scripture: A Dogmatic Sketch* (Cambridge: Cambridge University Press, 2003), p. 42.

[2] Webster, *Holy Scripture*, p. 42.

[3] John Webster, *The Domain of the Word: Scripture and Theological Reason* (London:
T&T Clark, 2012), p. vii.

[4] Kevin Vanhoozer, *The Drama of Doctrine: A Canonical Linguistic Approach to
Christian Theology* (Louisville: Westminster John Knox, 2005), p. 45.

[5] See, e.g. 2 Pet. 1.20-21; 2 Tim. 3.16-17.

[6] See, e.g. Augustine, *On Christian Teaching* 4.6.9.

[7] It seems probable that this tradition has its root in the first century Jewish
high view of Scripture, which assumed that the words of Scripture were exclama-
tions of the Holy Spirit intercepting the speaker – or, in other words, the work of
inspiration. See, e.g. Kaufmann Kohler, 'Inspiration', in Cyrus Adler and Isidore
Singer (eds.), *The Jewish Encyclopedia* (New York: Funk & Wagnalls, 1904), pp. 607-
609; Bruce Vawter, *Biblical Inspiration* (Philadelphia: Westminster, 1972), pp. 8-11;
Paul J. Achtemeier, *The Inspiration of Scripture: Problems and Proposals* (Philadelphia:

in the early centuries to explain what divine inspiration of the Scripture meant.[8]

Following the sixteenth century Reformation, however, the nature of the sacred text became a central point of argument. The Reformation theologians' insistence on divine inspiration as a basis of the authority, sufficiency, and clarity of Scripture triggered robust debates between the Reformers and the Catholic Church and even among the Reformers themselves. For instance, John Calvin, in his defense of the authority of Scripture against Catholic supremacy on the one hand and the radical wing of the Reformation on the other, was instrumental in laying the foundation for the doctrine of inspiration.[9] Despite the fact that Calvin's view is more in line with a dictation theory, his high view of Scripture as having originated with God shaped subsequent development of the doctrine of inspiration.[10] After the Reformation, the doctrine of inspiration became a significant locus in Christian theology. Particularly because of rising disputes regarding the authority of the Bible, the doctrine of inspiration received 'renewed interest' after the nineteenth century as well as in recent times in evangelical circles.[11]

In a broad sense, the doctrine of inspiration is for many the foundation for maintaining the authority of the Bible in Christian theology.[12] Many would agree with Paul Achtemeier's statement 'that some

---

Westminster, 1980), p. 107; N.T. Wright, *Scripture and the Authority of God: How to Read the Bible Today* (New York: HarperCollins, 2011), pp. 35-39.

[8] Gerald Bray, *Biblical Interpretation: Past and Present* (Downers Grove, IL: InterVarsity, 1996), pp. 195-97. Bray points out that some Church fathers defended a 'dictation theory' of inspiration with the assumption that the authors of the Bible functioned as nothing more than passive instruments, while others argued that human authors played more significant roles. See also Alister E. McGrath, *Christian Theology: An Introduction* (Oxford: Blackwell Press, 4th edn, 2007), pp. 134-36.

[9] Although Calvin's contribution is quite significant concerning divine inspiration and it has been well-discussed in Calvin scholarship, it is important to mention that Calvin never developed an independent discussion of his inspiration theory. See H. Jackson Forstman, *Word and Spirit: Calvin's Doctrine of Biblical Authority* (Stanford: Stanford University Press, 1962), p. 49.

[10] John Calvin, *The Institutes of the Christian Religion* 1.8; McGrath, *Christian Theology*, p. 134.

[11] Achtemeier, *Inspiration*, p. 76.

[12] For recent discussions of inspiration of Scripture, see, e.g. Achtemeier, *Inspiration*; William J. Abraham, *The Divine Inspiration of Holy Scripture* (Oxford: Oxford University Press, 1981); I. Howard Marshall, *Biblical Inspiration* (Vancouver: Regent College, 1982).

form of doctrine concerning the inspiration of the Scripture is a key issue for the Christian faith'.[13] The claim that the Bible has a divine origin functions as a decisive basis for the reliability and authority of the Bible. Christian theologians also hold that divine inspiration is a main factor that determines the distinctive quality of the Scripture. The special status that the Bible is given as *norma normans sed non normata* ('the norm of norms that is not normed') in the worship, life, and theology of the Christian community is established by the belief that it is inspired by God. In other words, Scripture is viewed as 'the word of God' by virtue of its nature as 'God-breathed' or as a divinely inspired product.

In discussions of divine inspiration, the role of the Holy Spirit in the formation of biblical texts has received important attention. In fact, the very idea of inspiration implies that the Spirit of God led and influenced the writings of human authors of the Bible.[14] Christians from various ecumenical circles believe that Scripture is God-breathed and the Holy Spirit is the principal agent of its production, but the locus of biblical inspiration is disputed among contemporary theologians.

For example, Karl Barth's doctrine of inspiration takes its own distinctive path in dealing with the Spirit's role in biblical inspiration. His understanding of the Bible as witness to revelation rather than revelation itself shapes his doctrine of inspiration.[15] Although he does not seem to be denying absolutely the objectivity of initial inspiration, Barth stresses the idea that the actual inspiration of the Holy Spirit occurs when the texts are being read faithfully. 'We have thought of the divine inspiration of the Bible as an actual decision which takes place in the mystery of God as His work and miracle, and which has to be recollected and expected in faith and obedience and in faithful exegesis.'[16]

---

[13] Achtemeier, *Inspiration*, p. 13.

[14] 2 Timothy 3.16-17, which speaks of Scripture as 'God-breathed' *(theopneustos)*, has had huge significance as a major source of the doctrine of inspiration. Marshall lays out a helpful summary of the Bible's own testimony in *Biblical Inspiration*, pp. 19-30.

[15] Karl Barth, *Church Dogmatics*, I/2, §19.2, (ed. G.W. Bromiley and T.F. Torrance; trans. G.W. Bromiley; Edinburgh: T&T Clark, 1958), p. 512.

[16] Barth, *CD* I/2, §19.2, p. 534.

In other words, Barth's theory gives emphasis to the subjectivity of inspiration as the act of the Holy Spirit in the reader rather than vis-à-vis the authors or the text itself. As G. W. Bromiley comments on Barth's doctrine of inspiration: 'It is all very well to say that we are dependent on God Himself speaking His Word, but the fact remains that if inspiration is not complete until it takes place in the individual, then God does not speak unless He speaks to me, and this means in practice that the only real or important act of "inspiration" takes place subjectively in the recipient'.[17] Nevertheless, Barth refers to inspiration to describe the relation between the Holy Spirit and the Bible.[18]

In his discussion of biblical inspiration, Achtemeier emphasizes the importance of canon formation. He claims that the existence of the Christian canon is the key to understanding the inspiration of Scripture. This is because the canon delineates the boundaries within which divine inspiration functions. 'God inspired the canonical books', Achtemeier writes, 'with no exception, and no noncanonical books are inspired, with no exception'; after all, it is the canon 'that tells us which Scriptures are inspired and which are not'.[19] Canon formation is the means by which the Church decided, through time, which books are inspired and which books are not, based on their responses to changing situations.[20] Achtemeier refers to the canon-making process to explain biblical inspiration, preferring it to a 'prophetic model' of biblical inspiration. For him, along with the authors or the final compilers of the texts, the Christian community that has preserved the tradition and formed the canon shares the inspiration that produced Scripture.[21]

William J. Abraham is another contemporary theologian to be mentioned in relation to biblical inspiration. Abraham argues for understanding inspiration in terms of everyday language before applying that language to Scripture.[22] He insists that the concept of inspiration ought to be perceived on the basis of common usage of the

---

[17] G.W. Bromiley, 'Karl Barth's Doctrine of Inspiration', *JTVI* 87 (1955), pp. 66-80.

[18] Barth, *CD* I/2, §19.2, p. 530.

[19] Achtemeier, *Inspiration*, p. 119.

[20] Achtemeier, *Inspiration*, p. 122.

[21] Achtemeier, *Inspiration*, p. 133.

[22] Abraham, *Divine Inspiration*, p. 44.

word in contemporary English. As I. Howard Marshall points out, Abraham seems to avoid dealing with the Greek term for inspiration and its usage in the context of Scripture.[23] In doing so, Abraham intends to avoid 'two fatal mistakes' committed by evangelical theologians, particularly their ultimate dependence on the doctrine of God in which 'they began, continued, and ended with God' and their exclusive focus on the mode of divine speaking to explain inspiration.[24] Attempting to clarify his theory of inspiration, Abraham uses the illustration of a good teacher who inspires his or her students without necessarily dictating the contents of the subject matter.[25] In this 'paradigm case of inspiration', what the students produce remains their distinct works, though they would have not generated them without the ingenious guidance of the teacher.[26] Without ignoring its limitations, Abraham believes that the analogy is comparable to the way that the Spirit of God inspired the writers of the Bible through his revelatory and saving acts.

Building on Abraham's theory of inspiration, Kern Robert Trembath claims that biblical inspiration does not primarily point to the Bible. Rather, it points to 'the Christian believers who have experienced salvation from God through the Bible'.[27] His theory of inspiration consists of a tripartite structure that involves an initiating agent, a medium, and a receiving agent. Based on this premise, he then constructs his definition of biblical inspiration as 'a mediated enhancement of human existence by God, through the Bible'.[28] He argues that his theory is consistent with a Thomistic doctrine of God, which maintains that the acts of God are mediated through the world rather than immediately happening in the world. Thus, according to him, only a human being can be a receiving agent of inspiration and the Bible functions merely as the medium of the process.

---

[23] Marshall, *Biblical Inspiration*, p. 40.

[24] Abraham, *Divine Inspiration*, p. 62.

[25] Abraham, *Divine Inspiration*, pp. 3-4. Abraham's arguments suggest his intense reaction against the dictation theory as well as against 'traditional conservative concepts of infallibility and inerrancy' (Marshall, *Biblical Inspiration*, p. 39).

[26] Abraham, *Divine Inspiration*, pp. 63-66.

[27] Kern Robert Trembath, *Evangelical Theories of Biblical Inspiration* (Oxford: Oxford University Press, 1987), p. 114.

[28] Trembath, *Evangelical Theories*, p. 115.

In sharp contrast to views that inspiration should be understood in light of its everyday meaning and connotations, John Goldingay insists that discussions regarding inspiration must proceed from material within Scripture itself.[29] Agreeing with Walter C. Kaiser Jr., who remarked on the strangeness of conversation about inspiration without an in-depth examination of key biblical texts, Goldingay expresses his disappointment with any approach, such as Trembath's, that determines the nature of inspiration while excluding engagement with biblical passages that relate to the question, such as 2 Tim. 3.16.[30] Goldingay's criticism of Abraham's view is aimed at the latter's emphasis on attempting to explain inspiration merely in terms of a natural process. Goldingay actually accuses both conservative and liberal approaches of denying and avoiding the supernatural involvement in the process and calls for understanding inspiration as an extraordinary activity of the Spirit of God.[31] Although he seems to consider Old Testament prophetic books as the basis for understanding inspiration, he argues that there are different forms of inspiration and the specific process varies from text to text. However, all Scripture shares the fundamental qualities of being objectively inspired. Scripture is inspiring not because it is a medium of inspiration, as Trembath would want to argue, but because it is itself inspired.[32]

For their part, both J.I. Packer and Marshall describe inspiration as a 'concursive action' of the Spirit.[33] Concursive action is explained in terms of the process of God's creation and providence in the universe. According to this theory, the creation event is understood from two perspectives – scientifically, as a cause and effect; and theologically, as an act of God. Both levels of explanation are true and complement each other as the natural and the supernatural. Similarly, the composition of biblical texts involves natural literary processes such as the gathering of oral and written information, while concurrently being inspired by the Holy Spirit. This concursive, inspiring activity

---

[29] John Goldingay, *Models for Scripture* (Grand Rapids: Eerdmans, 1994), p. 223.

[30] Goldingay, *Models for Scripture*, p. 13; cf. Trembath, *Evangelical Theories*, p. 6; Walter C. Kaiser Jr., 'A Neglected Text in Bibliology Discussions: 1 Corinthians 2.6-16', *WTJ* 43.2 (1981), p. 301.

[31] Goldingay, *Models for Scripture*, p. 223.

[32] Goldingay, *Models for Scripture*, pp. 217, 221-22.

[33] J.I. Packer, *'Fundamentalism' and the Word of God* (London: Inter-Varsity Press, 1958), pp. 80-82; Marshall, *Biblical Inspiration*, pp. 40-47.

of the Spirit is exercised 'in, through, and by means of the writers' own activity, in such a way that their thinking and writing was *both* free and spontaneous *and* divinely elicited and controlled, and what they wrote was not only their own work but also God's work'.[34]

In his contribution to the issue under discussion, Clark H. Pinnock asserts that inspiration is not a single activity. Rather, it is the broader superintendence of the Holy Spirit in the complex process of making the Scripture.[35] It is the Spirit's activity in the preparation and production of the Scriptures. He says, 'We are not privileged to observe how in hidden and mysterious ways the Spirit worked alongside the human agents in the creative literary work, but we can plainly see the result of what was done'.[36] Consequently, Scripture possesses a spiritual power that makes it effective for teaching, reproof, correction and training in righteousness (cf. 2 Tim. 3.16).[37]

Despite the diversity of views on biblical inspiration, the discussions mentioned above demonstrate that the role of the Spirit in biblical inspiration is widely acknowledged in Christian theology. Although these arguments offer wide-ranging viewpoints, they all recognize in some sense the central role the Spirit plays in biblical inspiration. This acknowledgement of the work of the Spirit in inspiration provides a relatively secure foundation to understand the nature of Scripture and its theological interpretation. It is the significance of the Spirit's work that requires proper attention and more assessment especially in relation to the concomitant role of the Spirit in theological interpretation.

Proponents of theological interpretation generally agree on the work of the Spirit in theological reading of Scripture. Many would affirm Pinnock's statement that it is naïve to think about understanding the Scripture without due attention to the Spirit.[38] Nevertheless, those who have written on theological interpretation since Pinnock

---

[34] Packer, *Fundamentalism*, p. 80.

[35] Clark H. Pinnock, *The Scripture Principle: Reclaiming the Full Authority of the* Bible (Grand Rapids: Baker Academic, 2006), p. 89. This is consistent with Webster, *The Domain*, p. 50: 'Inspiration is the narrower term, indicating the Spirit's superintendence and moving of the processes of Scripture's production: by the Spirit, these authors write these words'.

[36] Pinnock, *Scripture*, p. 90.

[37] Pinnock, *Scripture*, p. 89.

[38] Clark H. Pinnock, 'The Role of the Spirit in Interpretation', *JETS* 36.4 (1993), pp. 491-97.

have done little to address the substantial lacuna in constructive theological reflection on that dependency on the Spirit. This calls for a thorough study and critical examination of the subject. In brief, this monograph attempts to explore the significance and role of the Spirit in theological interpretation with the aim of presenting the issue within a constructive theological framework. Before doing so, though, it is necessary to come to a general consensus about how to define theological interpretation of Scripture.

Theological Interpretation: An Introduction

Reading biblical texts with a theological interest was a long-established practice among Jewish and Christian readers before it declined as a result of the modern era's fascination with critical biblical scholarship. However, the contemporary effort to retrieve this 'interested' reading from the hegemony of modernity's critical undertakings signals a fresh and promising trajectory in the field of biblical interpretation and theological method. Theological interpretation has become a growing concern among biblical scholars and theologians in the past two decades or more. The increasing number of publications on the topic – including a major dictionary, book series, journals, and commentary series – demonstrates the increasing interest in the conversation.[39]

---

[39] See, e.g. Kevin J. Vanhoozer (ed.), *Dictionary for Theological Interpretation of the Bible* (Grand Rapids: Baker Academic, 2005); Daniel J. Treier, *Introducing Theological Interpretation of Scripture: Recovering a Christian Practice* (Grand Rapids: Baker Academic, 2008); Stephen E. Fowl (ed.), *The Theological Interpretation of Scripture: Classic and Contemporary Readings* (Blackwell Readings in Modern Theology; Oxford: Blackwell, 1997); *idem, Theological Interpretation of Scripture* (Cascade Companions; Eugene, OR: Cascade, 2009); Joel B. Green, *Practicing Theological Interpretation: Engaging Biblical Texts for Faith and Formation* (Theological Explorations for the Church Catholic; Grand Rapids: Baker Academic, 2011); Craig G. Bartholomew and Heath A. Thomas (eds.), *A Manifesto for Theological Interpretation* (Grand Rapids: Baker, 2016). See also the *Journal of Theological Interpretation* (ed. Joel B. Green; Winona Lake, IN: Eisenbrauns), and commentary series such as the Brazos Theological Commentary on the Bible (ed. R.R. Reno; Grand Rapids: Brazos); Belief: A Theological Commentary on the Bible (ed. William C. Placher and Amy Plantinga Pauw; Louisville: WJKP); the Two Horizons New Testament Commentary (ed. Joel B. Green and Max Turner; Grand Rapids: Eerdmans); and the Two Horizons Old Testament Commentary (ed. J. Gordon McConville and Craig Bartholomew; Grand Rapids: Eerdmans). See also the book series: Journal of Theological Interpretation Supplement Series (Winona Lake, IN: Eisenbrauns) and Studies in Theological Interpretation (Grand Rapids: Baker Academic).

Although the core objective of Proponents of theological interpretation concur with the idea that the primary motivation behind theological interpretation is reading biblical texts as Scripture, that is, as the word of God or God's means of communication in the present to guide, edify, correct, and transform reader(s).[40] The underlying assumption in this approach is that the end goal of reading the Bible has everything to do with cultivating a profound relationship with God. Reading and interpreting Scripture is by any means indistinguishable from having an encounter with God. Thus, the notion of intimacy and communion with God and the readers' individual and/or communal transformation this approach is bringing about 'theologically interested interpretation' of Scripture, borrowing Robert Morgan's expression,[41] there are diverse agendas and proposals forwarded by advocates of theological interpretation. On the one hand, theological interpretation strives to recover the principal ancient practice of biblical interpretation prior to the dawning of the Enlightenment and its engagement in critical scholarship in an attempt to overcome the so-called control of dogma in biblical interpretation. Therefore, in many ways, theological interpretation is a reaction against modernism and the prestige given to historical criticism in biblical studies for more than two centuries. This explains the contemporary sentiment towards reclaiming precritical practices of biblical reading.[42]

On the other hand, theological interpretation deals with numerous contemporary theological, hermeneutical, and literary challenges largely motivated by postmodernism's reaction to the beliefs and assumptions of modernism and its concerns over the readings of

---

[40] When the phrase 'word of God' occurs in this work, small 'w' – 'word of God' – refers to the inscripturated word (the Bible or Scripture) and capital 'W' – 'Word of God' – to the Living Word (the incarnate Jesus), unless it is in a quotation, a title, or a beginning of a sentence.

[41] Robert Morgan, 'Can the Critical Study of Scripture Provide a Doctrinal Norm'? *JR* 76 (1996), pp. 206-32.

[42] Works like David C. Steinmetz's 'The Superiority of Pre-Critical Exegesis', *ThTo* 37.1 (1980), pp. 27-38, and Charles M. Wood's *The Formation of Christian Understanding: An Essay in Theological Hermeneutics* (Philadelphia: Westminster, 1981) illustrate contemporary attempts at recovering the premodern reading of Scripture in discussions of theological interpretation. See also Treier's first chapter, 'Recovering the Past: Imitating Pre-critical Interpretation', in *Introducing Theological Interpretation of Scripture*, pp. 39-55; and Fowl's introduction to *The Theological Interpretation*, pp. xvii-xviii.

biblical texts and systems of theological explanation. Consequently, the crucial impulse of theological interpretation centers on dealing with multiple and complex philosophical and literary challenges in biblical readings and theological understandings. Therefore, in order to deal with the topic carefully, it is necessary to have a common ground of understanding of what theological interpretation is and explain its vital sensibilities and objectives.

Generally, there is a consensus among some of the primary conversation partners that theological interpretation is not a well-crafted methodology of biblical interpretation to be handled with a particular form of procedure and system. It is not just one more method or a discreet technique along with, for example, literary criticism or rhetorical analysis of the Bible. The attempt to define theological interpretation of Scripture, therefore, is a complicated undertaking. Both its nature and the fact that it is an emerging movement make it categorically difficult to provide a full-fledged definition succinctly. Although most of the literature on the topic demonstrates outstanding efforts to define and explain what it means to interpret the biblical texts theologically, defining theological interpretation has always been a challenging task. Vanhoozer, a major contributor to the field, describes the problematic well when he recognizes that it is easier to talk about what theological interpretation is not than defining what it is.[43]

Regardless of the fact that it is challenging to have a consensual, simplified a definition, however, it is essential for this study to clarify issues concerning what it means to interpret biblical texts theologically so as to develop sound arguments pertaining to the Sprit's role in theological interpretation. One of the main contributions of the burgeoning publications on the topic is the vigorous attempt to provide a wide-ranging definition and explanation of theological interpretation by drawing attention to its specific interests and sensibilities. Therefore, I begin my discussion with presenting attempts provided by some of the main voices on the topic. After evaluating the proposed definitions, I will provide my own understanding of theological interpretation of Scripture.

---

[43] Kevin J. Vanhoozer, 'What Is Theological Interpretation of the Bible?' in Kevin J. Vanhoozer (ed.), *Dictionary for Theological Interpretation of the Bible* (Grand Rapids: Baker Academic, 2005), p. 19.

Key Voices on Theological Interpretation

Biblical Interpretation Driven by Theology and Ecclesiology: Stephen E. Fowl

The critical questions raised in the conversations of theological interpretation are inextricably linked with the primary purpose of biblical reading: reading the texts as Scripture. Although it is acknowledged that biblical texts can be read towards a variety of aims and objectives, theological interpreters would like to view the Bible primarily as Scripture that shapes the thoughts as well as the actions of the ones who read it. As one of the foremost dialogue partners in theological interpretation, Stephen E. Fowl argues for taking the Bible as Scripture, since it provides a 'normative standard' for faith, worship, and Christian practice among the believing communities.[44] Fowl insists that biblical interpretation needs 'to involve a complex interaction in which Christian convictions, practices, and concerns are brought and are shaped by it'.[45]

In his account of theological interpretation, Fowl emphasizes two core elements: the bearing of theological concerns in the interpretive practice and the Church as a significant interpretive community. In other words, he claims theology and ecclesiology as the driving forces of scriptural interpretation.[46] Simply, he defines theological interpretation of Scripture as the 'practice whereby theological concerns and interests inform and are informed by a reading of Scripture', or 'a reading aimed at shaping and being shaped by a community's faith and practice'.[47]

According to Fowl, biblical interpretation should not be treated as a discrete practice from theology. He actually argues that theology is a complex form of scriptural exegesis. Taking precritical interpretation practices seriously, Fowl asserts that bringing theological concerns to bear on Scripture ought to be relatively natural for theologians. In fact, this has to be a normative scriptural interpretive exercise

---

[44] Stephen E. Fowl, *Engaging Scripture: A Model for Theological Interpretation* (Challenges in Contemporary Theology; Oxford: Blackwell, 1998), p. 2.

[45] Fowl, *Engaging Scripture*, p. 8.

[46] Stephen E. Fowl, 'The Importance of a Multivoiced Literal Sense of Scripture: The Example of Thomas Aquinas', in A.K.M. Adam, Stephen E. Fowl, Kevin J. Vanhoozer, and Francis Watson (eds.), *Reading Scripture with the Church: Toward a Hermeneutic for Theological Interpretation* (Grand Rapids: Baker, 2006), p. 37.

[47] Fowl, *The Theological Interpretation of Scripture*, pp. xiii, xix.

for all Christians in all ages. From this vantage point, one of the huge
mistakes of the modern biblical study is the priority given to historical concerns over theological ones, whereas the premodern biblical
interpretation put theological concerns forward in understanding
biblical texts.[48] With this line of reasoning, Fowl contends that the
merits of modern biblical interpretation, such as theories of textual
meaning and philosophical hermeneutics, are not as crucial as theology is in reading biblical texts theologically. Evidently, this is the key
motivation behind Fowl's emphasis on the significance of premodern
biblical interpretation as a conversation partner in reading Scripture
theologically in the present.[49]

Theology does not have to be perceived as a process by which a
theologian attempts to distill the timeless truth or 'determinate meaning' from Scripture after treating the text as a human historical product like any other ancient text. Fowl identifies this approach with the
recent interpretive work of the 'biblical theology movement'.[50] This
approach treats biblical texts as relatively stable products and their
interpretation as a process to unearth and reconstruct meaning
from.[51] Rather, Fowl thinks, the set of theological interests and concerns have to come to the forefront to regulate the interpretive process. He says, 'One of the points I have tried to argue persistently
over the past several years is that the key to interpreting theologically
lies in keeping theological concerns primary to all others'.[52] He further states:

> If one's interpretive practice is governed by a general hermeneu-
> tical theory (of any type), then it is very hard to avoid the situation
> where theological interpretation of Scripture becomes the activity
> of applying theological concerns to interpretation done on other
> grounds. It seems all too easy to allow a general theory of textual
> meaning to provide the *telos* of theological interpretation. The key
> to interpreting theologically lies in keeping theological concerns

---

[48] Fowl, *Theological Interpretation*, p. 16.
[49] Fowl, *The Theological Interpretation of Scripture*, pp. xvii-xviii.
[50] Fowl, *Theological Interpretation*, p. 5.
[51] Fowl, *Engaging Scripture*, pp. 33-34.
[52] Fowl, 'Importance', p. 126; see also, *idem, Theological Interpretation*, p. xii.

and ends primary to all others. In this way, theology becomes a form of scriptural interpretation, not simply its result.[53]

Fowl's approach is also driven by his attention to the primary purposes for which Christians engage Scripture. Since the Church is a significant interpretive community, Christians engage Scripture theologically for it is an essential element to have a deeper communion with God and with one another. This is the end or *telos* of the Christian life and theological interpretation enables Christians, either individually or communally, to cultivate the intimacy with God by interpreting and personalizing the Scripture.[54] In other words, Scripture and its interpretation should not be viewed as the *telos* of the Christian life; rather, God uses the Scripture as a crucial means to draw the Church closer to him in a profound relationship.[55] Thus, theological interpretation has more to do with embodying the biblical texts than merely constructing their meanings. This embodiment of Scripture is to be taken seriously as the 'vocation' of Christians demonstrated in many ways and in diverse cultural and theological contexts.[56] Based on this argument, Fowl claims that scriptural interpretation is an ongoing assignment that involves discernment and guidance of the Spirit.[57]

Mutual Influence of Scripture and Doctrine in Christian Formation: Joel B. Green

The role of Scripture in the formation of the Christian life is a significant aspect in theological interpretation. Joel B. Green, one of the leading advocates of theological interpretation, distinguishes theological interpretation of Scripture from other readings of the Bible by its emphasis on faith and Christian formation particularly in a specific ecclesial location. Highlighting the fact that it is not a 'carefully defined method', Green states that theological interpretation is described by its certain sensibilities and aims like other kinds of 'interested' exegetical practices.[58]

---

[53] Fowl, *Theological Interpretation*, p. 39.

[54] Fowl, *Theological Interpretation*, p. 13.

[55] Fowl, 'Importance', pp. 49-50.

[56] Stephen E. Fowl and L. Gregory Jones, *Reading in Communion: Scripture and Ethics in Christian Life* (Grand Rapids: Eerdmans 1991), p. 1.

[57] Fowl, *Reading in Communion*, p. 31.

[58] Green, *Practicing*, p. 2.

J.B. Green's portrayal of theological interpretation is chiefly concerned with the goals and purposes of Christian Scripture. The
Christian Scripture mediates the voice of God and an encounter with
him that leads to the formation of individuals and ecclesial communities.[59] Christian formation for him has more to do with internalized
dispositions and mindsets shaped by the Scripture. Beyond the moral
actions emphasized by Christian churches and church-related institu-
tions, J.B. Green insists that the biblical texts are more concerned
with 'shaping our imaginations, our patterns of thinking, which, in-
evitably, find expression in transformed commitments and practices'.[60] Hearing the divine voice through Scripture creates a theological vision of God and his purposes that shapes the ways in which
individuals and Christian communities understand themselves and
others as well as interact with the world around them.[61]

Christian formation takes place through the mutual influence of
doctrine and Scripture. This mutual influence of doctrine and Scripture, according to J.B. Green, has a circular nature. He writes, 'We
discern God's character and will in Scripture, but it is God's character
and will that guide our reading of Scripture'.[62] J.B. Green makes a
distinction between 'doctrine' and 'theology' in his description of
theological interpretation. Whereas 'theology' suggests the ongoing
critical thinking of the Church, 'doctrine' refers to the relatively stable
set of affirmations shaped by the overall narrative of the Church that
enables it to interpret and serve as a frame of reference to restrict its
communal life and practice. In other words, he uses doctrine as the
Rule of Faith, particularly as it is embedded in the structures of the
ecumenical creeds of the early Church.

J.B. Green argues that the Rule of Faith is not merely taken from
the Old and New Testaments or there is no ground to claim that the
Church has received its doctrine from the Bible. He constructed his
argument on historical facts that indicate the New Testament texts
were not canonized at the time when the Rule of Faith was being
formulated. In fact, the agreement of the texts with the Rule of Faith

[59] Green, *Practicing*, p. 5.
[60] Joel B. Green, *Seized by Truth: Reading the Bible as Scripture* (Nashville: Abingdon, 2007), pp. 19-20.
[61] Green, *Seized*, p. 23. See also, *idem*, 'The (Re-)Turn to Theology', in *JTI* 1.1
(2007), pp. 1-3.
[62] Green, *Seized*, p. 62.

was one of the crucial determining factors in canon formation.
Moreover, J.B. Green asserts that Christological reading was the primary lens through which the early Christians read the Old Testament
texts in ways different from other contemporary readings. Based on
these historical and theological grounds, J.B. Green claims that 'theological interpretation cannot escape the question of the relationship
between those ecumenical creeds that define the faith of the Church
and this canonical collection that we embrace as Scripture'. Doctrine,
as the Rule of Faith, provides the interpretive community with certain hermeneutical assumptions and viewpoints to practice faithful
interpretation.[63]

The relationship between history and theological interpretation is
another concern in Green's account. Given the modern dominance
of historical critical method in biblical studies, it is commonly perceived that the contemporary recovery of theological interpretation
has an ill-disposed relationship to historical criticism. This perception
stems partly from inadequate understanding of both approaches. In
order to clarify apparent misconceptions, Green provides three 'interpretive agendas' pertaining to historical criticism – reconstruction
of past events to recount the past, excavation of traditional materials
to explain how the past events became textualized, and historical
study of the setting within which the biblical texts were formed. Utterly rejecting the first approach and welcoming the second one with
caution when it serves rhetorical purposes, Green underscores the
third approach to historical criticism as an important tool in theological interpretation. This involves the study of historical context and
the socio-cultural norms of the day for interpretive purposes. In
other words, theological interpretation is interested in the kind of
historical work that helps to elucidate the biblical message for listening to God's voice in the present. The study of history in theological
interpretation, therefore, is not an end in itself; rather, it serves the
purpose of forming faith and practice of Christians today.[64]

Biblical Interpretation in Theological Perspective: Francis Watson

The notion of biblical interpretation in theological perspective is at
the center of contemporary conversations concerning theological

---

[63] Green, *Practicing*, pp. 71-74.
[64] Green, *Practicing*, pp. 43-45.

interpretation of Scripture. Francis Watson is a prominent scholar to be mentioned in connection with this issue. His contributions to advance the conversation include his major monographs: *Text, Church, and World* (1994) and *Text and Truth* (1997).[65] In the first, Watson offered an outline for the practice of biblical interpretation in theological perspective. His aims were to clarify the essence of biblical theology in relation to theological hermeneutics of biblical texts and to reformulate theological responsibilities in biblical interpretation. He writes,

> Biblical interpretation should concern itself primarily with the theological issues raised by the biblical texts within our contemporary ecclesial, cultural and socio-political contexts. At a time when many former hermeneutical certainties are encountering sustained and effective challenge, the familiar but still controversial claim that biblical interpretation should no longer neglect its theological responsibilities is due for reformulation and restatement.[66]

In his effort to return theological concerns to biblical interpretation, Watson deals with biblical textuality reflecting on the significance of the final canonical version of the text as a basis for theological interpretation. 'To think of a "text", is to focus on the finished product, abstracted from its relation to a progenitor and considered in terms of its *use*'.[67] Watson's critical interaction with Hans Frei and Brevard Childs enable him to develop a canonical interpretation that takes the canon as literary unity, although he criticizes Frei's 'narrative realism'[68] and Childs's failure to acknowledge that the canonical texts were established by ideological conflicts from within and outside the Church.[69] Given the nature of the canonical texts, Watson expands what he regards as the incomplete approaches of Frei and Childs by arguing for the inevitability of engaging with historical and ethical concerns. Establishing a considerable critique of conventional

---

[65] Francis Watson, *Text, Church, and World: Biblical Interpretation in Theological Perspective* (Grand Rapids: Eerdmans, 1994); *idem, Text and Truth: Redefining Biblical Theology* (Grand Rapids: Eerdmans, 1997).

[66] Watson, *Text, Church, and World*, p. vii.

[67] Watson, *Text, Church, and World*, p. 2.

[68] Watson, *Text, Church, and World*, pp. 19-29.

[69] Watson, *Text, Church, and World*, pp. 30-45.

historical-criticism, he then proceeds to interact with postmodern theories of interpretation and textuality, feminist critiques, and how theology relates to hermeneutics and exegesis.

Watson develops his position further in a second book, in which he attempts to redefine biblical theology. This redefinition focused on dismantling the barriers that separate biblical studies and Christian theology, so that biblical theology is now 'an interdisciplinary approach', that is, 'a theological, hermeneutical and exegetical discipline, and its hermeneutical and exegetical dimensions are placed at the disposal of its overriding theological concern'.[70] Watson also claims that the existing separation between Old Testament and New Testament studies has the same origin that divided biblical studies and systematic theology. He advances his hermeneutical positions in the rest of the book by exercising exegesis on the Gospel narratives and the doctrine of creation vis-à-vis natural theology. In a sharper and more consistent approach, Watson expands his position outlined in the previous book and emphasizes the significance of theology in biblical interpretation.

Watson's theological perspective on biblical interpretation is highlighted by his emphasis on interdisciplinarity. According to him, the current demarcations of biblical and theological disciplines restrict theological engagement with biblical texts and create a 'systematic distortion' in biblical interpretation. Firmly challenging the mutual exclusivity of academic theology and biblical studies, Watson calls for a 'biblical theology' that integrates biblical scholarship and systematic theology in biblical interpretation. His biblical theology is 'biblical' in the sense that it is concerned with the entirety of the Bible and does not view the Old Testament and New Testament theologies as separate and exclusive disciplines to each other. It is also 'theology' in that it cannot be limited in its descriptive capacity.[71] It is a biblical theology that involves working on both lines of demarcations of disciplines. Despite its own risks and dangers, proper integration and dialogue between biblical and theological studies are necessary components for theological interpretation.

Contemporary hermeneutical discussion for Watson is a critical element, in fact 'a prerequisite' in rethinking the relationship between

---

[70] Watson, *Text and Truth*, p. vii.

[71] Watson, *Text and Truth*, p. 8.

exegesis and theology.[72] This is mainly because of the nature of the Bible as a text. Emphasizing its textuality, Watson shows the importance of focusing on the biblical text in theological interpretation. It is necessary to maintain that 'truth is textually mediated', and even our access to the reality of Jesus is mediated to us through the text. Therefore, a textually mediated theology is necessary in theological hermeneutics.[73] On the basis of this assertion, Watson's vision of theological hermeneutics attempts to interact with the best of current hermeneutical discussions including historical criticism.

Proposing a full outline of his ecclesial hermeneutics, Watson shows that he takes the reading community seriously in theological interpretation. 'The primary reading community within which the biblical text is located is the Christian Church.'[74] In the first place, the purpose of biblical texts is to be read in public in the context of communal worship, and one of the functions of the Church as a Christian community is to read, interpret, and embody the biblical texts. The world is the primary location where the Christian Church functions. This relationship between the text, Church, and world, described as a 'concentric circle', is hermeneutically significant in theological interpretation of Scripture.[75] However, as much as he believes the Church is the primary reading community, Watson does not seem to give much emphasis to the ultimate purpose of reading Scripture or the practices of reading as a Christian community. In consequence, as Fowl comments, Watson's work reads more like contemporary systematic theology rather than a theological interpretation account.[76]

Theological Interpretation as Experiential Knowledge of God: Kevin J. Vanhoozer

As one of the primary contributors to contemporary discussions of theological interpretation, Vanhoozer articulates his definition of theological interpretation of Scripture in his editorial introduction to the *Dictionary for Theological Interpretation of the Bible*.[77] His main focus is the experiential knowledge of God. Vanhoozer writes, 'Theological

---

[72] Watson, *Text, Church, and World*, p. 223.

[73] Watson, *Text and Truth*, p. 1.

[74] Watson, *Text, Church, and World*, p. 3.

[75] Watson, *Text, Church, and World*, p. 11.

[76] Fowl, *Engaging Scripture*, pp. 22-23.

[77] Vanhoozer, 'What Is Theological Interpretation?', pp. 19-25.

interpretation of the Bible is biblical interpretation oriented to the knowledge of God'. This knowledge is not simply described in terms of an academic pursuit. Rather, having experiential and relational orientation, it simultaneously involves 'an intellectual, imaginative, and spiritual exercise'. 'To know God as the author and subject of Scripture requires more than intellectual acknowledgement. To know God is to love and obey him, for the knowledge of God is both restorative and transformative.'[78]

Vanhoozer's account entails clarification of potential misconceptions about theological interpretation. First, theological interpretation is not 'an imposition of theological system' in biblical interpretation. It is not subject to a particular confessional framework like, for example, Lutheran or Reformed or Catholic theology. Second, it is not 'an imposition of a general hermeneutic or theory of interpretation onto the biblical text'. In other words, it avoids reading the Bible as any other book and demands a theological approach to biblical exegesis. Third, theological interpretation is not 'a form of merely historical, literary, or sociological criticism preoccupied with (respectively) the world "behind", "of", or "in front of" the biblical text'.[79] Although these critical tools are helpful and have their place in the interpretive process, theological interpretation ought to work beyond their limits to disclose divine action in and through the biblical texts.

In an earlier article, Vanhoozer offers two possibilities to explain what makes theological interpretation 'theological'. It is theological, first, because it appeals to God as Scripture's 'author', and, second, on account of its aim and outcome for reading Scripture, which is 'living faithfully with others before God'.[80] Theological interpretation is a practice of the Church with the purpose of spiritual formation and building up the body of Christ. It focuses on what Vanhoozer calls 'the *theological* natural sense' of Scripture. The 'natural sense' refers to the way human authors of the Bible use words in different ways and literary contexts, whereas the 'theological sense' refers to

---

[78] Vanhoozer, 'What Is Theological Interpretation?', p. 24.

[79] Vanhoozer, 'What Is Theological Interpretation?', p. 19.

[80] Kevin J. Vanhoozer, 'Body-Piercing, the Natural Sense, and the Task of Theological Interpretation: A Hermeneutical Homily on John 19:34', *ExAud* 16 (2000), p. 8.

what God, as divine author, does with the words of the human authors in the canonical context of the biblical texts.[81]

In defining theological interpretation, Vanhoozer points out three important elements. First, theological interpretation belongs to the whole people of God and involves all theological disciplines, including biblical and theological scholarship. This obviously means filling the gap created by 'the ugly ditch' in modern biblical interpretation between theology and exegesis, faith and reason, or even the Church and the academy.[82] Second, theological interpretation is a theological criticism marked by its highest priority and interest in God. In this approach to biblical interpretation, God is not an 'afterthought' or 'simply a function of a certain community's interpretative interest'. Rather, 'God is prior to both the community and the biblical texts themselves'. [83] Finally, theological interpretation comprises wide-ranging ecclesial concerns and academic approaches. Given various types of interpretive approaches and theological interests, there is no single exclusive model to pursue theological interpretation. It may incorporate diverse perspectives and broad theological concerns in interpretation practices that involve 'faith, hope, and love' with the ultimate aim of knowing 'the triune God by participating in the triune life, in the triune mission to creation'.[84]

Ancient Theological Practice of Reading the Bible as the Word of God: Daniel J. Treier

Daniel J. Treier is another important voice in advancing the recovery of theological interpretation. In his account, *Introducing Theological Interpretation of Scripture*, Treier recognizes contemporary theological interpretation as a movement by offering its major themes and development as well as addressing questions and challenges that specify its future directions. This movement 'seeks to reverse the dominance of historical criticism over churchly reading of the Bible and to redefine the role of hermeneutics in theology'.[85] As a Christian spiritual practice of reading Scripture, theological interpretation orients the

---

[81] Vanhoozer, Body-Piercing', pp. 1-2.

[82] Vanhoozer, 'What Is Theological Interpretation?', pp. 20-21.

[83] Vanhoozer, 'What Is Theological Interpretation?', p. 23.

[84] Vanhoozer, 'What Is Theological Interpretation?', pp. 22-24.

[85] Treier, *Introducing*, p. 14.

Church in a deeper and meaningful way towards seeking the knowledge of God.[86]

Theological interpretation is a Christian interpretive practice that has always existed, until its decline as a result of modern, critical biblical scholarship. The current movement is a considerable attempt to recover this ancient practice.[87] Precritical biblical reading approaches the Bible religiously with referencing to Christology for practical Christian application in light of the Rule of Faith as criteria for interpretation.[88] As a dominant premodern biblical interpretive practice, theological hermeneutics has had an enormous impact on Christian interpretation for centuries. It was a theological practice that viewed the Bible as the word of God for life and faith; hence, it was a practice equivalent to an encounter with God.[89]

Surveying the most recent recovery of theological interpretation, Treier reflects on Barth's programmatic theological exegesis as a critical impetus to the movement. Although he cannot be taken as a single model, Barth's inspiration for contemporary theological interpretation plays a very significant role. Treier enumerates the influence of Barth's theological exegesis in some of the key theological voices in current critical biblical scholarship such as Childs, David Kelsey, Frei, George Lindbeck, Stanley Hauerwas, and Watson. For Treier, Barth's theological interpretation provides a crucial stimulus to cross Lessing's 'ugly ditch' and checks the dominance of historical criticism in modern biblical interpretation.[90]

In describing contemporary theological interpretation of Scripture, Treier indicates that there is a clear distinction between theological interpretation and the existing critical biblical studies in the academic discipline. The primary aim for modern biblical criticism is closing the historical gap between the contemporary readers and the biblical text. It is a methodological approach of biblical interpretation grounded on a flawed model of neutrality and objectivity. The current movement attempts to reverse this approach, although critical

---

[86] Treier, *Introducing*, p. 205.

[87] Treier, *Introducing*, p. 11.

[88] Treier, *Introducing*, p. 41.

[89] Treier, *Introducing*, pp. 11-14.

[90] Treier, *Introducing*, pp. 14-20.

biblical scholarship can still serve a significant use in theological interpretation.

Trier underlines the importance of employing insights from general hermeneutics in theological interpretation by what he calls 'plundering the Egyptians'. Works of Martin Heidegger, Hans Gadamer, and Paul Ricoeur on philosophical hermeneutics have important contributions in improving the deficiencies of modern historical and literary perceptions as well as the interpretive role of the reader. Although there are diverse approaches to dealing with questions in relation to the author, text, and reader, Treier highlights the importance for theological interpreters of giving appropriate emphasis to each of the segments in the triad of biblical interpretation. He writes,

> Emphasis on the author tends to privilege historical (and grammatical) methods; focus on the texts usually fits with prioritizing literary methods. Those who pursue theological interpretation of Scripture must give attention to what should be the proper role of the reader, yet they do not necessarily have to adopt reader-response hermeneutics. For, instead, theological hermeneutics involves thinking about the nature and nurture of interpretation in light of God, whose action puts reader, text, and author in a larger context that decisively alters the character of their interaction.[91]

Another important issue that Treier mentions in restoring theological interpretation is imitating precritical interpretation. 'Recovering the most significant aspects of theological exegesis requires imitation of precritical Christian exegetes.'[92] For Treier, the virtues of spiritual interpretation demonstrated in our forebears, for example, piety in reading or Christ-centered approach in biblical interpretation has been practically missing from the late modern biblical studies. Despite the imperfections in their practices, Treier insists, 'the ancients do have much to teach us about reading the Bible ultimately as one book from one Author'.[93] Contemporary theological interpretation also appeals to the early reactions to modern approaches of biblical interpretation. For instance, regardless of their apparent

---

[91] Treier, *Introducing*, pp. 135-36.
[92] Treier, *Introducing*, p. 40.
[93] Treier, *Introducing*, p. 55.

differences, Treier refers to the reactions of Barth and Rudolf Bultmann against the modern ideological assumptions concerning history and faith. This can at least inform contemporary theological interpreters about the limitations of the historical critical approach to
biblical interpretation.[94]

Reading the Bible towards Transformation through Enduring Truth: R.W.L. Moberly

Transformation of the reader(s) is one of the primary goals of reading Scripture theologically. As one of the advocates of theological
interpretation, R.W.L. Moberly acknowledges the intrinsic correlation
between the practice of theological reading of Scripture and Christian transformation. In his article 'What Is Theological Interpretation
of Scripture?' Moberly attempts to provide a working definition of
theological interpretation.[95] Theological interpretation is 'reading the
Bible with a concern for the enduring truth of its witness to the nature of God and humanity, with a view to enabling the transformation of humanity into the likeness of God'.[96]

Theological interpretation, according to Moberly, is concerned
with making a meaningful connection between the study of the Bible
and the existential issues that relate to the Christian faith and life. The
primary concern for theological interpreters, then, is 'to reengage the
questions of *truth* posed by the biblical account of God and humanity, as received and practiced by Jews and Christians down the ages'.[97]
Moberly thinks that the nature of theological interpretation is inherently ecumenical, interfaith in its reach, and interdisciplinary.

Summarizing his understanding of theological interpretation,
Moberly discusses the concept of applying one's whole self to the
text and applying the whole subject matter to one's self, borrowing
the well-known line from Johann Albrecht Bengel in the eighteenth
century.[98] Moberly refers to Deut. 6.5 and its Christian usage as a

---

[94] Daniel J. Treier, 'Theological Interpretation, Contemporary', in *Dictionary for
Theological Interpretation of the Bible* (ed. Kevin J. Vanhoozer; Grand Rapids: Baker
Academic, 2005), p. 788.

[95] R.W.L. Moberly, 'What Is Theological Interpretation of Scripture?', *JTI* 3.2
(2009), pp. 161-78.

[96] Moberly, 'Theological Interpretation', p. 163.

[97] Moberly, 'Theological Interpretation', p. 164.

[98] It reads, *Te totum applica ad textum, rem totam aplica ad te* – 'Apply your whole
self to the text; apply the whole subject matter to yourself'.

bedrock for theological interpretation. He writes: 'head and heart and energy all together are to be applied in theological interpretation ... [T]here is to be no separation between head and heart, between thought and life, between the intellectual and the existential.'[99] At the same time, when one applies to oneself the whole subject matter of the text, the result is a life transformed by an encounter with God's enduring truth that results in changing the lives of others.

Approaching and Understanding Scripture with Eyes of Faith: Richard B. Hays

Richard B. Hays is another important voice in recovering theological interpretation of the Bible. In his article 'Reading the Bible with Eyes of Faith: The Practice of Theological Exegesis', Hays calls attention to the significance of *faith* as the 'epistemological precondition' for biblical interpretation.[100] Using visual imagery as an entryway to his view of theological interpretation, Hays affirms that faith is a necessary ingredient in reading Scripture theologically. Hays defines theological interpretation as 'a way of approaching Scripture with eyes of faith and seeking to understand it within the community of faith'.[101]

Hays describes theological exegesis as 'a complex *practice*' for which he proposes twelve identifying marks.[102] This complex practice is 'a practice of and for the Church' in which the texts of the Bible are esteemed more than a collection of pieces of ancient writings. Theological reading of the Bible is also a practice of worship and a confessional act that involves taking the texts to be addressed to self as a reader. Nevertheless, this does not stop the theological interpreter from historical engagement, since historical study of Scripture is at the heart of the practice of theological exegesis.

Theological interpretation attends to the literary wholeness of Scripture as well as its canonical coherence. For Hays, 'theological exegetes will seek the big picture, asking how any particular text fits into the larger biblical story of God's gracious action'.[103] Reading the biblical texts as *testimony* is another feature of theological

---

[99] Moberly, 'Theological Interpretation', p. 168.

[100] Richard B. Hays, 'Reading the Bible with Eyes of Faith: The Practice of Theological Exegesis', *JTI* 1.1 (2007), pp. 5-21.

[101] Hays, 'Reading', p. 11.

[102] Hays, 'Reading', pp. 11-15.

[103] Hays, 'Reading', p. 13.

interpretation, in which texts point to God as a primary focus of attention. Hays also uses the terms *intratextuality* and *intertextuality* as identifying marks of theological exegesis. Whereas the former implies that theological interpretation works within the particularity of Scriptural framework, the latter indicates the significance of correspondence between the two testaments in theological reading.

Hays suggests that theological interpretation involves taking *multiple senses* of biblical texts into consideration. 'Texts have multiple layers of meaning that are disclosed by the Holy Spirit to faithful and patient readers.'[104] Learning from the wisdom of the Church accumulated in its *tradition* is also an important element in theological exegesis. Nevertheless, theological readers need to generate *fresh readings*, learning from traditional interpretations and guided by the Holy Spirit who continues to speak today. Hays writes that 'the Spirit-led imagination, an imagination converted by the word, is an essential faculty for the work of theological exegesis'.[105] With this recognition of the Spirit's role, prayer and humility have an essential place in theological exegesis. Using these identifying marks, Hays urges that theological interpretation is faith-seeking understanding through interaction with Scripture as God's instrument for transforming his people into Christ's image.

Theological Interpretation as a Practice of the Community of Faith: J. Todd Billings

J. Todd Billings' description of theological interpretation focuses on its nature as a practice of the community of believers. His book, *The Word of God for the People of God*, is aimed at widening the extent of scholarly discussions on theological interpretation to readers who 'love Scripture and Christian ministry' and serves as an 'entryway' to engage in this interpretive practice. Billings defines theological interpretation of Scripture as 'a multifaceted practice of a community of faith in reading the Bible as God's instrument of self-revelation and saving fellowship. It is not a single, discrete method of discipline; rather, it is a wide range of practices we use toward the goal of knowing God in Christ through Scripture.' Scripture is a means through which God reshapes the Church into the image of Christ by the power of the Spirit. Theological interpretation, therefore, is a practice

---

[104] Hays, 'Reading', p. 14.
[105] Hays, 'Reading', p. 15.

of reading Scripture from a specified location in the context of the triune God's redemptive activity.[106]

Billings portrays reading Scripture as a 'Trinitarian-shaped' journey of faith seeking understanding. Given the fact that interpretations are shaped and biased by the location and preunderstanding of the reader, the readers' theological presupposition is a vital element in this journey.[107] The Rule of Faith that arises out of Scripture and yet offers extrabiblical guidelines to read Scripture plays a crucial role in determining the theological decisions Christians make in interpretation. For Billings, the Rule of Faith is not straightjacket for interpreting Scripture; rather, it is a functional rule to read Scripture in a Trinitarian way. With the Rule of Faith, 'Christian scriptural interpretation takes place on the path of Jesus Christ, empowered by the Spirit to transform God's people into Christ's image, anticipating a transformative vision of the triune God'.[108]

Expounding his Trinitarian hermeneutic, Billings argues that the theological perception of God and his relationship with humans considerably colors the way Scripture is interpreted. He offers two either/or expressions to clarify theological presuppositions about God's revelation – either revelation is based on intrinsic, universal human capacities and understood through a Deistic hermeneutic or it is grounded in God's specific action with Israel and in Jesus Christ and interpreted through a Trinitarian hermeneutic. Preferring the latter, Billings asserts that Trinitarian theology of revelation provides the necessary context to understand the inspiration and canonicity of Scripture properly. The affirmation of the doctrine of inspiration and canonicity entails the recognition of Scripture to be the Spirit's instrument for shaping the people of God into Christ's image. He writes,

> The Spirit uses Scripture in our journey of faith seeking understanding, mediating the self-presentation of the Word, Jesus Christ, through Scripture. This journey of reading Scripture is not just about texts, meaning, and interpretation. It is about receiving Scripture as the Spirit's word that unites God's people ever deeper

---

[106] J. Todd Billings, *The Word of God for the People of God: An Entryway to the Theological Interpretation of Scripture* (Grand Rapids: Eerdmans, 2010), pp. xii-xiii.

[107] Billings, *The Word of God*, pp. 19-20.

[108] Billings, *The Word of God*, p. xiv.

to Jesus Christ and his ways, mortifying sin while vivifying the community for service in Christ. Scripture is not God; it is an instrument in the triune God's work.[109]

The practice of reading Scripture theologically is participation in the work of the Holy Spirit that involves a life of prayer, worship, and community. Although methodological approach plays its own part in historical and linguistic analysis of the text, reading the Bible cannot be reduced to a simple method or technique. It should not be considered as reading other books. Rather, through the practices of reading Scripture, believers participate in the drama of God's redemptive action and enter into an encounter with a mysterious triune God.[110]

Main Themes and Relevant Issues in Theological Interpretation

We have reviewed some of the significant voices in contemporary conversations of theological interpretation of Scripture. The surveyed literature demonstrates the fact that theological interpretation is a remarkable enterprise that cannot be ignored or marginalized in current biblical and theological scholarship. The literature indicates not only the increasing sensibilities towards reading Scripture theologically, but also that they imply the difficulties in providing a categorical definition to theological interpretation of Scripture due to the nature of its own approach. They nevertheless provide helpful information to understand its characteristics, locate its place in current biblical and theological studies, and specify the directions of its development. Moreover, with respect to the main objective of this work, the literature serves as a starting point to deal with issues in relation to the role of the Spirit in reading Scripture theologically. In this section, I attempt to tease out some of the overriding themes and relevant issues that emerge from the discussions of key voices toward the direction of developing a constructive approach to understand the Spirit's interpretive role in theological reading of Scripture.

---

[109] Billings, *The Word of God*, p. 103.
[110] Billings, *The Word of God*, pp. 195-96.

Reading the Bible as Scripture – One of the compelling issues the key voices maintain in the conversation is that theological interpretation undoubtedly recognizes the Bible as Scripture. They all affirm the Church's confession from the early days that *sacra scriptura est verbum Dei* ('Holy Scripture is the word of God'). This affirmation is a substantial basis for a theological approach in biblical interpretation. In the first place, acknowledging the Bible as Scripture, which is taking it more than a collection of ancient pieces of writings and recognizing its sacredness, is a clear and landmark theological assumption. At least two implications derive from this assumption. First, it points to God as the source and origin of sacred Scripture and recognizes that he uses it as a means of self-communication. Second, it draws attention to the importance of the readers' dispositions and beliefs in relation to reading Scripture. In both cases, it becomes clear that reading the Bible as Scripture is not reading it 'like any other book', to mention Benjamin Jowett's famous saying which turned into a common axiom in the conventional modernist approach of biblical studies.[111]

Reading for a Communion with God – Reading Scripture oriented toward a specific purpose of communion and intimacy with God (Fowl) that leads to experiential knowledge of him (Vanhoozer and Treier) and transformation (Moberly) or Christian formation (Green) is another theme that runs throughout the discussions. The purpose of reading biblical texts as Scripture is to have an encounter with God and that encounter takes place through the hearing of God's voice in the texts. It is a theological assumption to believe that God speaks through texts and theological interpreters bring this assumption to the reading in order to hear God speaking. The *telos* of theological interpretation is for the Church to hear God's address and be transformed into the image of Christ, so it can be salt of the earth and light of the world.

Doctrine and Rule of Faith – The influence of doctrine in biblical interpretation and the Scripture's influence in Christian doctrine is also a significant theme in the discussions. Christian doctrine in

---

[111] Benjamin Jowett's programmatic claim that demands the Bible to be read as any other book was instrumental in propagating the modern disengaged approach towards the Bible. See his 'On the Interpretation of Scripture', in Victor Shea and William Whitla (eds.), *Essay and Reviews: The 1860 Text and Its Reading* (Charlottesville: University Press of Virginia, 2000), p. 482.

theological interpretation is considered to be a shared interpretation of the witness of Scripture. Theological interpreters approach Scripture with the sort of doctrinal and theological presuppositions they gathered from Christian practices and traditions of the Church, which are in some way formed and informed by the Rule of Faith through time. In the same way, the reading of the biblical texts shapes the doctrinal approaches of the readers in a continuous circularity. Rule of Faith (*regula fedie*), as a confession of faith mostly for public use in worship, facilitates the practice of faithful interpretation by providing hermeneutical assumptions and guidelines to the interpretive community. As a communal faith of the Church received from the apostolic teaching and preaching traditions, the Rule of Faith holds a key hermeneutical part in theological interpretation of Scripture.

Canonical Approach – Although there are diverse approaches among proponents of theological interpretation of Scripture, understanding both the Old Testament and the New Testament as unified sections of the Bible is a common theme. In fact, canon is a crucial element in theological interpretation as the source and basis for its entire operation. The canonical understanding of Scripture as a coherent narrative is a significant approach within the interpretive framework of reading Scripture theologically. The underlying assumption in the canonical approach is that the final form of the biblical texts bears witness to God's communicative address. Although both the writings of the two testaments originated in certain historical contexts among a specific people, times, and occasions, theological interpretation proponents agree that they were intended to address all people regardless of cultural and temporal differences. The two testaments, within one canon, provide the interpretive context for the believing community to approach Scripture as a means of encountering the living God through Jesus Christ.

Ecclesial Location – The importance of ecclesial location in theological interpretation is a shared emphasis especially among some (such as Fowl and Green). Theological interpretation of Scripture does not occur in a vacuum; rather, it is located within the individual and collective practices of piety, worship, and prayer of the community of faith. In general, faith, as an 'epistemological precondition' (Hays), governs the way biblical texts are interpreted theologically and lived practically. The Church, as the community of God's people, is the main context for the reception, interpretation, and practical embodiment of the Bible as Scripture. As the primary audience addressed by the contents of Scripture, the ecclesial community is summoned to hear God's voice through the biblical texts for an ultimate life changing response and experience. Given both the nature of Scripture as a means through which God speaks and the Church as people who are called to hear his voice, an ecclesially located approach is a key aspect of theological interpretation of Scripture.

The main themes and issues in theological interpretation as observed in these discussions draw attention to limitations of humanly devised interpretive methods and the need for divine guidance to the interpretation of Scripture which significantly shapes our focus on the importance of reflecting on role of the Holy Spirit in this interpretive practice. This is not unfounded consideration. If theological interpretation assumes the biblical texts to be treated as Scripture, namely as God's means of self-revelation and self-communication, and designed to shape and transform readers who approach them faithfully to have a meaningful encounter with the living God, the proper implication is that interpretive exercise is not predominantly an academic human enterprise. Demanding and primarily involving the actions of the divine agent, that is, the Holy Spirit, this consideration shapes the direction of biblical and theological scholarship to practices performed to hear the voice of the Spirit through the written texts of Scripture. This makes a thorough reflection on *pneumatic hermeneutics*, or the role of the Spirit in theological reading of Scripture, inevitable.

Organization of the Study

Although a few have approached the issue in their writing, the Spirit's interpretive role in theological interpretation needs to be thoroughly addressed. This study is an effort to grapple with questions in relation to *pneumatic hermeneutics* in theological reading of Scripture so as to develop a constructive theological contribution to the broader conversation. I have discussed in this chapter the contemporary sensibilities toward reading Scripture theologically and the essential elements of this approach by way of dealing with key voices and their unique emphases with regard to theology and biblical interpretation. Chapter 2 continues the discussion by narrowing the focus on those who specifically approach the Spirit's interpretive role from the vantage point of theological interpretation of Scripture. The Pentecostal interpretive tradition has a key importance for this study given the fact that it places a considerable emphasis on the person and work of the Holy Spirit and hence, it has more to say on the topic in discussion. Therefore, the literature review extends to include several Pentecostal approaches on the Spirit's interpretive role in the second half of the chapter.

Following the literature review of contemporary conversations on theological interpretation and Pentecostal scholarship, we explore interpretive practices of mainstream Christian traditions in order to understand diverse approaches and perspectives of the Spirit's role in theology and biblical interpretation. Thus, chapter 3 discusses some basic theological perspectives from the Eastern Orthodox and Roman Catholic traditions on the interplay between the Spirit and biblical interpretation. The significance of mysticism and church tradition as a context of scriptural interpretation within the theology of Eastern Orthodoxy is discussed in the first section. The second section deals with the Roman Catholic dogmatic constitution on divine revelation (*Dei Verbum*), Henry De Lubac's spiritual sense of Scripture, and the practice of divine reading (*Lectio Divina*). The role of ecclesial practices and the dogmatic theologies on the Holy Spirit and Scripture help us understand the way the Spirit's work in biblical interpretation is perceived in these mainline Christian traditions.

In the same manner, I will discuss *pneumatic hermeneutics* within Protestant Christian tradition in chapter 4, giving a specific emphasis to the thoughts of three important theologians. Since Protestant theology is shaped by the sixteenth century Reformation, understanding its approaches in relation to Spirit and biblical interpretation through the writings of prominent Protestant theologians whose thoughts were formed by the Reformation ideals and values would benefit this research. After offering introductory remarks on divine illumination and internal testimony of the Spirit, which is a significant Protestant concept on the Spirit's interpretive role, the chapter will discuss the approaches of John Calvin, John Owen, and John Wesley to the role of the Spirit in scriptural interpretation. This is helpful for understanding Protestant perspectives on the Spirit's role in biblical interpretation, given the importance of this theological and/or ecclesial locus for most of contemporary proponents of theological interpretation; additionally, this will provide an appropriate contextual setting for the emergence of the Pentecostal interpretive tradition, which is a major emphasis in this study.

Given its key importance in this discussion, it is crucial to explore Pentecostal hermeneutics carefully to hear voices from within the tradition and understand its interests in *pneumatic hermeneutics*. Chapter 5 articulates an in-depth analysis on the thoughts of three prominent Pentecostal theologians and their theological and/or historical contributions to conversations on the Spirit's interpretive role. In the first section of the chapter, I discuss Pentecostalism – its passion and commitment to the Holy Spirit and Christian spirituality that shapes the theological culture and scholarship within the Pentecostal-charismatic traditions. The remaining sections explore Pentecostal hermeneutical approaches and Pentecostal understandings of the Spirit's interpretive role through the writings of Kenneth J. Archer, Amos Yong, and L. William Oliverio. Although Pentecostal literature on the topic is growing now, analyzing these theological approaches helps us reasonably identify characteristic features of Pentecostal proclivities to the Spirit's interpretive role and assess its contributions to the general conversations on theological interpretation of Scripture.

The final chapter offers a theological reflection pointing a way toward a model for the Spirit's role in theological interpretation of Scripture. Primarily dealing with questions raised concerning Pentecostal hermeneutics and the significance of a pneumatological approach to biblical interpretation, the chapter attempts to offer a theological interpretive strategy that integrates the roles of the Spirit and community in understanding sacred texts. The first section identifies the interpretive community as people of the Spirit who listen to God's address through Scripture and ongoing fresh experiences to provide a basis for a theological interpretation permeated by the Spirit. The second section deals with the Spirit's role in community formation particularly focusing on the way that the Spirit was shaping the early Church communities in the book of Acts. The final section highlights the Spirit, as the starting point, is mediated through the Christian community's theological and hermeneutical practices.

2

THE HOLY SPIRIT IN THE READING OF SCRIPTURE: A REVIEW OF LITERATURE

The previous chapter examined critical issues and key representatives of contemporary conversations in the theological interpretation of Scripture. By analyzing the nature of theological interpretation and its significance in current biblical and theological scholarship, it served this study in providing prominent ideas that help us to understand better what sort of interpretive practice it is and to identify what distinguishes it from other approaches to biblical interpretation. We saw that the contemporary recovery of theological interpretation raises issues in relation to the nature of biblical texts and the location and disposition of readers, as well as overall theological interpretive practices. We noted, too, that this interpretive practice opens space to reflect on divine activity in understanding biblical texts, activity that takes us beyond human-oriented engagement.

This general analysis suggests that exploring the Spirit's work in reading Scripture should be given crucial attention in theological interpretation. In fact, awareness of the role of the Holy Spirit in interpretation is growing among proponents of theological interpretation. In the first place, the theological interpreters' insistence on viewing the biblical texts as Scripture, as the word of God – that is, as God's self-revealing communicative tool – requires that biblical interpretation be understood as more than the employing of certain literary and/or historical techniques. As Treier points out, theological interpretation demands that we 'discern how the Holy Spirit leads members of the Christian community to discover the meaning of

Scripture, and in particular how different parts of the body of Christ connect with each other in that process'.[1] It is also clear that the purpose of reading the Bible, as perceived by many theological interpretation advocates, has to do with the transformation of individuals and communities. In order for this to happen, theological interpretation proponents claim that the work of the Spirit in reading Scripture theologically is indispensable. J.B. Green, for instance, argues as follows:

> If theologically, we recognize that we turn to the Bible to attune our ears to God's address and if we recognize that Christian formation, whether of persons or of ecclesial communities, is divine work after all, then our conversation needs to extend beyond what we human beings bring to the table of biblical interpretation. Particularly, we require, more reflection on the role of the Holy Spirit in theological interpretation.[2]

Given this sort of broad recognition of the importance of the Spirit's work in theological interpretation of Scripture and increased attention to critical treatments of this issue, it is alarming to find so little written on the subject. Although the significance of the Spirit for theological interpretation is mentioned in some works and a few studies have broached the question, this area of theological inquiry remains largely underdeveloped in contemporary, mainstream accounts of theological interpretation. This lack of adequate pneumatological orientation in conventional discussions of theological interpretation demonstrates a considerable lacuna and the need for further reflection on the topic.[3]

Examining conversations on the Spirit's role in biblical interpretation from the Pentecostal tradition can help to close the scholarly gap in contemporary theological interpretation discourses.[4] Because of

---

[1] Treier, *Introducing*, p. 80.

[2] Joel B. Green, 'Response: Theological Interpretation on Display: Trajectories and Questions', in Joel B. Green and Tim Meadowcroft (eds.), *Ears That Hear: Explorations in Theological Interpretation of the Bible* (Sheffield: Sheffield Phoenix Press, 2013), pp. 253-57 (256).

[3] For a brief overview of the history of this topic, cf. John Christopher Thomas, 'The Holy Spirit and Interpretation', in S.E. Porter (ed.), *Dictionary of Biblical Criticism and Interpretation* (London: Routledge, 2007), pp. 165-66.

[4] The global movement and scholarship within Pentecostal and charismatic ecclesial traditions is simply referred to as 'Pentecostal' in this work, which is recently

the emphasis on the Spirit and his works within these ecclesial communities, the Holy Spirit is given a primary role in the hermeneutics of Pentecostal tradition. Recent academic attention given to a distinct pneumatic hermeneutic within Pentecostalism has the potential to make a significant contribution in current hermeneutical debates. In this chapter, I will survey some of the literature on the Spirit's interpretive role among the contemporary proponents of theological interpretation of Scripture, then turn to introduce a few primary voices and literature on the question from within the Pentecostal tradition as an introduction to a more detailed analysis of selected Pentecostal theologians in a later chapter. In order to put this into a wider context, it is necessary first to introduce some contemporary approaches to the role of the Holy Spirit in biblical interpretation.

Spirit and Interpretation: Contemporary Approaches

Recent theological study demonstrates a mounting interest in the person and work of the Holy Spirit. This renewed interest, which is witnessed in global ecclesial and individual Christian practices, has spawned fresh attention in academic theological studies. Veli-Matti Kärkkäinen observes how this recent curiosity is echoed 'everywhere from new theological studies in the academy to publications of popular books to the emergence of new spiritual orientations and movements'.[5] Although still largely ignored in contemporary hermeneutics, the current development of pneumatological concerns, predominantly stirred by Pentecostal and charismatic movements, has influenced some theologians to address the Holy Spirit's role in biblical interpretation.

For more than three decades, Clark Pinnock was one of the influential theologians who maintained the significance of the Spirit's role in biblical interpretation.[6] He adamantly criticized evangelicalism's

---

identified as a 'renewal tradition'. It includes classical Pentecostals (the first wave), charismatics in the mainline churches (the second wave), and non-Pentecostal, non-charismatic mainline church renewal (the third wave). See Kevin L. Spawn and Archie T. Wright, *Spirit and Scripture: Examining a Pneumatic Hermeneutic* (London: T&T Clark, 2012), p. xvii.

[5] Veli-Matti Kärkkäinen, *Pneumatology: The Holy Spirit in Ecumenical, International, and Contextual Perspective* (Grand Rapids: Baker Academic, 2002), p. 11.

[6] Clark H. Pinnock, *The Scripture Principle* (San Francisco: Harper & Row, 1984); *idem*, 'The Work of the Holy Spirit in Hermeneutics', *JPT* 2 (1993), pp. 3-23; *idem*,

neglect of Spirit-hermeneutics and insisted on due attention to the Spirit's work in biblical interpretation. According to Pinnock, attending to the Spirit's guidance in biblical interpretation is essential to our understanding and contextualizing the biblical message in contemporary cultures. The Spirit enables readers to convey the message of Jesus with meaningful expressions.[7] Reflecting his somewhat more conservative approach, Pinnock considers the work of the Spirit in drawing readers deeper into the world of the text, which, he urges, draws readers deeper into the Kingdom of God and closer to God's heart.[8]

Contemporary biblical scholar Gordon D. Fee has attempted to bring Spirit and interpretation together.[9] His works on biblical exegesis and the Spirit focus on converging the academic exercise of biblical interpretation with the 'spirituality' of the readers.[10] Despite his heavy emphasis on the historical-critical approach to biblical interpretation, Fee highlights the significance of the presence and power of the Holy Spirit in understanding the biblical texts. For him, the purpose of exegesis is 'to produce in our lives and the lives of others true Spirituality, in which God's people live in fellowship with the eternal and living God, and thus in keeping with God's own purposes in the world'; hence, 'the ultimate aim of all true exegesis is spirituality, in some form or another'.[11]

John W. Wyckoff's extensive study, *Pneuma and Logos: The Role of the Spirit in Biblical Hermeneutics*, is also important to this conversation.

'The Role of the Spirit in Interpretation', *JETS* 36.4 (1993), pp. 491-97; Clark H. Pinnock with Barry L. Callen, *The Scripture Principle: Reclaiming the Full Authority of the Bible* (Grand Rapids: Baker Academic, 2nd edn, 2006); Clark H. Pinnock, 'The Work of the Spirit in the Interpretation of Holy Scripture from the Perspective of a Charismatic Biblical Theologian', *JPT* 18 (2009), pp. 157-71.

[7] Pinnock, 'The Role of the Spirit', p. 491.

[8] Pinnock, 'The Role of the Spirit', p. 494.

[9] Gordon D. Fee, *Gospel and Spirit: Issues in New Testament Hermeneutics* (Peabody, MA: Hendrickson, 1991); *idem*, *God's Empowering Presence: The Holy Spirit in the Letters of Paul* (Peabody, MA: Hendrickson, 1994); *idem*, *Listening to the Spirit in the Text* (Grand Rapids: Eerdmans, 2000).

[10] Fee defines 'spirituality' in relation to the Pauline usage of the Greek term *pneumatikos* ('spiritual'), for which the Holy Spirit is a primary referent. 'In the New Testament, therefore, spirituality is defined altogether in terms of the Spirit of God (or Christ). One is spiritual to the degree that one lives in and walks by the Spirit.' Fee, *Listening to the Spirit in the Text*, p. 5.

[11] Fee, *Listening to the Spirit in the Text*, pp. 6-7.

In this informative monograph, Wyckoff analyzes the relationship of the Holy Spirit to the interpretive process of the biblical texts. The book's central argument is rooted in the ontological chasm between God and humanity, which makes biblical hermeneutics challenging and underscores the pivotal nature of the Spirit's role in bridging the gap so as to make it possible for humans to understand Scripture. The question for those who affirm the Spirit's interpretive role is how to provide valid descriptions of how the entire process takes place – or in other words, *how* the Spirit guides the reader into spiritual understanding of Scripture. By exploring historical backgrounds and present positions, Wyckoff proposes a metaphorical teacher-pupil model to understand the mystery of his pneumatic hermeneutics paradigm.[12]

A few other studies also demonstrate the growing attention to the work of the Spirit in relation to biblical interpretation. Roy B. Zuck attempted to show how the Holy Spirit guides and directs Christians in the biblical interpretive process by suggesting fourteen propositions.[13] He suggests the importance of 'salvation, spiritual maturity, diligent study, common sense and logic, and humble dependence on the Spirit for discernment'.[14]

Gary L. Nebeker challenges the common perception of the Spirit's role either in the exegesis of Scripture or in its application. He proposes the christocentric character of truth as a third alternative in which the Spirit enables the reader to understand the text in relation to the reader's being transformed into the image of Christ.[15] He uses the Pauline parallel between the christocentricity of the gospel and its transforming effect in the new covenant ministry of the Holy Spirit (2 Cor. 3.1-4.18) in his proposal. According to him, the goal of biblical interpretation is the work of the Spirit in the service of the 'relational-transformational knowledge of Christ'.[16]

---

[12] John W. Wyckoff, *Pneuma and Logos: The Role of the Spirit in Biblical Hermeneutics* (Eugene, OR: Wipf & Stock, 2010). This was initially a PhD dissertation: The *Relationship of the Holy Spirit to Biblical Hermeneutics* (PhD diss., Baylor University, 1990).

[13] Roy B. Zuck, 'The Role of the Holy Spirit in Hermeneutics', *BSac* 141.562 (1984), pp. 120-30.

[14] Zuck, 'The Role of the Holy Spirit', p. 129.

[15] Gary L. Nebeker, 'The Holy Spirit, Hermeneutics, and Transformation: From Present to Future Glory', *ERT* 27.1 (2003), pp. 47-54.

[16] Nebeker, 'The Holy Spirit', p. 53.

Myk Habets has recently taken up the relationship between the Spirit and interpretation to propose what he calls 'a retroactive hermeneutic'. 'A retroactive hermeneutic recognizes that the experienced presence of Christ in the Spirit, post-Easter, brought to mind the life of Jesus; thereby reawakening remembrances of his life, words, and deed. In this sense, the present and the past correspond such that the present does not contradict the past, nor vice versa. This same retroactive process is available for the exegete today.'[17] Habets states that there are two common approaches to understanding the Spirit's role in interpretation: what the Spirit does with the text and what the Spirit does with the exegete. While the former is rejected, the latter is favored by Habets's retroactive hermeneutics, which draws attention to what the Spirit does in guiding the Christian community into correct understanding of the text. 'The *locus* of the Spirit's re-creative work is not the letter of the text ... Rather the Spirit's re-creative work centers on the life of the interpreter.'[18] Therefore, 'the text of Scripture, the life of Christ, and the ongoing illumination of the Holy Spirit are equal participants in the Church's ongoing task of understanding and articulating the Word of God for today'.[19]

Exploring these contemporary approaches on the role of the Holy Spirit in biblical interpretation provides a helpful contextual framework that serves as a starting point to examine discussions on the topic among advocates of theological interpretation. In the next section, I will examine some of the mainstream accounts within the sphere of contemporary theological interpretation in order to show how the Spirit's role in interpretation has been considered.

Approaches by Proponents of Theological Interpretation

Although the Spirit's interpretive work is well recognized and affirmed by proponents of contemporary theological interpretation of Scripture, only a few have begun to develop their understanding of it. In this section, I discuss three studies that deal with the Spirit's role

---

[17] Myk Habets, 'Reading Scripture and Doing Theology with the Holy Spirit', in Myk Habets (ed.), *The Spirit of Truth: Reading Scripture and Constructing Theology with the Holy Spirit* (Eugene, OR: Wipf & Stock, 2010), pp. 89-104 (90).

[18] Habets, 'Reading Scripture', pp. 94-95.

[19] Habets, 'Reading Scripture', p. 104.

in theological interpretation. As prominent advocates of theological interpretation, Fowl, Green, and Billings each attempt to broach the Spirit's work as a crucial subject matter in reading the Bible theologically. Despite their apparent differences in approaching the issue, these three studies markedly represent the general position of contemporary theological interpretation with regard to the role of the Holy Spirit in interpreting the Bible as Christian Scripture.

The Spirit's Reading and Reading the Spirit: Stephen E. Fowl
As we have seen, Fowl's main emphasis in theological interpretation lies with the theological concerns that readers bring to biblical interpretation and the significance of the Church as the interpretive community. The convictions and practices that Christians bring to reading have a significant bearing on the way they understand and embody biblical texts in their diverse contexts. Fowl suggests that theological convictions about the Holy Spirit are among the various beliefs and practices that shape and are shaped by Christian interpretation. In his chapter, 'How the Spirit Reads and How to Read the Spirit', Fowl deals with the Spirit's role in Christian interpretive practices.[20] He basically seeks to address the complex nature of interaction between the ways Christians attempt to interpret the Spirit's work and the ways the Spirit guides their interpretive tasks. This interaction depends on Christians' participation in practices that allow them to offer and listen to testimonies about the Spirit's ongoing work. Although it is relatively easy to judge the Spirit's role in interpretation in hindsight, by evaluating the longterm effects of those interpretations, Fowl contends that such a position eschews the importance of discussing the role of the Spirit in specific, existing disputes over scriptural interpretation. Therefore, in order to read the Spirit within Scripture, Christians need to understand first how the Spirit reads Scripture. It is only when Christians understand how the Spirit reads that they can be effectively guided by the Spirit in the interpretation process.

Fowl begins his argument by looking at the promise of the Spirit as depicted in Jesus' farewell discourse in chapters 13-17 of the Gospel of John. Jesus has promised the Spirit to his followers in order for them to be able to continue being faithful to him even after his departure. The interpretive work of the Spirit is crucial for the disciples to complete the mission begun by Jesus and carried forward by

---

[20] Fowl, *Engaging Scripture*, pp. 97-127.

them. After Jesus returns to his Father the promised Spirit would be sent to guide them into all truth and to bring all the things that Jesus was teaching while he was with them to their remembrance. The Spirit's activities of 'reminding' them of what Jesus has told them and 'speaking' what they were unable to bear at the time were the main features of his guidance and direction to the followers of Jesus.[21] The disciples' mission to abide in the true vine and to bear fruit that glorifies the Father would be achieved only by the Spirit's acts of reminding and speaking.

Fowl provides a Trinitarian foundation for his discussion of the significance of the Spirit's role in understanding and embodying Scripture. Although Fowl does not say much about it and it needs to be further developed, laying a Trinitarian foundation in the discussion is important for showing that the Spirit speaks in agreement with the Father and the Son. This certifies that the Spirit's role in interpretation is in harmony with the will of the Triune God. As Fowl states, this prevents misconstruals of the Spirit's work as a 'free-floating entity operating in distinction from the other persons of the Trinity'.[22]

In his discussion of the Spirit's enabling the disciples to remember the things they were taught, Fowl observes that remembrance of the past is not merely repeating the words of Jesus. Rather, it is a 'Spirit-directed-understanding' of the past in light of Jesus' death and resurrection. Fowl contends that the disciples' remembrance in different instances in John's Gospel was more of an interpreting of past events from a Spirit-given perspective on Jesus' death and resurrection than a simple recollection of events. 'The past does not simply exist as an uninterpreted collection of sense data. The past is always a particular sort of remembering. In this context, this specific "past" only exists by means of the subsequent work of the Spirit.' The Spirit-directed understanding also has a lot to do with interpreting past events in new ways, depending on changing circumstances. Fowl states:

> The Spirit's role is to guide and direct this process of continual change in order to enable communities of Christians to 'abide in the true vine' in the various contexts in which they find themselves. In terms of John's gospel, this is the 'more', which Jesus speaks to the disciples through the Spirit. Because the Spirit

---

[21] Fowl, *Engaging Scripture*, p. 99.
[22] Fowl, *Engaging Scripture*, p. 98.

speaks this 'more' in unison with the Father and the Son, believers can act in ways that are both 'new' and in continuity with the will of God.[23]

In a closer examination of Acts 10-15, Fowl then attempts to show the Spirit's decisive role in interpreting Scripture to resolve disagreements concerning a specific practical matter. Despite the general agreement by Christians regarding the Spirit's role in biblical interpretation, it is always challenging to explain the ways the Spirit is involved in interpretation in more concrete and practical ways. In fact, many would agree that one of the difficulties in dealing with the complexity of the Spirit's role in scriptural interpretation is lack of adequate practical materials. Fowl's choice of this text is warranted for its practical demonstrations of how to read the works of the Spirit and understand his role in interpreting biblical texts. Accordingly, Fowl claims that Luke's narrative provides a realistic account of the Spirit's role in interpreting biblical texts. He further argues that the viewpoints and practices of the main characters in the storyline, shaped by their presuppositions about the work of the Spirit in textual interpretation, can serve as suitable models for contemporary theological interpretation of Scripture. In short, for Fowl, this passage deals with questions in relation to interpreting Scripture and interpreting the work of the Spirit in light God's will and purpose. Hence, he wants to draw out implications from this narrative about identifying, understanding, and performing the work of the Spirit.

Fowl grants that using an account from Acts for the practical purpose of discovering the Spirit's hermeneutical significance is not unproblematic. Questions raised by historical critics about the historicity of Acts in general and this passage in particular, together with the absence from this account of any miraculous occurrences (since signs and wonders are generally taken to validate and discern the Spirit's presence and work in Acts), generate significant objections. Fowl insists, however, that the prescriptive value of this passage is more important than its historical accuracy, and argues that the presence or absence of miraculous signs cannot be a necessary, determining factor in discerning the Spirit's activity. For him, as much as signs confirm the work of the Spirit, they also require the Spirit's interpretive role to understand them.

---

[23] Fowl, *Engaging Scripture*, p. 101.

With these preliminary concerns addressed, Fowl uses Acts 10-15 as a model to highlight the importance of reading the Spirit and his works in order to be guided by the Spirit in interpreting biblical texts. The dispute regarding Gentile inclusion that runs through this section of Acts was settled through a set of practices, including listening to testimonies about the work of the Spirit, referring to and confirming the words of the prophets, and sending out the decree of the Apostolic Council. This decision was made only after Luke's narrative of a significant interplay between interpretations of the Spirit's work and Spirit-inspired interpretation and application of Scripture. Based on this model, Fowl argues that these interactions are necessary components of the Spirit's role for Christian communities to interpret and embody the Scripture.

Fowl deals with the implications of the narrative with regard to recognizing, interpreting, and acting on the work of the Spirit by drawing on Luke Timothy Johnson's assessment that the interpretation of the biblical texts in this passage was confirmed and illuminated by the present activities of the Spirit (as opposed to an alternative view, namely, that Scripture confirmed these narratives).[24] The present activity and experience of the Spirit provide the lenses through which Scripture is interpreted. Unlike a core presumption in modern biblical exegesis, which relies exclusively on abstract principles to understand experience, Fowl offers a view that allows present experience of the Spirit's work to be used as lenses through which Scripture is interpreted. He states:

> Understanding and interpreting the Spirit's movement is a matter of communal debate and discernment over time. This debate and discernment is itself often shaped both by prior interpretations of scripture and by traditions of practice and belief. This means that in practice it is probably difficult, if not impossible, to separate and determine clearly whether a community's scriptural interpretation is prior to or dependent upon a community's experience of the Spirit. Experience of the Spirit shapes the reading of scripture, but scripture most often provides the lenses through which the Spirit's work is perceived and acted upon. Even here the notion of an 'experience of the Spirit' should not be taken as a

---

[24] Cf. Luke Timothy Johnson, *Scripture and Discernment: Decision Making in the Church* (Nashville: Abingdon, 1996), pp. 89-108.

reference to an internal mental transaction, immediately perceived and understood by isolated individuals.[25]

Fowl admits that it is often difficult to read the Spirit. However, he argues that the difficulty of distinguishing between instances of scriptural interpretation and instances of interpretation of the Spirit's activity is insufficient reason to shy away from reflecting on the Spirit's work in order to focus only on the written text. Instead, debates and reflections need also to involve attention to the Spirit's present activities. Fowl writes, 'Such reduction will leave us merely paying lip-service to the hermeneutical significance of the Spirit'.[26] Therefore, it is crucial that Christians learn from Acts 10-15 to discern the works of the Spirit and read the Scripture with the Spirit or as the Spirit reads.

Fowl highlights two interpretive practices that Christian readers learn from this narrative: the practice of testifying or bearing witness and the practice of wise listening to testimonies of the Spirit's work. Those who have seen and have firsthand experience of the Spirit need to testify to their experience, and thus demonstrate how their experience of the Spirit's ongoing work confirms God's will and purpose. In this case, the testimony of Peter along with that of Paul and Barnabas about the work of the Spirit among uncircumcised Gentiles played a pivotal role in confirming God's will and purpose. The accounts by Paul and Barnabas confirm and assist the council's decision making, so that their decision is based on God's recurring interventions rather than a single encounter witnessed by Peter. The testimony was neither about what they have done nor what had been done to them; rather, they bore witness to what they have observed God doing to others – the Gentiles.

Reading the Spirit involves testifying to what the Spirit is doing in the lives of others. Fowl writes, 'Christians have no choice but to struggle, argue, and debate with one another over how best to extend our faith, worship, and practice in the present and into the future while remaining true to our past. In this struggle, testimony about the Spirit's work in the lives of others must become as central to contemporary Christians as it was to the characters in Acts.'[27] The

---

[25] Fowl, *Engaging Scripture*, p. 114.

[26] Fowl, *Engaging Scripture*, p. 115.

[27] Fowl, *Engaging Scripture*, p. 117.

character of those who give testimonies about the works of the Spirit has a significant bearing on their testimonies.[28] The eyewitness's prior experience and knowledge of the Spirit before what they witness about the Spirit's work in the lives of others render their account valid and acceptable. Listening wisely to these testimonies is another important Christian practice in reading the Spirit and with the Spirit. The final decision in the dispute over Gentile inclusion was made based on careful listening to the testimonies of the Spirit's creative movement, which led to understanding Scripture in a different way.

The skill of testifying concerning what the Spirit is doing among 'others' generates a willingness and openness on the part of Christians to enter into relationship with them. Knowing these others and forming friendship with them is a crucial move in detecting the Spirit's work in the lives of the others and in enabling Christians to be wise hearers of testimonies about it. Using a courtroom analogy, Fowl writes, 'Unlike the adversarial nature of a law court, where we look for jurors who do not have connections to either the defendant or witnesses, wise listening in the Church is usually founded on friendships between witnesses and listeners'. These testimonies are contingent on friendships that allow openness to others so that the Spirit's working is observed. Since the whole process takes time, Fowl insists on the importance of patience and the ability to refrain from hasty conclusion over the issues. 'It is only within communities that both sustain and nurture certain types of friendship and exhibit patience in discernment that we will find the sort of consensus emerging that is narrated in Acts.'[29]

Fowl's argument based on the text in Acts 15, pertaining to the importance of giving testimony to the work of the Spirit and of careful listening to these testimonies as essential Christian practices in dealing with the Spirit's role in scriptural interpretation, is compelling for its emphasis on the nature of theological interpretation as a practice of Christian community. Fowl practically demonstrates how the Spirit assists Christians to interpret biblical texts in light of his present deeds. As important an insight as this may be, Fowl discusses the issue as a generic Christian practice without reflecting on the

---

[28] In another chapter, 'Who Can Read Abraham's Story?' in *Engaging Scripture*, pp. 128-60, Fowl argues that the character of the interpreter is a vital constituent in the process of reading the Spirit and reading with the Spirit.

[29] Fowl, *Engaging Scripture*, p. 118.

diversified nature of contemporary Christian traditions. However, we cannot overlook the fact that a Christian community's openness to reading the Spirit and reading with the Spirit will vary depending on its particular tradition. Given the diversity of contemporary Christian communities, Fowl's treatment of 'the' Christian community raises questions yet to be resolved.

Spirit-Imbued Interpretation: Joel B. Green

As one of the key voices in theological hermeneutics, J.B. Green devotes a section in one of his books to the pivotal role that the Holy Spirit plays in reading Scripture theologically.[30] Here, he claims that 'Reading Scripture Must be Spirit-imbued', thus identifying the Holy Spirit as a central resource in reading the Bible as Scripture – along with other resources and procedures: 'ecclesial location', 'theological approach', and 'critical engagement'.[31] J.B. Green states that the Spirit's role in biblical interpretation is related to his ongoing role in biblical inspiration, which involves the generation, canonization, and transmission of the biblical texts. Despite the fact that it is relatively easy to affirm the Holy Spirit's role in interpretation, J.B. Green admits that explaining the way in which the Spirit is involved in biblical interpretation is a challenging task.

To approach the Spirit's interpretive role in understanding Scripture, J.B. Green develops four claims that allow him to examine the issue carefully. His first claim pointedly challenges the essence of modern identity shaped by the humanist system of thought that assumes the autonomous self. Based on this assumption, identity is perceived in self-referential terms and human dignity is established on self-sufficiency and self-determination. From the outset, bringing a discussion concerning the Holy Spirit into biblical interpretation militates against the postulation of modern identity, which in turn has had a substantial influence on modern biblical scholarship. In fact, to understand that the Bible as Christian Scripture destabilizes this misguided representation of humanity in terms of the autonomous self. J.B. Green states:

> To invite the Holy Spirit into the interpretive process is to deny our autonomy as readers of Scripture and to affirm our

---

[30] Green, *Seized by Truth*, pp. 94-101.
[31] Green, *Seized by Truth*, p. 66.

dependence on the Spirit and on the community of God's people generated by the spirit ... To seek the assistance of the Spirit in our reading of the Scriptures – our interpretation and embodiment of them – is even further to engage in a practice that flies in the face of our former, typically unspoken but tightly held, claims of self-sufficiency.[32]

Given the presupposition in theological interpretation that the Bible is Scripture, the Spirit's crucial interpretive role in the reading of Scripture ought to be intimate to the conversation. In other words, as Green articulates, identifying the Bible as Scripture demands discernible recognition of an authority – that is, the Holy Spirit – external to the autonomous self.

Like Fowl, Green uses Acts 15 as a biblical model to understand the Spirit's role in scriptural interpretation. The question of whether it is necessary for Gentiles to be circumcised according to the tradition in the Torah was dealt with wisely, first by summoning a council and listening to the works of the Spirit among the Gentiles in the mission of Peter, Paul, and Barnabas; and second by a process of decision-making that involved biblical interpretation. We find a considerable difference between Fowl and Green in their respective analyses of the Spirit's role in this passage, however. Whereas Fowl assumes that what happened among the Gentiles was something completely new, Green argues that the Gentile inclusion was not an unprecedented act of the Holy Spirit. The interpretation of the Scripture was not about discovering a new revelation not already present in Israel's Scriptures. Rather, based on testimonies with regard to the Spirit's present work through the mission of the apostles, the Jerusalem Council was pressed in the direction of 'attending to aspects of the biblical message that had been hidden in the shadows of the faith and life of God's people'.[33] In James's use of the Old Testament, what we see the Spirit doing is generating a new understanding among the Council members about how to read the scriptural witness concerning the inclusion of Gentiles in the promise of God, which is confirmed by the Spirit's witnessed actions. For Green, this is similar to the work of the 'Pentecostal Spirit' who enables the Church to embody and broadcast the interpreted Scriptures as demonstrated in

---

[32] Green, *Seized by Truth*, p. 95.
[33] Green, *Seized by Truth*, p. 96.

Peter's interpretation of Joel's prophecy in Acts 2.17-21 to explain the dramatic event orchestrated by the Spirit. He comments:

> Their [the disciples'] minds having been opened by the risen Lord to understand the Scriptures, and now, recipients of the Pentecostal Spirit, the disciples are empowered by the Spirit both to fathom the significance of the dramatic events that have transpired at this feast and to communicate their significance in ways that draw those events into the ancient purpose of God. They weave together Pentecostal phenomena, the story of Jesus, and the witness of Israel's Scriptures. The result is a community generated by the Spirit, shaped by the proclaimed Word.[34]

For Green, then, the Spirit's interpretive role works within the parameters of the biblical testimony in confirming and agreeing with its message as opposed to generating new revelation as in, for example, Fowl's affirmation of practicing homosexual Christians.

Green's second claim has to do with the Spirit's work as the divine agent of sanctification. We have seen that Green emphasizes reading Scripture as a means of Christian formation. The Spirit plays an important role in shaping readers to read the Bible as Scripture with dispositions of openness and invitation so that Christian formation occurs in their lives. The Spirit enables Christians to bear the fruit that allows them to participate in a life of devotion and intimacy with God by being involved in prayer and repentance-oriented biblical reading. Green writes, 'The Spirit teaches us to affirm *both* the knowability *and* unfathomability of God – the God who would be known and yet the God whose depths can never be plumbed'.[35] Openness to divine guidance and dependence on the Spirit in biblical interpretation involves a necessary risk, for it challenges the attitudes of skepticism and independence characteristic of modern biblical scholarship. Nevertheless, it has a positive impact in guiding biblical reading and engendering long-term effects in the Church's interpretation and embodiment of Scripture.

The Spirit who inspired the generation of Scripture and who is now involved in their interpretation is the Spirit of Christ, who is now engaged in pointing readers of Scripture to Christ. This is J.B.

---

[34] Green, *Seized by Truth*, p. 33.
[35] Green, *Seized by Truth*, p. 97.

Green's third claim as he explores the Spirit's role in scriptural interpretation. Affirming the notion of Trinitarian hermeneutic in the discussion, Green states that 'the Spirit reveals the identity of Christ and the character of God's missional agenda' and in doing so, 'he pulls us into the life of the Triune God'.[36] In fact, Green argues based on the New Testament witness itself that the Spirit, as 'the Spirit of Christ', is the same Christ whom Christians worship as Lord and who revealed God's ways in the written texts. This Spirit is the same Spirit who worked in Jesus' earthly life from his conception to his anointing and ministry in power. Green insists, 'The Spirit and Christ are related so forcefully that the two seem at times virtually to be identified'. On this basis, 'whatever work is attributed to the Sprit, including the work of reading and embodying the Scriptures, is identifiable as an expression of Jesus of Nazareth, Christ, the Son of God, and so must conform to him'.[37]

Green's final claim draws attention to an essential part of the Holy Spirit's work in reading Scripture – forming the interpretive community. The ongoing work of the Spirit through history and across the globe includes shaping the believing community to be the people of God who are engaged in reading and embodying the biblical message. Green clarifies this claim by pointing out three issues. First, the Spirit's action to build up interpretive communities cultivates participation of the entire people of God in interpretive commitment that prevents individualized or secluded readings of the Bible. Second, this allows the contemporary Church to attend to, and to be nurtured by the Spirit's interpretive guidance through, biblical interpretation across time and among churches in other geographical locations around the world. Third, the Spirit's work in forming an interpretive community enables readers to appreciate and understand the significance of the tradition of the Church. For Green, the 'Scripture only' principle needs amendment, since the tradition of the Church is a critical platform on which the Spirit allows discernment of authentic Christian interpretation. He writes, 'To proclaim the work of the Spirit in the ongoing life of the church is to recognize the importance

---

[36] Green, *Seized by Truth*, p. 97.
[37] Green, *Seized by Truth*, p. 98.

of reading Scripture in relation to the historic faith of the church and those expressions of the church that have stood the test of time'.[38]

J.B. Green's articulation of what the Spirit does and how he does it interpretively affirms the divine origin of the Bible and its nature as Scripture; therefore, in reading Scripture we need the assistance of the Holy Spirit to understand its message and to attune our ears to hear God's voice through it. By demonstrating the significance of extending the scope of conversations in biblical interpretation beyond methodological commitments, typically the focus of modern biblical scholarship, what J.B. Green does inspires more reflection on the Spirit's work in reading Scripture. Although discussing the issue takes more than a few pages and there is a significant challenge in dealing with the mystery of the Spirit's *modus operandi* in relation to biblical interpretation, J.B. Green's attempt to reflect on the issue provides helpful fodder for further reflection.

The Spirit's Varied-Yet-Bounded Work: J. Todd Billings
Billings describes theological interpretation as a practice of the believing community to read Scripture from a specified location in the context of the redemptive activities of the triune God. Since reading Scripture is perceived as a journey of faith seeking understanding shaped by a Trinitarian principle as well as biased by the location and preunderstanding of the reader, the Holy Spirit plays a substantial part in this communal interpretive practice. In his chapter, 'Discerning the Spirit's Varied Yet Bounded Work', Billings expounds the indigenizing yet transforming work of the Spirit.[39] The main question he engages concerns how the contextual location of the interpreter influences the way that God speaks through Scripture, with all the implications this has on scriptural interpretation that occurs within culturally conditioned milieus.

Drawing attention to the inevitability of contextual manifestations of Christianity in both the global South and West, Billings argues that all scriptural interpretation is shaped and conditioned by the location of the interpreter. The sociocultural context of the interpreter, either in the academic environment or in the church setting, shapes the practice and outcome of interpretation. It is important, however, to pay attention to the fact that the significance of

---

[38] Green, *Seized by Truth*, p. 100.
[39] Billings, *Word of God*, pp. 105-48.

contextual location in biblical interpretation might lead to differing normative claims, depending on the circumstances. Two normative claims that might be drawn out of the descriptive observation of culturally conditioned nature of interpretation are mentioned to illustrate this statement. One can simply determine that 'all interpretation of Scripture must be equally valid' or 'one culture never has the right to criticize another culture's interpretation of Scripture', based on the culturally conditioned nature of scriptural interpretation.[40]

Billings rejects both conclusions since they are not aligned with the premise that all interpretation is culturally conditioned, though they sound as though they are in agreement with it. He believes that the two normative claims lead to a cul-de-sac for Christians who affirm Scripture's instrumentality in transforming God's people into the image of Christ. This stimulates a significant cultural relativism and mutes genuine discussions in biblical interpretive practice toward the goal of knowing God in Christ through Scripture. However, how to deal with the implications of biblical interpretation that occurs within culturally conditioned contexts still remains a significant issue that needs to be addressed carefully. In order to tackle the issue, Billings proposes three concepts that together indicate how the Spirit works in scriptural interpretation: the Spirit's work in indigenizing the Word, the Spirit's work in ongoing cultural and individual transformation, and the Spirit's work in spiritual discernment.

The Holy Spirit plays a significant role in indigenizing God's word in Scripture in diverse cultural contexts. Billings argues that this contextual reception of Scripture is inherent to the way God reveals himself to human beings. He writes:

> Just as the Word became flesh and inhabited a human culture in Jesus Christ, God's word is properly received in a culture only

---

[40] Billings offers good examples of the contextual interpretation of German Christians in Nazi Germany and the Barmen Declaration's protest against Nazi Christians to explain the theological fallacy of these conclusions regarding scriptural interpretation. These normative claims led to conclusions that approve both the Nazi's interpretation of Scripture to exterminate the Jews, based on the understanding that Jesus was the first and greatest anti-Semite, as well as to the theological declaration of Barmen that rejects the subordination of the German Church to the state and the subordination of the Word and Spirit to the Church. Billings says, 'If we really hold to normative claims one and two, we have no choice but to say that the Nazi interpretation and the Barmen interpretation are equally valid and beyond criticism'. See Billings, *Word of God*, pp. 106-107.

when it comes to inhabit that culture by the Spirit's indwelling power. As such, the cultural differences manifested in various interpretations of Scripture are God's gift to the church, a product of the Spirit's work in animating God's word in various cultures of the world. The dynamic of the Spirit's work is one of 'indigenizing' of the Christian story in various cultures.[41]

The development of Christianity throughout the world confirms that indigenization is fundamental to the Christian message itself. Using the distinctive portraits of Jesus in varied cultural contexts as an example, Billings attributes the diverse range of scriptural interpretation around the globe to the indigenizing work of the Holy Spirit who enables the gospel to be received and become a living message in divergent sociocultural contexts. For him, the cultural variety in the scriptural reception and gospel expression is essentially the work of the Spirit. 'The Spirit enables the reception of the Christian faith in a way that makes the gospel a living message in various cultural contexts'.[42]

Billings offers a biblical and theological rationale to substantiate the claim that the variegated cultural manifestation of the Christian message is in fact the work of the Spirit. Scripture confirms that God revealed himself from the beginning in particular, culturally specific ways. The way that God was making himself known in the Old Testament was always related to the covenantal promises to Noah, through the descendants of Abraham, and then to the people of Israel. God's self-disclosure did not begin by giving lists of propositions or transcendental truths about God. Instead, we find narratives about God and his dealings with particular individuals, families, and people. This cultural specific communication of God and his blessing to the people of Israel is extended to all the families of the earth in the New Testament through the coming of Jesus Christ, the eternal Word who became flesh and took on all the particularity of human culture. The cultural particularity of the gospel message is also demonstrated as the early Christians were witnessing it with the remarkable reception of their message in diverse cultures. As Billings contends, this cross-cultural transmission of the gospel is only explained in terms of the explicit work of the Spirit. He states, 'There

---

[41] Billings, *Word of* God, pp. 106-07.
[42] Billings, *Word of God*, p. 112.

is a Spirit-enabled knowledge of Jesus Christ that takes place through Scripture. This does not require one voice in interpretation, for the Spirit is also the bond that hold together Jews and gentiles in the Christian community as one body.'[43]

The Spirit's work that enables different receptions of Scripture toward the knowledge of God through Jesus Christ continues to be demonstrated in the contemporary global mission of the Christian Church. The translation of Scripture into diverse languages illustrates the cultural plurality of gospel reception as the working of the one Spirit. Billings asserts that it is the Spirit who inspires the Church's missional commitment from the very beginning to translate the Bible into other languages. In contrast to other religions, such as Islam, which aggressively rejects the vernacular expression of its sacred text, 'the Christian tradition has generally worked with an assumption that holds unity and plurality together in biblical interpretation: the Spirit will use Scripture in various languages to bring people to the knowledge of God in Jesus Christ – and the unity therein'.[44] The Spirit's role in translating the Christian message is also closely tied to the contextual interpretation of Scripture, contrary to the assumption of Enlightenment biblical interpretation, which tends to perceive cultural particularity as an obstacle to be eliminated in order that an unbiased understanding of Scripture might occur. This indigenization of biblical interpretation is a sign of the Spirit of Pentecost that breaks through the languages and practices of diversified cultures. 'There is no such thing as noncontextual reading of Scripture, just as there is no such thing as an untranslated manifestation of Christianity.'[45]

As much as the Spirit plays a significant role in allowing interpretation of Scripture to be indigenized and fashioned by the contextual culture of the reader, it is crucial to recognize the Spirit's role in using Scripture as a powerful instrument to transform and shape individuals and communities into the image of Christ. This is Billings's second proposal in relation to the Spirit's work in theological interpretation. He argues that the Spirit uses Scripture to identify and challenge various forces and idols in the contextual culture that seek to claim

---

[43] Billings, *Word of God*, p. 116.

[44] Billings, *Word of God*, p. 120.

[45] Billings, *Word of God*, p. 122.

incarceration and captivity of the biblical message under the influences of their concerns and priorities. The Spirit's work to indigenize
Scripture is not merely compared with the postmodern sympathy to
'the other' and undifferentiated celebration of 'difference'. It is a
work of transforming individuals and cultures into the identity
shaped by the Holy Spirit through the power of the living and active
word of God. Billings writes:

> Our reading of Scripture is part of our continual transformation
> into the image of Christ. Yet this transformation involves both a
> death to our old self – a mortification of some of our cherished
> cultural wishes and conceptions – as well as rising again in Christ.
> The Spirit animates both aspects of our reading of Scripture in
> union with Christ: mortification and vivification. The Spirit uses
> Scripture as an instrument in this process of dying, rising, healing,
> and restoration in Christ.[46]

The New Testament teachings maintain that there is no culture
that is beyond the need for the transforming power of the Spirit
through Scripture. In fact, as Billings argues, the New Testament emphasizes the Spirit's work of converting people and cultures into a
different way of thinking and living that is informed by the gospel.
Despite the fact that the Spirit works to indigenize and preserve the
diversity of gospel reception, the New Testament teaches the superiority of God's work in Jesus Christ that extends beyond the multiplicity of cultures to establish boundaries around diverse cultural expressions of the gospel. This bounded diversity is the central stimulus behind the numerous ethical warnings and admonitions in the
New Testament. In the same sense, the Spirit works in the present
day to shape the Church through Scripture into a bounded-yet-spec-
ified character. Rather than conforming people to a single, uniform
cultural expression, the Spirit generates a bounded diversity that
transforms them into the image of Christ. For Billings, this is a paradox that needs to be carefully maintained. He states, 'The incarnate
Word speaks through Scripture so that our faith can become our
own, amidst all of our cultural particularity; yet the incarnate Word

---

[46] Billings, *Word of God*, p. 123.

calls his disciples to a continuing conversion, wherein the Spirit uses Scripture to reshape God's people into Christ's image'.[47]

Maintaining the dialectical paradox of the Spirit's work in culture through Scripture demands significant spiritual discernment. Billings's third proposal deals with how Christians need to engage in discerning either the Spirit's indigenizing or culture-transforming work through Scripture. Spiritual discernment is an aspect of faithful reading of Scripture as a Church that seeks to distinguish between the varied and bounded work of the Spirit in using Scripture to transform the Church into the image of Christ. Billings discusses three issues in order to clarify the concept of spiritual discernment in understanding Scripture and the works of the Spirit. First, he argues that direct appeal to experience is insufficient as a criterion for discerning the Spirit's work in Scripture. Participating in the Spirit's work to contextualize the gospel does not necessarily entail making the gospel 'relevant' to the cherished experiences of a certain culture. This leads to improper attempts of contextualization that reinforce esteemed cultural values in ways that may conflict with the aims and purposes of the Spirit. Billings states, 'Experiences must always be interpreted, and they are frequently *re*-interpreted in light of our encounter with Scripture and Christian teaching'.[48]

Second, Billings recognizes the crucial importance of the Christian Church in discerning what the Spirit says through Scripture. It is unsafe to engage in interpreting Scripture in an abstract way, detaching it from the Church's creedal tradition, its culture, and experience. Here again, Billings points out two sides of a paradox. On the one hand, hearing what the Spirit speaks today through Scripture involves careful attention to what the Spirit has been saying through history and across cultures in the Church's debates and struggles over scriptural interpretation. On the other hand, this involves openness to the fresh guidance of the Spirit who preserves the right not to be restricted and constrained in the established and venerated tradition of the Church. Billings explains:

> The Spirit always calls the church beyond itself, to its identity as God's new creation. But it is false to assume that this fresh calling of the Spirit is contrary to affirming the Spirit's work in the

---

[47] Billings, *Word of God*, p. 126.
[48] Billings, *Word of God*, p. 129.

Christian community of the past ... In Enlightenment-influenced Christianity, interpretation of Scripture is frequently seen as the task of the individual; thus is the Spirit like an ethereal little voice in the head speaking to the individual. But that is not how Scripture portrays the Spirit's work. The Spirit forms believers into a community that has its own checks and balances, both in a given local church and across time and cultures. The community of the Spirit is the church both living and dead, the church of cultural multiplicity held together in oneness in Jesus Christ.[49]

The third issue in discerning what the Spirit says has to do with the significance of reading or exegeting one's own culture. This involves a hermeneutics of suspicion with respect to one's own cultural captivities on the one hand, and relying on the Spirit's power to transform people and their culture through Scripture on the other. Billings insists that every culture has its own idols that resist the transforming work of the Spirit through Scripture. Since culture is the lens through which the world is perceived, culture is a strong determining factor in the way the Bible is received in a given culture. Billings suggests that cross-cultural encounters are a helpful way to address the liabilities of cultural exegesis, since these '[provide] both illumination and criticism of how one receives the Bible in one's own culture'.[50] Reading the Bible as Scripture does not require only exegesis of the text, but also careful analysis of one's own culture. Interaction with other historical, cultural, and social settings enables us to have a proper cultural exegesis and to discern how the Spirit works in the encounter of Scripture and culture.

Billings's examination of the Spirit's work in indigenizing the Christian message sheds light on the contextual nature of scriptural interpretation; it also works to balance identifying and appreciating the multicolored reception and embodiment of the biblical message within diverse cultural contexts without simply confirming the validity of every interpretation. Given that all cultures have the marks of human sin, the Spirit's role in dealing with cultures towards conversion and transformation is a crucial insight for the study of the Spirit in relation to theological interpretation of Scripture. To discern the Spirit's work in scriptural interpretation, whether it is indigenizing or

[49] Billings, *Word of God*, p. 134.
[50] Billings, *Word of God*, p. 137.

transforming, is a practical skill that the Church needs to develop along with its primary mission of spreading the gospel message throughout the globe. Although Billings does not deal with it sufficiently, the ongoing, fresh spiritual experience of the Spirit accompanied by what he calls 'living under the Spirit's word through Scripture' (since Scripture functions as the final theological authority) plays a significant role in developing skills for discerning what the Spirit says and does in interpretation.

Summary
Our survey indicates that the Spirit's interpretive work is recognized among at least some contemporary proponents of theological interpretation of Scripture. The essential affirmation that the Bible is God's Scripture has a robust influence on how the Spirit is perceived vis-à-vis the Spirit's interpretive role in theological reading of Scripture. To read Scripture theologically entails the conviction that the Spirit maintains an ongoing role that has begun in the generation of the writings, formation of their canon, and transmission of the texts. This recognition inspires the understanding in theological interpretation that the Spirit continues to have a central interpretive role as those texts are being read. Given the prevalent acknowledgment in theological interpretation that the purpose of reading Scripture is to hear God's voice through these texts in the service of individual and communal transformation, the Spirit's work in biblical interpretation seems vital.

Despite their own ways of approaching the issue, Fowl, J.B. Green, and Billings agree far more than they may disagree, and their voices are largely complementary as they discuss the Spirit's interpretive work. They all affirm that Scripture is God's way of communicating with the aim of conforming and transforming believers into the image of Christ. Therefore, Christians have every reason to embrace the ideas that the Spirit plays a key role in scriptural interpretation and that a priority of the believing community is to read Scripture under the guidance of the Spirit. This, of course, requires discipline so as to mitigate the forces behind the skepticism of modern biblical scholarship and its influence on a reading of the Bible dependent on the autonomous self and overdependence on humanly designed methods of reading. Theological interpretation of Scripture involves the Spirit's work beyond our human efforts to understand the biblical texts and to be drawn by the Spirit into transformed

Christian life. Dispositions of belief, convictions of truth, and prayerful openness and willingness to be shaped by the divine voice we hear through Scripture are essential elements in facilitating the Spirit's guidance to scriptural interpretation.

They also affirm the crucial role of the Church as a believing community in witnessing and discerning the Spirit's work. The Church as an interpretive community of Scripture has an important part in discerning the present work of the Spirit in light of its ongoing experiences and established traditions of interpretation as well as interpretive undertakings around the globe. Discerning the Spirit's work through time and across cultures provides substantiated guidance for theological interpretation of Scripture. The Christian community across time and space is profoundly used by God to discern and hear what the Spirit speaks through Scripture. Nevertheless, the Church's voice is not the ultimate voice it seeks to hear, since the Spirit can speak afresh beyond the Church's tradition and present-day experiences.

Therefore, the Church needs to cultivate vigilance and attentiveness through observing and hearing testimonies of what the Spirit is actively doing among believers as well as the larger world in order to discern and understand the will of God disclosed in Scripture. Despite differences in its interpretation and implications among the theological interpretation advocates, the narrative of Acts 10-15, in particular the Jerusalem Council, proves to be a key scriptural model for reflecting on the Spirit's role in interpretation. As the experience of the Spirit's work gave the early Church a primary lens for interpreting Scripture, openness and willingness to hear testimonies of the Spirit's active involvement play an important role in the Church to understand Scripture in a fresh way.

At the same time, the significance of these ongoing, fresh spiritual experiences and this openness to hear testimonies of what the Spirit is doing need further exploration. Obviously, experiences vary across the contemporary Church, which has diverse and manifold traditions. On the one hand, some churches are more attentive to well-established and time-honored traditions as a foreground in understanding Scripture – for example, the Roman Catholic and the Eastern Orthodox churches. On the other hand, others, especially in the Western reformed traditions, tend to form their biblical and theological understanding based on the results of historical-grammatical readings of the Bible. Other church traditions are more open to ongoing, fresh experiences of the Spirit and are concerned with listening to what the Spirit is doing in the present as a way to understand scriptural testimony. Pentecostal and charismatic church traditions can illustrate the emphasis given to the ongoing, fresh experiences of the Spirit and to this openness to listen to what God is doing as a primary lens through which Scripture is interpreted. Discussion of the Spirit's role in theological interpretation of Scripture can be supplemented by considering how the Spirit's interpretive role is treated in these traditions.

Approaches within the Pentecostal Tradition

Pentecostal Interpretation: Introduction

The global movement and scholarship within Pentecostal ecclesial traditions are known mainly for their enthusiasm, commitment to the person and work of the Holy Spirit, and intense passion and love for the Bible.[51] This emphasis on the Spirit is reflected in both the religious experiences and the distinctive hermeneutical approaches of those within the tradition. The pneumatological interest in this renewal tradition has considerable methodological implications that inform the way Scripture is interpreted by Pentecostal/charismatic biblical scholars and theologians. Biblical interpretation and theological engagements within this group are profoundly shaped by the attention given to the Holy Spirit in the interpretive and reflective processes.

Because of its emphasis on the importance of depending on the Holy Spirit and the value of spiritual gifts for the entire Christian experience, Pentecostalism's vigorous appeal to the Spirit and his active interpretive role is a crucial feature of its distinctive hermeneutical approach. Given charismatic faith experiences, this tradition provides a productive ground to cultivate and nurture the understanding of the Spirit's role in theological interpretation.[52] John Christopher

---

[51] Walter J. Hollenweger notes this passionate commitment to Scripture when he partly dedicates his great study, *The Pentecostals*, to his friends and teachers in the Pentecostal movement who taught him to love the Bible ([London: SCM, 1972], p. xvi).

[52] For a detailed argument regarding what the charismatic renewal as a distinct faith experience can offer to biblical hermeneutics, see Francis Martin, 'The

Thomas, for instance, argues that Pentecostal interpretation functions with this kind of pneumatological prominence. He states, 'Unlike many of their Christian siblings, Pentecostals have had a keen interest in, and a place for the role of, the Holy Spirit in the interpretive process. For Pentecostals, it is indeed one of the oddities of modern theological scholarship that across the theological spectrum approaches to Scripture have little or no appreciation for the work of the Holy Spirit in interpretation'.[53]

Despite a rising attentiveness to the works of the Spirit in theology and scriptural interpretation, there remains a relative vacuum of scholarly research on this topic among leading voices in the contemporary theological interpretation movement. This dearth of pneumatological reflection on biblical interpretation can be addressed by examining the theological method and pneumatic biblical hermeneutic within the Pentecostal ecclesial tradition. By exploring hermeneutical contributions from Pentecostalism, we will be able to address the lacuna concerning the Spirit's interpretive role and provide a sound contribution to the conversation in theological interpretation of Scripture. Distinctive Pentecostal hermeneutical approaches from the very beginning of the movement in its classical form are being invigorated and claimed by Pentecostal theologians and biblical scholars who attempt to take Pentecostal hermeneutics out of the shadow of modern evangelical, higher-critical interpretive traditions. In this section we introduce some key voices and literature that deal with hermeneutical practices and the Spirit's interpretive role from within the Pentecostal scholarship. A few of them will be treated in depth in a separate chapter.

Key Voices in Pentecostal Interpretation

Rickie D. Moore

Rickie D. Moore was one of the earliest Pentecostal scholars to articulate Pentecostalism's distinctive hermeneutic. In his 1987 article, 'A

Charismatic Renewal and Biblical Hermeneutics', in John C. Haughey (ed.), *Theological Reflections on the Charismatic Renewal: Proceedings of the Chicago Conference October 1-2, 1976* (Ann Arbor, MI: Servant, 1978), pp. 1-37.

[53] John Christopher Thomas, 'Reading the Bible from within Our Traditions: A Pentecostal Hermeneutic as Test Case', in Joel B. Green and Max Turner (eds.), *Between Two Horizons: Spanning New Testament Studies and Systematic Theology* (Grand Rapids: Eerdmans, 2000), pp. 108-22 (109).

Pentecostal Approach to Scripture', Moore claims that Pentecostals have a unique approach to Scripture, which is closely tied to their emphasis on life in the Holy Spirit.[54] Moore points out four key aspects of reality of life in the Spirit and its significance in Pentecostals' interpretive approach. First, the Spirit addresses us through Scripture in ways that transcends human reason and often works in unpredictable manner. Since the Spirit flows in ways that humans cannot control or dictate, it is essential to approach Scripture not as an object to interpret, but as a living Word to be interpreted by it. Coming to Scripture with an open heart and readiness for surprises characterizes the Pentecostal reading approach.

Second, experience plays a crucial role in knowing the truth. Although Pentecostalism is not exclusively experience-based faith, as some would want to perceive it, Pentecostals do give a strong emphasis to experience to understand reality. In fact, knowledge and lived-experience are intimately linked to each other in Pentecostal understanding. Bringing the Hebrew word *yada*, used for 'knowledge' in the Old Testament, into the discussion, Moore argues that knowledge is more of an actualization of a relationship than a mere conceptualization of an object.[55] Pentecostals' inclusion of testimony in their gatherings around the Word is an indication that they recognize the significance of lived-experience to understand Scripture for transformation more than acquisition of information.

The third key aspect of reality of life in the Spirit has to do with the Spirit's call on every individual believer to be a witness for truth. Moore draws this from the biblical accounts of priesthood (1 Pet. 2.5, 9) and prophet-hood of all believers (Num. 11.27-29; Joel 2.28-32; Acts 2.16-20). Although the Spirit bestows a special gift of teaching to some, every believer is called to walk in the light and to be a Christ-like witness before others. Pentecostals believe that every

---

[54] Rickie D. Moore, 'A Pentecostal Approach to Scripture', in Lee Roy Martin (ed.), *Pentecostal Hermeneutics: A Reader*, (Leiden: Brill, 2013), pp. 11-13; first published as 'A Pentecostal Approach to Scripture', *Seminary Viewpoint* 8.1 (1987), pp. 4-5, 11.

[55] Moore, 'A Pentecostal Approach to Scripture', p. 12. He notes that the term *yada* is used in Gen. 4.1 for marital lovemaking and in Jer. 1.5; 22.16; and 31.34 for covenantal intimacy; this allows him to conclude that knowledge is more relational than conceptual. He also indicates how this was carried forward to the teachings of the NT, referring to the verse 'he who does not love does not know God' (1 Jn 4.8) as an example.

believer has an actual responsibility and contribution in teaching the word of God and spreading the good news for those who need to hear.

Finally, Moore mentions the importance of corporate experience of faith for Pentecostals by pointing out the fact that knowing the truth involves an active participation in localized body of Christ. Gathering together as believers is a fundamental Pentecostal expression in which the Spirit is believed to speak and operate through the gifts among the members for the edification of the body. With the emphasis on life in the Holy Spirit, theology of praxis, and community's interpretive role, the Pentecostal hermeneutical approach maintains a practical view in which the Spirit takes a significant part in the practice of scriptural interpretation.

French L. Arrington

French L. Arrington is a classical Pentecostal scholar who contributed to the development of a distinct Pentecostal hermeneutics. Two of his articles, 'The Use of the Bible by Pentecostals', and 'Hermeneutics', stand out as a Pentecostal reflection on hermeneutical approaches and the importance of the Holy Spirit in the interpretive process.[56] Arrington provides a well-defined description of the indispensability of the Spirit in Pentecostal interpretation. The basis for the Spirit's interpretive role rests on a deep conviction within classical Pentecostalism that affirms the Bible as a reliable revelation of God through which the Holy Spirit intends to convey a message.[57] The Pentecostal understanding of the Spirit's role in biblical interpretation, Arrington maintains, goes beyond the conventional evangelical concept of illumination. He basically argues that Pentecostals engage Scripture with a unique perception of the biblical texts and a unique approach to interpretation.

For Arrington, beyond the grammatical and historical analysis of the texts, Pentecostal hermeneutics involves pneumatic and experiential dimensions of spiritual understanding of Scripture. This understanding is essentially pneumatic or charismatic in that the reader

---

[56] French L. Arrington, 'The Use of the Bible by Pentecostals', *Pneuma* 16.1 (1994), pp. 101-07; *idem*, 'Hermeneutics, Historical Perspectives on Pentecostal and Charismatic' in Stanley M. Burgess and Gary B. McGee (eds.), *Dictionary of Pentecostal and Charismatic Movements* (Grand Rapids: Zondervan, 1988), pp. 376-89.

[57] Arrington, 'Use of the Bible', p. 101.

relies on the Spirit's illumination to comprehend fully the significance of the biblical text.[58] Arrington identifies three crucial elements that regulate the Pentecostal pneumatic hermeneutic. First, pneumatic interpretation is rooted in Pentecostalism's high view of divine inspiration. The assumption is that, as the Spirit guided the human author in the writing of Scripture, the human interpreter needs the same guidance and illumination of the Spirit to understand the written text. Second, this hermeneutic is shaped by an epistemology that perceives knowledge in terms of one's relationship with God; hence, this knowledge transcends a merely cognitive recognition of a set of principles. Pentecostal epistemology insists that deeper insight into Scripture is realized only through a Christian walk in fellowship with the Spirit. Arrington writes, 'The believer comes to understand the Word of God only in his relationship with its ultimate author, the Spirit of God'. Third, Pentecostal pneumatic hermeneutics is guided by a concern to achieve harmony in interpretation. Clarifying this Pentecostal concern of seeking a biblical unity that is only attained by the Spirit, Arrington states, 'As there is one God and this one God is the embodiment of all truth, then the conclusion of the early Pentecostals was that there was one truth and therefore one correct interpretation of Scripture'.[59]

On the experiential dimension of Pentecostal hermeneutics Arrington points out two distinct but interrelated issues. First, biblical experiences that are directly drawn from the reading of Scripture deeply impact personal and corporate experiences of the readers. The Pentecostal interpretation of Scripture is a practice of existential continuity with apostolic believers through which believers draw experiences from biblical models and patterns. More than a historical record of God's workings among the ancients, Scripture is a primary source book for living the Pentecostal life. Arrington argues that Pentecostal hermeneutic perceives the study of the Bible as a subjective sharing of biblical experiences rather than a detached, objective reading of the texts. Second, experiences also inform and shape the process of Pentecostal hermeneutics. Pentecostals believe not only the contemporary experience of glossolalia, but also all the miraculous works of the Holy Spirit provide a parallel experience with the

---

[58] Arrington, 'Hermeneutics', p. 382.
[59] Arrington, 'Hermeneutics', p. 382.

Church of the New Testament. This similarity allows Pentecostals to identify with the biblical narratives and interpret Scripture in light of their existential experiences.

John Christopher Thomas

John Christopher Thomas takes his part in the discussion of Pentecostal hermeneutics by offering essays on the interpretation of Scripture. In 'Women, Pentecostals, and the Bible: An Experiment in Pentecostal Hermeneutics' and 'Reading the Bible from within Our Traditions: A Pentecostal Hermeneutic as Test Case', Thomas explores a New Testament interpretive paradigm to exemplify the Pentecostal hermeneutical tradition that gives a significant place for the role of the Holy Spirit in the interpretive process.[60] Pentecostalism, according to Thomas, has a real contribution to the Christian Church's hermeneutical understanding and the Spirit's interpretive role in the process of scriptural interpretation in the same way that it has been helping the Church rediscover numerous biblical truths concerning pneumatology.[61] Although western modern thinking, which grew out of the eighteenth century Enlightenment, presupposes pure reason as the key to interpretation of any literature, including the Bible, the fact that this interpretive conjecture resulted in uncontrolled rationalism suggests that there is more to interpretation than reason alone. The discontent with this hermeneutical assumption as well as the emergence of recent paradigm-shifts in the field of hermeneutics that confirm the importance of Pentecostal insights, such as the role of interpretive community, experiential presuppositions, and narrative theology in biblical interpretation, boosts the confidence of Pentecostal biblical scholars and theologians to contribute critical reflections on the interpretive role of the Holy Spirit.

Thomas highlights three important elements that explain the Pentecostal understanding of the Spirit's role in biblical interpretation. First, he considers the Pentecostals' extremely high view of Scripture and its normative value for life and experience as important aspects of their biblical interpretation practices. This view is the result of a

---

[60] John Christopher Thomas, 'Women, Pentecostals, and the Bible: An Experiment in Pentecostal Hermeneutics', *JPT* 5 (1994), pp. 41-56; *idem*, 'Women in the Church: An Experiment in Pentecostal Hermeneutics', *ERT* 20 (1996), pp. 220-37; *idem*, 'Reading the Bible from within Our Traditions', pp. 108-22.

[61] Thomas, 'Women, Pentecostals, and the Bible', p. 42.

strong awareness of the direct ministry of the Holy Spirit within Pentecostalism through various manifestations in relation to Spirit baptism and spiritual gifts. The possibility of the Spirit's manifestation through ordinary men and women makes it easier for Pentecostals to believe the Spirit inspired human beings to write Scripture and to affirm the need for the same Spirit to understand it. Second, the significance of the Pentecostal emphasis on community in general and the community's interpretive role in particular is worth mentioning. This emphasis in Pentecostalism plays an important role in producing the necessary interpretive accountability within the Christian community and resisting the tendency of extensive individualism in biblical interpretation. Finally, he points to the positive aspects of experiential presuppositions and the role of narrative theology in the process of Pentecostal hermeneutics, which is aligned with the growing concern within the Christian Church's interpretive tradition.

Thomas uses the deliberation of the Jerusalem Council in Acts 15 to illustrate the Pentecostal hermeneutical approach. As the text indicates how the early Church came to understand Gentile inclusion to the promises of God, Thomas seeks to explore the role of women in the ministry of the Church using the procedures taken in the Jerusalem Council, according to this text. Three important concepts are deduced from the model of the Jerusalem Council in the process of Pentecostal biblical interpretation: the role of the Christian (Pentecostal) community in discerning the Spirit's move through hearing testimonies and examining the ongoing experiences, the work of the Holy Spirit about which testimonies are witnessing to confirm God's intention on a particular issue (in this case, the role of women in the ministries of Pentecostal churches), and the role of the biblical texts as evidence to confirm the work of the Holy Spirit as experienced and witnessed by the community. The Pentecostal biblical interpretation, according to Thomas, has much in common with the interpretive paradigm in Acts 15 that involves the community, the activity of the Spirit, and Scripture.

Kenneth J. Archer

Kenneth Archer is one of the leading voices in the study of Pentecostal hermeneutics and its contribution to the hermeneutical undertakings of the Church in the twenty-first century. Primarily identifying early Pentecostal interpretive strategies and considering their significance in contemporary hermeneutical discussions, Archer argues in his monograph, *A Pentecostal Hermeneutic: Spirit, Scripture, and Community*, for the authenticity of early Pentecostalism and the influence of its interpretive approach in current biblical interpretation.[62] On the basis of early Pentecostalism, Archer offers a critically informed, contemporary Pentecostal hermeneutic that is embedded in the stories, beliefs, practices, and identity of the Pentecostal community. He claims that the Pentecostal interpretive approach is 'rooted in and guided by Pentecostal identity which can be retrieved and critically reappropriated within the current postmodern context'. In this sense, this approach to biblical interpretation is 'anchored in Pentecostal identity and informed by contemporary concern'.[63]

Throughout the book, Archer develops three major categorizations of Pentecostal hermeneutics, namely, an early Pentecostal hermeneutic, a modernized evangelical hermeneutic, and a postmodern and narrative-based hermeneutic. In his view, the modernized evangelical hermeneutic is Pentecostals' attempt to gain recognition by the mainstream evangelicalism, which compromises the major tenets of early Pentecostalism. Therefore, he argues that this move to the modern evangelical hermeneutic was a critical mistake for Pentecostalism. Maintaining a hermeneutical approach that is firmly established by the tenets of Pentecostal identity, Archer follows Thomas in articulating a tridactic negotiation for theological interpretation that involves Spirit, community, and Scripture.

Amos Yong

As an Asian American, constructive, Pentecostal theologian, Amos Yong is another important scholar whose significant contributions are receiving growing attention in North America and around the globe in discussions of pneumatological theology from the Pentecostal tradition. In his important work on theological hermeneutics, *Spirit-Word-Community: Theological Hermeneutics in Trinitarian perspective*, Yong focuses on a theological interpretation that is informed by a Trinitarian pneumatological approach.[64] The main contribution of

---

[62] Kenneth J. Archer, *A Pentecostal Hermeneutic: Spirit, Scripture, and Community* (Cleveland, TN: CPT, 2009).

[63] Archer, *A Pentecostal Hermeneutic*, p. 3.

[64] Amos Yong, *Spirit-Word-Community: Theological Hermeneutics in Trinitarian Perspective* (Eugene, OR: Wipf & Stock, 2002).

this monograph is an approach to theological interpretation that integrates a philosophical understanding of the world with pneumatology and Trinitarian ontology.

Having a larger vision that involves constructing a Pentecostal theology guided by pneumatology, Yong proposes a pneumatological theology that brings diverse voices to a 'consensual hermeneutic' that aims to 'develop a Trinitarian theological hermeneutic and method from a pneumatological starting-point'.[65] He engages a pneumatological starting point to explain a Trinitarian approach using metaphysical and epistemological categories. Yong expounds the Pentecostal interpretive and theological engagement as a hermeneutical trialectic of the Spirit, Word, and community. In doing so, he explains the way in which the Holy Spirit engages with the hermeneutical process mainly by illuminating human imagination to inspire liberative practices in the world.

In a more recent contribution, Yong elaborates his vision by cogently engaging in contemporary theological interpretation conversations, proposing an alternate interpretive approach within the framework of apostolic spirituality and practices from a Pentecostal perspective.[66] Building on what he started in his previous works on theological hermeneutics, Yong suggests that the Pentecostal interpretive tradition is deeply entrenched in post-Pentecost Christian reading, that is, a reading after the outpouring of the Spirit on the Day of Pentecost. He precisely argues that all Christian theological interpretation of Scripture is 'pentecostal' in the sense that it is formed and informed by the presence and activity of the Spirit poured out on all flesh at the event of Pentecost. Although the global Pentecostal-charismatic movement has a significant bearing to this hermeneutical viewpoint, Yong's understanding of Pentecostal theological interpretation is not necessarily provincial to the modern Pentecostal movement that began in the Azusa Street Revival and expanded to become a worldwide phenomenon. Yong insists that the Trinitarian theme evident in contemporary arguments of theological interpretation can be significantly reinforced and enhanced by a Pentecostal pneumatology from the vantage point of Pentecost detailed in Acts 2.

---

[65] Yong, *Spirit-Word-Community*, p. 1.

[66] Amos Yong, *The Hermeneutical Spirit: Theological Interpretation and Scriptural Imagination* (Eugene, OR: Cascade, 2017).

L. William Oliverio

As an emerging Pentecostal theologian, L. William Oliverio takes part in hermeneutical contributions to the dialogue concerning the Spirit's work in theology and biblical interpretation from the Pentecostal ecclesial tradition. In his *Theological Hermeneutics in the Classical Pentecostal Tradition: A Typological Account*, Oliverio provides an account of the development of Pentecostal theology and theological hermeneutics since the beginning of modern Pentecostalism at the turn of the twentieth century. Rather than dealing with its development chronologically, however, Oliverio seeks to use a typological approach to the different categories in Pentecostal theological hermeneutics.

Oliverio's hermeneutical project results in a typological account that identifies four types of Pentecostal hermeneutics: the original classical Pentecostal hermeneutic, the evangelical type Pentecostal hermeneutic, the contextual-Pentecostal hermeneutic, and the ecumenical-Pentecostal hermeneutic. He recognizes that these are tentative categories of Pentecostal interpretation, since all approaches may not fit into the broad categories provided. With these classifications, though, Oliverio seeks to show how different kinds of Pentecostal hermeneutical engagement began and developed so as to establish a hermeneutical realism for the sustained development of Pentecostal theological hermeneutics. The hermeneutical realism Oliverio proposes includes Scripture, culture, and tradition, through the guidance of the Spirit who makes a way for the possibility of human theological understanding.

Chris E.W. Green

A recent work by a Pentecostal theologian Chris E.W. Green, *Sanctifying Interpretation: Vocation, Holiness, and Scripture*, is another contribution to Pentecostal hermeneutics.[67] The interpretive proposal that C. E.W. Green puts forward in this constructive monograph begins with soteriological and practical concerns rather than the conventional evangelical models of Scripture and a hermeneutical strategy that begins with the typical epistemological questions about the nature of the Bible. Attempting to bring classical Pentecostal theology and interpretive tradition into conversation, C.E.W. Green argues for a

---

[67] Chris E.W. Green, *Sanctifying Interpretation: Vocation, Holiness, and Scripture* (Cleveland, TN: CPT Press, 2015).

dramatic shift away from epistemological to soteriological conceptions of Scripture. Having scriptural interpretation as the main concern of his work, C.E.W. Green suggests that reading Scripture is inextricably linked with Christian vocation and sanctification. In other words, before dealing with the nature of Scripture it is important to deal with how God wants to use it to transform the readers since the purpose of reading Scripture is not merely gaining cognitive knowledge, but being transformed by it for the sake of loving God and neighbor.

Reading the Bible is primarily a means through which the Spirit works to shape the Christian community in the image of Christ and have them participate in his priestly vocation. More than a means to gaining knowledge, Scripture reading is a practice that allows us 'to be moved by and toward wisdom that comes in truly loving God and neighbor'.[68] C.E.W. Green is critical of the historical-critical method of interpretation, claiming that it fails to accomplish this sanctifying work of the Spirit intended in the practice of reading Scripture. His proposal for a Christocentric reading of Scripture maintains that the whole Scripture, including the Old Testament, witnesses to Jesus.

Early Pentecostal hermeneutics was mainly concerned with reading for Christ and encountering him through the Scriptures. Those early Pentecostals shared a common conviction with precritical readers in seeking and finding the prefigured Christ in the Old Testament. Because of their belief that Scripture is the word of God, early Pentecostals understood the impossibility of biblical interpretation without the divine guidance and illumination of the Spirit. 'Only the inspiring Spirit can "open up" the Scriptures in ways that make a saving difference for the readers. Only through the aid of the Spirit can the Scriptures "unfold" their endless christic significance(s).'[69] Reading in the Spirit does not necessarily mean that readers are either free or bound to make a text say whatever they want it to say. Since the chief purpose of Scripture is for God to complete his sanctifying work in the believers, reading in the Spirit is rather a faithful reading that involves interpreters in quieting their own voices so they can hear what God speaks through the texts.

---

[68] Green, *Sanctifying Interpretation*, p. 147.

[69] Green, *Sanctifying Interpretation*, p. 118.

Craig S. Keener

A recent Pentecostal contribution to contemporary conversations on the Spirit's role in scriptural interpretation comes from the renowned biblical scholar Craig Keener. Keener's *Spirit Hermeneutics: Reading Scripture in Light of Pentecost* is an in-depth critical examination of biblical interpretation that offers experiential, eschatological, and missional analysis of Pentecostal-charismatic hermeneutical approaches.[70] Originally intended to be included in the Pentecostal Manifesto series published by William B. Eerdmans and coedited by James K.A. Smith and Amos Yong, *Spirit Hermeneutics* exceeded the manifesto's page requirement and came out as a 'stand-alone volume', as Yong stated in its forward.[71] Keener offers his biblical theological and epistemological reflections on the significance of experiential and global reading of Scripture in light of Pentecost in this fresh volume. He addresses the questions of the Spirit's interpretive role in an exegetically responsible way, but with a significant emphasis on dynamic nature of reading Scripture shaped by the experience of the Spirit. His understanding of the Pentecostal features of interpretation involves the significance of the Bible and the illumination of the Spirit in interpretation.

Although this monograph deals with Pentecostal and charismatic traditions, it is deliberately intended particularly to address the Christian theological context in general by taking the sectarian, in-house conversation on Pentecostal hermeneutics to a dialogue that involves a wider ecumenical community.[72] Since the original vision of Pentecostalism was a renewal of Christianity as a whole, the invitation of Spirit hermeneutics in this book is to all believers regardless of their tradition or denominational affiliations. Keener's reference to Pentecostal experience is inclusive of the Christian experience with God modeled in Acts 2. He writes, 'The Pentecostal emphasis on the Spirit in interpretation has a long history before Pentecostals; it is thus historically a wider Christian hermeneutic'.[73] He argues that this inclusive approach prompts all Christians to engage the Spirit's work in

---

[70] Craig S. Keener, *Spirit Hermeneutics: Reading Scripture in Light of Pentecost* (Grand Rapids: Eerdmans, 2016).

[71] Keener, *Spirit Hermeneutics*, p. xvii.

[72] Keener, *Spirit Hermeneutics*, pp. 1, 4, 53, 287-88.

[73] Keener, *Spirit Hermeneutics*, p. 287.

interpretation in order to properly hear and embrace God's message through Scripture.

The overarching argument that Keener offers in this volume is that Spirit-guided interpretation involves experiential appropriation that engages concrete literary and cultural contexts that are inherent in Scripture itself. He maintains that 'biblical texts are *texts*, communicated in real language, history, culture, and genres that at least resemble identifiable genres from their historical context. The shape of these texts invites interpretive approaches appropriate to their shape.'[74] Critical biblical study is necessary in Spirit hermeneutics to understand the biblical texts in the way that they were designed to communicate engaging their linguistic, cultural, and historical circumstances. Therefore, Keener's approach significantly relies on historical-critical hermeneutics, which grounds meaning in the original text and the communication of biblical authors.

Despite his awareness that the original meaning of a text cannot be perfectly reconstructed in historical criticism, Keener insists that a responsible reconstruction of the biblical narratives is necessary to understand the message of the inspired text. This is a reasonable approach for him to hear the voice of the Spirit that speaks in contemporary setting through the texts beyond merely examining them objectively. Biblical interpretation from the vantage point of Pentecost, therefore, develops a humble attitude toward reading Scripture that involves the knowledge of God's heart and a Spirit-filled experience with eschatological and missional perspectives. Spirit hermeneutics emphasizes charismatic experience, as an experience of all Christians, to facilitate a living encounter with the God of the text. In other words, Keener's understanding of Pentecostal hermeneutic is simply a Christian hermeneutic that magnifies the invitation of the Scripture to experience God's living voice in the text.

Summary

We have reviewed several important works from theologians and biblical scholars within the Pentecostal ecclesial tradition in this survey. The main contribution of the Pentecostal interpretive approaches to the wider conversations on theological interpretation has to do with

---

[74] Keener, *Spirit Hermeneutics*, p. 3.

the experiences of the interpretive community and the Spirit's primary role in our understanding of biblical texts. The emphasis on the person and work of the Holy Spirit shapes and cultivates the Pentecostal religious experiences and hermeneutical perspectives. Discerning the pneumatological prominence in the Pentecostal hermeneutics is a significant step toward filling the considerable gap in contemporary discussions by broadening our understanding of the Spirit's role in theological reading of Scripture.

For the most part, the Pentecostal scholarship tends to define Pentecostalism primarily in its classical form, although history indicates that there have been challenges to maintain its identity and the important tenets in the form of its early expression with efforts to blend with mainstream evangelicalism. The recent appeal to return to the roots of its authentic identity in the classical form of Pentecostalism emphasizes narrative-based and experience-oriented hermeneutics. The notion of the Spirit's interpretive role in the Pentecostal tradition goes far beyond the evangelical concept of illumination and focuses on the interpretive community and its experiential presuppositions as a means that the Spirit inspires biblical interpretation.

The extremely high view of Scripture and the passion to encounter God through the reading of the Bible are key motivations in Pentecostal hermeneutics. It is a shared conviction within this interpretive tradition that Scripture is God's way of addressing us beyond our human reason and intellect. This is the basis that Pentecostalism, as a paramodern movement, is highly critical of the approaches of historical criticism, although its importance is not refuted. This Pentecostal perception is reverberated in these studies with the exception of Keener who seems to be far removed from the others on the issue of playing by modern historical critical assumptions and rules. In general, these writings show the Pentecostals' strong view that the ultimate purpose of reading Scripture is an immediate divine encounter and experience of the transforming power of the Spirit to be shaped in the image of Christ. This suggests the indispensability of a robust hermeneutical approach that integrates the interpretive role of the Spirit.

3

SPIRIT AND SCRIPTURE IN EASTERN ORTHODOX AND ROMAN CATHOLIC TRADITIONS

The previous chapter discussed issues pertaining to theological reading of Scripture and the Spirit's interpretive role as suggested by contemporary advocates of theological interpretation and theologians from the Pentecostal tradition. Reading the biblical texts as Scripture, with a theological approach aiming to cultivate a meaningful encounter with the Triune God as a practice that involves the Spirit's guidance, attracts considerable attention in the interpretive proposals suggested by voices from the proponents of theological interpretation of Scripture and from Pentecostal scholars. The surveyed literature identifies the importance of the work of God's Spirit in theological interpretation, and shapes how we discern the ways in which the Spirit works in theological understanding of Scripture. That is, these studies both suggest the crucial need for attention to pneumatology in contemporary discussions of theological interpretation, call attention to certain trajectories, and provide some guidelines that help us outline an approach to the role of the Spirit in theological reading of Scripture.

Our literature survey also suggests that a Pentecostal hermeneutical approach has particular significance for this project, in that it expands the aims and sensibilities of contemporary conversations on theological interpretation of Scripture, given the tradition's emphasis on the Spirit's interpretive role. In fact, it is basic to a Pentecostal hermeneutic that it demands an accounting of the Spirit's direct involvement in interpreting the biblical texts. Central characteristics of the Pentecostal understanding of life in the Holy Spirit inherently influence Pentecostal interpretive approaches to Scripture. Scripture is considered as a living Word through which the Spirit flows in ways beyond an anthropocentric set of hermeneutical principles, interpretive practices, and/or methodological advances. This feature of a Pentecostal interpretive approach contributes to a better understanding of the Spirit's role in theological reading of the biblical texts. Taking this into consideration, the main task in this chapter and the next involves systematically exploring and engaging with Pentecostal hermeneutical contributions vis-à-vis wider conversations in theological interpretation, particularly related to the Spirit's role in the interpretive practices.

The way forward involves examining Pentecostal theological hermeneutics alongside and in light of wider theological and interpretive ecclesial contexts in which the Pentecostal tradition participates. This includes exploring the theological interpretative approaches and understandings of the Spirit's role within the major streams of Christian tradition. Although Pentecostal hermeneutical presuppositions are typical of Pentecostalism, they are not necessarily unique to that tradition.[1] As Pentecostalism is an emerging movement, its interpretive approaches have been and continue to be, in one way or another, shaped by the developments of a range of Christian hermeneutical activities. Therefore, other ecclesial traditions concerned with the Spirit and scriptural interpretation help us to identify more clearly the Pentecostal interpretive perspectives.

With this in mind, the following two chapters specifically deal with three main streams of Christian tradition as a suitable framework for our subsequent articulation of the Pentecostal hermeneutical tradition.[2] The Spirit in scriptural interpretation within the Eastern Orthodox and the Roman Catholic traditions is discussed in this chapter.

---

[1] R.W.L. Moberly, for instance, points out that the Pentecostal concerns for pneumatic biblical hermeneutic are also shared by other traditions, including the early Church fathers. R.W.L. Moberly, 'Pneumatic Biblical Hermeneutics: A Response', in Kevin L. Spawn and Archie T. Wright (eds.), *Spirit and Scripture: Examining a Pneumatic Hermeneutic* (New York: Bloomsbury, 2012), pp. 161-62.

[2] I am following Douglas Jacobsen, who categorizes the primary Christian traditions as Eastern Orthodoxy, Roman Catholicism, Protestantism, and Pentecostalism, in *The World's Christians: Who They Are, Where They Are and How They Got There* (Chicester: Wiley, 2011).

Chapter 4 takes up the Protestant tradition's understanding(s) of the Spirit's interpretive role. Because of the distinctive historical and theological heritages that shape their particular religious expressions, these ecclesial traditions have diverse approaches to the Spirit in biblical interpretation and theological tasks. The spiritual experiences and the pneumatological perspectives within the churches are main determining factors for the way each tradition perceives the Spirit's work in relation to theology and reading biblical texts. By analyzing some representative works from each tradition, we will examine the role of the Holy Spirit in relation to Scripture and its interpretation. This will provide useful resources for analytical treatment of Pentecostal hermeneutical contributions that point the way toward a model of theological interpretation that reflects on the Spirit's interpretive role in ways imbued with insightful theological concerns and appropriate ecclesial needs.

Perspectives in Eastern Orthodoxy

Biblical interpretation and theological understanding in the Eastern Orthodox tradition are overwhelmingly infused with the Church's pneumatological sensibilities. Pneumatology is one of the key features in Eastern Orthodoxy that distinguishes it from Western Christian traditions. Stanley M. Burgess rightly comments that pneumatology is located at the center of Eastern Christian theology, not as a separate doctrine but as an integral aspect of its teaching.[3] The mystical experiences and the 'spirit-sensitive theology', using an expression from Kärkkäinen, decisively shape Eastern Orthodox Christianity and inspire its understanding of the Spirit in relation to Scripture and the collaborative role the Spirit and Scripture have in its doctrine, particularly the doctrines of salvation and ecclesiology.[4] The

---

[3] Stanley M. Burgess, *The Holy Spirit: Eastern Christian* Traditions (Peabody, MA: Hendrickson 1989), p. 1. Eastern Orthodoxy's emphasis on pneumatology contrasts with Western theology, which is more influenced by its Christological interests. According to Burgess, this pneumatological emphasis in the Eastern tradition is often disapproved by its Western counterpart as 'pneumocentrism', to indicate a disproportionate stress on the Spirit at the expense of the incarnate Word.

[4] Kärkkäinen, *Pneumatology*, pp. 67-69. Kärkkäinen points out that one of the significant differences between the theology of the East and the West is the strong pneumatological orientation in the East that influences all theological foci, including Christology, soteriology, and ecclesiology.

fundamental Eastern Orthodox doctrine of *theosis* centers on the ultimate end of the whole Christian life, and scriptural hermeneutics has major significance in the tradition's teachings on deification or divinization. In this section, we explore the Eastern Orthodox understanding of the Spirit's work in the theological reading of Scripture by dealing with its mystical approach as well as the priority given to the Church and its tradition as the proper context of theology and scriptural interpretation.

Mysticism in Orthodox Biblical Interpretation

As an integral part of the Eastern Church's thoughts and practices, mysticism plays a major role in the way Scripture is perceived and interpreted. This mystical approach shapes the Church's understanding of the Spirit's role in theology and biblical interpretation in a significantly different way to the Western Christian traditions. It is a fundamental belief in the Eastern Orthodox tradition that divine knowledge cannot be established on what may be obtained on a strictly rational basis. Rather, a concrete and experience-oriented mystical theology warrants exceptional consideration of the Spirit and his work in scriptural interpretation and theological reflection.

Understanding the wisdom and mysteries of the divine is attained only through mystical experiences that involve prayer and meditation as well as ascetic experiences and otherworldliness – all emphases of the Eastern Orthodox contemplative spirituality. Explaining mysticism as the very air of Orthodoxy, Sergius Bulgakov states, 'The whole life of Orthodoxy is bound up with visions of the other world. Without that vision Orthodoxy would not exist.'[5] He describes mysticism as an interior perception and experience that leads to the spiritual and divine world. Life is inextricably linked with this mystical realism and with visions of divine spiritual world, which function as a foundation for worship, theology, and service in Orthodox Christianity. The mystical approach in the Eastern Orthodox tradition does not necessarily lose sight of the empirical realities of this world. It rather provides a means for seeing the divine sphere behind the realities of this world; both domains are real, though they have a hierarchically different value.[6]

---

[5] Sergius Bulgakov, *The Orthodox Church* (Crestwood, NY: SVSP, 1988), p. 145.

[6] See Alexander I. Negrov, *Biblical Interpretation in the Russian Orthodox Church* (Tübingen: Mohr Siebeck, 2008), pp. 140-42.

The mystical approach of the Orthodox tradition has a vigorous impact in theological reflection and interpretive practice. In fact, the very act of theology and scriptural reading are explained more in terms of mystical, contemplative experiences than as abstract intellectual activities. Vladimir Lossky describes the Eastern Church's spiritual attitude toward theology and biblical reading as a mystical experience. His main work on the mystical theology of the Eastern Church is widely recognized as an authoritative presentation of Eastern Orthodox theology.[7] For him, 'mystical theology' quite simply denotes 'a spirituality which expresses a doctrinal attitude'.[8] Contrary to the way mysticism is often perceived, in opposition to theology, Lossky views them complementing each other.[9] 'The eastern tradition has never made a sharp distinction between mysticism and theology; between personal experience of the divine mysteries and the dogma affirmed by the Church.'[10]

The mystery of the divine, as revealed in the sacred texts, is not intended to be assimilated to the ways of human intellectual understanding. Rather, it is to be experienced mystically through contemplation that generates profound change and inner transformation of the human spirit. Christian mysticism as spirituality signifies a personal working out of the biblical truth and a deeper encounter with God, whereas theology provides the necessary objectivity that inner

---

[7] Vladimir Lossky, *The Mystical Theology of the Eastern Church* (London: Plymouth, 1957). Insofar as the mystical theology of the Eastern Church as presented by Lossky is well-recognized by many as an authoritative account of Eastern Orthodox theology, as well as the degree to which it informs Eastern Christianity, it is considered as a challenge to Western theologizing and scriptural approaches, given the fact that, at its center, Western theology is more Christological than pneumatological.

[8] Lossky, *Mystical Theology*, p. 7.

[9] Often, Protestant historians and theologians disregard Eastern Christian mysticism as mere 'religiousness', rather than 'spirituality'. See, for instance, Jürgen Moltmann's comment on Orthodox spirituality as blurring the sense of the term as mere religiousness in *The Spirit of Life: A Universal Affirmation* (Minneapolis: Fortress, 2001), p. 83.

[10] Lossky, *Mystical Theology*, p. 8. The absence of a sharp distinction between mysticism and theology (in the Western understanding of the term) in Eastern Christianity can be illustrated by the title given to the Byzantine mystic and spiritual writer Symeon (949-1022): 'New Theologian'. See Burgess, *Holy Spirit*, pp. 53-65. The Eastern Orthodox Church's recognition of Symeon as a 'theologian' has nothing to do with the modern academic sense of the term. Rather, the title was given to him because of his love for piety, prayer, ascetic life, and his direct mystical experience of God accompanying his numerous writings and teachings.

experiences need. Therefore, as Lossky states, 'far from being mutually opposed, theology and mysticism support and complete each other'; 'there is no Christian mysticism without theology; and there is no theology without mysticism'.[11] In other words, mysticism in the Eastern Orthodox tradition is 'theology *par excellence*', the perfecting and crowning of all theological activities.[12]

Genuine knowledge and understanding of Scripture, according to the Eastern Orthodox tradition, is only achieved through the Holy Spirit. Since the Bible was written under the guidance of the Holy Spirit, proper understanding of Scripture and an accurate theological approach are guaranteed only through the work of the Spirit who permanently indwells the church. This is demonstrated in Lossky's understanding of true knowledge. Explaining scriptural knowledge as an encounter with the living God that occurs when intelligence is illuminated and transformed by the Spirit, Lossky begins the prologue to his book *Orthodox Theology* by stating, 'Authentic *gnosis* is inseparable from a charisma, an illumination by grace which transforms our intelligence. And since the object of contemplation is a personal existence and presence, true gnosis implies encounter, reciprocity, *faith* as a personal adherence to the personal presence of God Who reveals Himself'.[13] This encounter takes place in the life of prayer along with other ascetic experiences in the Eastern tradition. In this sense, as mediums through which encounter and illumination take place, prayer and other spiritual disciplines are crucial elements within the Orthodox Church for proper interpretation of Scripture. Using an axiom from the fourth-century monk Evagrius Ponticus – 'The one who has purity in prayer is true theologian, and the one who is true theologian has purity in prayer' – Lossky stresses the prayerful reading of Scripture as an essential practice in Orthodox hermeneutics.[14]

Church and Its Tradition as the Context of Interpretation

The self-understanding of Eastern Orthodox tradition is heavily influenced by the central claim that it is the one true Church of Christ,

---

[11] Lossky, *Mystical Theology*, pp. 8-9.

[12] Lossky, *Mystical Theology*, p. 9.

[13] Vladimir Lossky, *Orthodox Theology: An Introduction* (Crestwood, NY: SVSP, 1978), p. 13.

[14] Lossky, *Orthodox Theology*, p. 13.

with an unbroken lineage of apostolic succession to the original apostles in the first century. This understanding profoundly shapes the Eastern commitment to drawing from and deeply rooting itself in early patristic exegesis and theological reflection.[15] The perception that its theology is patristic theology, in a strong ecclesial sense of the term, shapes the understanding that the Orthodox Christianity received the revelation of Pentecostal fullness for the present time in the way that the early Church fathers expressed the ecclesial experience of God for their times. The purpose of biblical interpretation in the premodern writings of the ancient Church fathers was firmly tied to the mission of the Church to proclaim the word of salvation; this contrasts with providing a scientific analysis of biblical texts, as has become common in Western post-Enlightenment exegetical engagement. The emphasis on spiritual reading of the sacred texts, which is reading based on the inspirational activity of the Holy Spirit within the Church, is a significant aspect of patristic hermeneutics and theological reflection. The Orthodox tradition continues to use this patristic practice as a lens through which it reads Scripture and constructs theology.

Eastern Orthodox Christianity emphasizes the Church as the appropriate context in which biblical interpretation and theological activities take place. The Church, as the body of Christ, is endowed with the capability and responsibility to interpret the Bible faithfully. In his introduction to the life and faith of the Orthodox Church, Anthony M. Coniaris points out that the Church in the Orthodox tradition is esteemed as 'the custodian', 'the caretaker', and 'the proper interpreter' of the Bible.[16] Coniaris highlights the conviction in Eastern Orthodoxy that the Holy Spirit is the one who guided and continues to guide the Church through the centuries, not only in its endeavor to interpret the Scriptures properly, but also in discerning the genuinely inspired books among the many books in circulation and warranting them as God's authentic revelation. Given the strong affirmation within the Orthodox tradition that the Spirit of truth

---

[15] For an introduction to the influence of patristic thought on contemporary Eastern Orthodoxy, see Constantine N. Tsirpanlis, *Introduction to Eastern Patristic Thought* and *Orthodox Theology* (Theology and Life 30; Collegeville, MN: Liturgical Press, 1991).

[16] Anthony M. Coniaris, *Introducing the Orthodox Church: Its Faith and Life* (Minneapolis: Light and Life, 2007), p. 156.

indwells the Church, infallibility of interpretation with the guidance of the Holy Spirit is granted to the entire body of Christ and not to individual readers of Scripture. The belief that the Church provides the favorable and conducive environment for proper interpretation of Scripture with the guidance of the Holy Spirit is built on the conviction that the Bible is the book of the Church. Eastern Orthodox scriptural reading and ecclesial theology, often performed in contemplative, liturgical, and spiritual settings, are intertwined with the life of the Church where vital experience of God is attained and cherished.

In his discussion of the aims and methods of Eastern Orthodox biblical hermeneutics, John Breck underlines the work of the Holy Spirit that enables the Church both to generate and interpret its own canon and rule of faith.[17] Breck claims that Jesus' farewell discourse in John 14 and 16 provides the foundation for Orthodox biblical interpretation. The Holy Spirit, identified as the Paraclete in these passages, glorifies Jesus by bringing the words and acts of Jesus to the remembrance of each new generation of believers as the source of faith and new life. Breck states, 'An Orthodox hermeneutic proceeds from the premise, grounded in the biblical understanding of *anamnesis*, that "remembrance" is more than a simple "recalling" of past events. *Anamnesis* signifies *reactualization*, a reliving of the event within the community of faith. Yet beyond that, the work of the Spirit in bringing the Word to remembrance also *fulfills* that Word.'[18]

The primary referent of the Word of God in the Orthodox tradition is the eternal Logos, the incarnate Jesus of Nazareth, the glorified member of the Holy Trinity. The word of God in the form of Scripture and proclamation is also understood as a divine-human reality on the analogy of the incarnate Jesus. As the Spirit within the Church signifies the presence of the risen and glorified Jesus, he continues the revealing, saving, and sanctifying work of Christ through guiding believers into all truth, as emphasized in the Johannine tradition. This involves the Spirit's ongoing inspirational work to illumine scriptural truth in revealing the Father and the Son. Breck underlines this inspirational work of the Spirit as 'nothing other than an

---

[17] John Breck, *Scripture in Tradition: The Bible and Its Interpretation in the Orthodox Church* (Crestwood, NY: St Vladimir's Seminary Press, 2001).

[18] Breck, *Scripture in Tradition*, p. 12.

actualization *of the Word of God* through preaching and hearing with faith'.[19] He argues, 'If our ecclesial experience confirms that Christ, the Son of God, dwells within us to work out our salvation, it is only by virtue of the Spirit which he, Christ, has given to us'.[20]

Breck contends that modern literary criticism has its place in Eastern Orthodox biblical interpretation. This is because of the dynamic nature of biblical texts as well as the need for the reader's response to read and interpret them. Obviously, a radical reader-response approach to biblical interpretation is vehemently rejected in the Orthodox Christian tradition. However, there is a sensible reader-response approach that affirms the Spirit's inspirational work in guiding the interpretation of biblical texts within the life of the Church.[21] Breck maintains that there is a 'literal sense' of the texts that refers to the meaning intended by the biblical author and a 'spiritual sense', which is the message that God seeks to convey through the text. Whereas the literal sense indicates the author's own understanding of the historical significance of the reality, the spiritual sense denotes 'the higher, transcendent meaning discernible in that same reality by the later interpreter through the inspirational guidance of the Spirit'.[22]

Eastern Orthodox Christianity considers church tradition as a key element in its interpretation of the sacred texts. Bulgakov recognizes tradition as the 'living memory' of the Church that contains the true doctrine of God manifested in history and transmitted from generation to generation. As a living stream and power intrinsic to the life of the Church, tradition carries forward the life of the Church from the past to the present. Bulgakov claims, 'The Church has a unique life, guided at all times by the Holy Spirit; the historical form changes, but the Spirit remains unchanged. Thus belief in Church tradition as the basic source of Church doctrine arises from a belief in the unity and self-identity of the Church.'[23] Lossky also defines tradition as 'the life of the Holy Spirit in the Church, communicating to each member

---

[19] Breck, *Scripture in Tradition*, p. 209.

[20] Breck, *Scripture in Tradition*, pp. 209-10.

[21] For a helpful suggestion on the difference between 'radical' and 'sensible' approaches, see Kevin J. Vanhoozer, 'The Reader in New Testament Interpretation', in Joel B. Green (ed.), *Hearing the New Testament: Strategies for Interpretation* (Grand Rapids: Eerdmans, 2nd edn, 2010), pp. 259-88.

[22] Breck, *Scripture in Tradition*, p. 90.

[23] Bulgakov, *Orthodox Church*, p. 10.

of the Body of Christ the faculty of hearing, of receiving, of knowing the Truth in the Light which belongs to it, and not according to
the light of human reason'.[24]

Scripture and tradition are not regarded as two conflicting aspects
of the Church in the Eastern Orthodoxy. The synergy between human authors and the Spirit as the divine author in generating Scripture as well as in preserving and transmitting the written texts involves various elements of tradition and the inspirational work of the
Holy Spirit. In fact, as Breck suggests, 'rather than see Scripture as
the original and primary medium of revelation, and Tradition as mere
human reflection upon its witness, we need to give full weight to
Scripture as written text born of Tradition'.[25] Rather than perceiving Scripture and tradition juxtaposed to one another as in, for example, the
Protestant Reformation, or giving tradition priority over Scripture as
in medieval Roman Catholicism, Eastern Orthodoxy recognizes that
Scripture exists within the tradition of the Church and is an essential
component of the Church's written tradition. On this basis, it is the
tradition of the Church that provides the hermeneutical key and perspective to allow the interpretive work of the Holy Spirit. In other
words, the dynamic work of the Spirit in relation to scriptural interpretation is recognized as operating in and through the written and
oral traditions of the Church.

Perspectives in Roman Catholicism

The Roman Catholic tradition integrates the work of the Spirit in
biblical interpretation and theological reflection in its own way. The
basic assumption that Scripture is inspired by the Holy Spirit makes
the Spirit's work in interpretation essential. Three important elements
help us understand pneumatic hermeneutics within the Roman Catholic ecclesial tradition. First, we examine the official Second Vatican
Council document known as *Dei Verbum* or the Dogmatic Constitution on Divine Revelation, which represents the Roman Catholic position on Scripture, theology, and the Spirit's work in interpretation.
Second, we discuss the traditional spiritual sense of Scripture or

---

[24] Vladimir Lossky, 'Tradition and Traditions', in Leonid Ouspensky and Vladimir Lossky (eds.), *The Meaning of Icons* (Crestwood, NY: SVSP, 1982), p. 15.
[25] Breck, *Scripture in Tradition*, p. 10 (emphasis original).

spiritual exegesis based on the works of the prominent Catholic theologian Henri de Lubac. Finally, dealing with the ancient Christian practice of reading Scripture identified as *Lectio Divina* or Divine Reading helps us to understand the nature of Roman Catholic perceptions of the Spirit's work in the practice of biblical reading. By exploring these three approaches, we will be able to understand basic perspectives concerning the Spirit's role in the hermeneutical and theological engagements of the Roman Catholic tradition.

Dei Verbum: The Dogmatic Constitution on Divine Revelation

The Second Vatican Council (1962-65) was one of the remarkable and decisive incidents in the history of the Roman Catholic Church. It was a critical moment in the renewal and transformation of the life and theology of Roman Catholicism, and its significance continues to reverberate in twenty-first century global Christendom.[26] Among the sixteen ecclesiastical documents issued by the Council, *Dei Verbum: Dogmatic Constitution on Divine Revelation*, is one of the only two dogmatic constitutions, the other being *Lumen Gentium: The Dogmatic Constitution of the Church*.[27] As one of these two fundamental and authoritative documents of the Council, *Dei Verbum* represents the official perspective of the Roman Catholic Church concerning Scripture and its interpretation. Affirming that the written word of God

---

[26] The Second Vatican Council has a huge significance in relation to the Holy Spirit for it was officially recognized by Pope John XXIII as 'a new Pentecost' in his announcement of the Council and by Pope Paul VI as the 'Council of the Holy Spirit'. See Thomas Hughson, 'Interpreting Vatican II: "A New Pentecost"', *TS* 69.1 (2008), pp. 3-37; Edward D. O'Connor, *The Pentecostal Movement in the Catholic Church* (Notre Dame, IN: Ave Maria, 1971), p. 184. However, observers from Orthodox, Protestant, and Anglican Churches frequently criticized the documents for their lack of pneumatology. Yves M.J. Congar admitted the legitimacy of the criticism, although he noted that the lack of pneumatology had more to do with the nature of pneumatology expressed – which is more Christocentric and ecclesiological, given the recognition that the Church is the body of Christ and the expression of the principle of the Holy Spirit, than pneumatocentric. Nevertheless, it is obvious that despite the fresh pneumatological awareness that shapes the Roman Church's Council and its decisions, it did not exhibit a fully developed pneumatology. For a summary of the Council's pneumatological perspective, see Yves M.J. Congar, *I Believe in the Holy Spirit* (3 vols.; New York: Crossroad Herder, 1997), I, pp. 167-73.

[27] Second Vatican Council, *Dei Verbum* [Dogmatic Constitution on Divine Revelation], Vatican Website, November 18, 1965, accessed 12 July 2013,
http://www.vatican.va/archive/hist_councils/ii_vatican_council/documents/vat-ii_const_19651118_dei-verbum_en.html

is the bedrock for theology, *Dei Verbum* gives high importance to the study and interpretation of Scripture as 'the soul of sacred theology'.[28]

> Sacred theology rests on the written word of God, together with sacred tradition, as its primary and perpetual foundation. By scrutinizing in the light of faith all truth stored up in the mystery of Christ, theology is most powerfully strengthened and constantly rejuvenated by that word. For the Sacred Scriptures contain the word of God and since they are inspired, really are the word of God; and so the study of sacred page is, as it were, the soul of sacred theology. By the same word of Scripture the ministry of the word also, that is, pastoral preaching, catechetics and all Christian instruction, in which the liturgical homily must hold the foremost place, is nourished in a healthy way and flourishes in a holy way.[29]

As *Dei Verbum* specifies, the Catholic Church regards sacred Scripture as the word of God for it is inspired by the Holy Spirit and it makes the voice of the Spirit resound in the words of the prophets and apostles. Insofar as the Spirit inspires the sacred texts, the document instructs that their interpretation ought to be guided by the Holy Spirit. Given their nature as spiritual texts, *Dei Verbum* prescribes spiritual interpretation as the principle to read and understand the sacred texts. It requires that Scripture 'must be read and interpreted in the sacred Spirit in which it was written'.[30]

However, *Dei Verbum* distinctly emphasizes that the Spirit's guidance in interpretation does not work in a vacuum space that is neutral and independent of the Church. Rather, it firmly ties the decisive role that the Church plays to the work of the Spirit in correctly reading and understanding the sacred texts. Avery Dulles puts the Roman Catholic Church's understanding of Scripture as stated in *Dei Verbum* this way: 'The Bible is not self-sufficient. It does not determine its own contents, vouch for its own inspiration, or interpret itself. The Bible is God's gift to the Church, which is its custodian and

---

[28] *Dei Verbum*, p. 24.

[29] *Dei Verbum*, p. 24.

[30] *Dei Verbum*, p. 12.

authoritative interpreter'.[31] The Church, as the magisterium, is given interpretive authority, and is the proper context within which the living voice of the Holy Spirit resonates to lead the world into all truth and make Christ abundantly dwell in the hearts of people.[32] *Dei Verbum* states, 'The bride of the incarnate Word, the Church taught by the Holy Spirit, is concerned to move ahead toward a deeper understanding of the Sacred Scriptures so that she may increasingly feed her sons with the divine words'.[33] Thus, Scripture, tradition, and the magisterium 'are so linked and joined together that one cannot stand without the others'.[34]

Based on the teachings of *Dei Verbum*, understanding the role of the Holy Spirit in guiding the Church's interpretive task entails further considerations of at least three issues that shape the work of spiritual exegesis in gaining access to the meaning of Scripture. First, the document insists that spiritual interpretation requires giving attention to the contents and unity of the entire Bible. The principle that unifies the entire Bible is the knowledge of Jesus Christ and it is Christ who gives unity to the whole of Scripture and their contents. Since Scripture emanates from Christ and is given to lead us to Christ, this Roman Catholic document claims that 'ignorance of the Scriptures is ignorance of Christ', and prayerful and spiritual reading of Scripture leads to 'excellent knowledge of Jesus Christ'.[35] It recognizes that the unity of Scripture found in Christ is a crucial outcome of the Spirit's work in relation to Scripture.

Second, taking the sacred tradition of the whole Church into account is a significant issue in pneumatological reading of Scripture. Tradition, identified as the apostolic teachings handed down and entrusted to the Church, plays a significant role in spiritual interpretation of Scripture. Although orally transmitted tradition has a considerable overlap with the teachings contained in the written Scriptures, *Dei Verbum* indicates that it is through the sacred tradition of the Church that the full canon of the written books of the Bible came to

---

[31] Avery Dulles, 'Vatican II on the Interpretation of Scripture', *Letter and Spirit* 2 (2006), pp. 17-26 (17).

[32] *Dei Verbum*, p. 8.

[33] *Dei Verbum*, p. 3.

[34] *Dei Verbum*, p. 10.

[35] *Dei Verbum*, p. 25.

be identified, preserved, and interpreted.[36] Since it is the Holy Spirit who guided the transmission of both the written Scripture and the oral tradition, the spiritual sense of Scripture is found through the living tradition of the ecclesial worship, life, and expressed beliefs.

The third issue that *Dei Verbum* addresses in relation to the Spirit's work in biblical interpretation is the 'analogy of faith' or 'rule of faith'.[37] The Church's 'analogy of faith', as the established faith of the Church, is a key principle in the spiritual interpretation of the sacred Scripture. The analogy of faith indicates the importance of God's definitive revelation and the essential faith in the Church to understand biblical texts as well as Christian beliefs. To put it another way, the analogy of faith upholds the task of theology as 'faith seeking understanding'. Pneumatological reading and interpretation of Scripture are identified in the harmony they generate with the tradition of the Church, as well as the existing elements of Christian faith.

In brief, based on the teachings in this dogmatic constitution on divine revelation, Roman Catholicism understands pneumatological interpretation to be shaped by Christological, ecclesial, and theological concerns. There is a mutual influence on the pneumatological interpretation and the Christological, ecclesial, and theological concerns. On the one hand, the Holy Spirit, as the source of divine inspiration and illumination, leads the Church to Christ by shaping her understanding of Scripture in light of Christian practices and the definitive elements of faith. On the other hand, the Christological, ecclesial, and theological perspective influences the Church's understanding of the works of the Spirit and prepares her to listen to his voice through Scripture.

The Spiritual Sense of Scripture and Henri de Lubac

Spiritual exegesis in the Catholic Church is mainly identified with the 'New Theology' (French: *Nouvelle Théologie*) or *Ressourcement* ('returning to the original sources'), the most influential renewal movement in Catholic theology that arose in the mid-twentieth century. Mainly developed among certain French and German Jesuit theologians,

---

[36] *Dei Verbum*, pp. 8, 12.

[37] *Dei Verbum*, p. 12. The 'analogy of faith' – *analogia* (Greek), refers to 'proportion'. The phrase is taken from Rom. 12.6: 'in proportion to our faith'. It is mainly understood in the Roman Catholic tradition in terms of its being a rule or a guide for the scriptural exegesis and associated with the one unchanging faith of the Church, the 'proportion' of the inner unity of the entire Christian revelation.

'New Theology' was an important catalyst in preparing the ground-work for the Second Vatican Council by informing and shedding light on the hermeneutical perspectives that would come to expression in the Council. The central objective of the theologians in the move-ment was bringing about a fundamental reform in Catholic theology largely dominated by the thoughts of Neo-Scholasticism and Tho-mistic philosophy through returning to the primary sources of the Christian faith and theology, namely, Scripture and patristic literature. The movement generated significant influence in the spiritual reading of Scripture and theology of the Roman Catholic Church.[38]

Henry de Lubac (1896-1991), a French Jesuit priest who became a Cardinal by Pope John Paul II, was one of the forerunners in *Ressourcement* theology and a leading voice in spiritual exegesis of the Roman Catholic interpretation. De Lubac, one of the most influen-tial theologians in the twentieth century, contributed to the renewed interest in the patristic and medieval practices of spiritual exegesis of Scripture.[39] His three-volume groundbreaking study, *Medieval Exegesis*, originally published in French as *Exégèse medieval* (1959-61), revitalized interest in the spiritual exegesis of Scripture and provided a major inspiration to the development of Roman Catholic covenantal theol-ogy.[40] This multivolume work is considered as one of the most sig-nificant studies in medieval exegesis and theology. De Lubac provides a comprehensive historical and literary analysis of scriptural

---

[38] For a detailed discussion of the 'New Theology', see Jürgen Mettepen-ningen, *Nouvelle Théologie – New Theology: Inheritor of Modernism, Precursor of Vatican II* (London: T&T Clark, 2010).

[39] De Lubac was appointed as a consultant and theological expert to the Pre-paratory Theological Commission for the Second Vatican Council and had a well-recognized influence on *Lumen Gentium* and *Dei Verbum*, the two dogmatic Consti-tutions of the Council. He conveyed his theology through his more than forty volumes and numerous articles as well as smaller works. Precisely characterizing de Lubac's theology as this is expressed in his immense volumes as having organic unity rather than systematic arrangement, Hans Urs Von Balthasar comments, 'This seeming jungle reveals the order of an organic whole, far from a textbook theology, that unfolds an eminently successful attempt to present the spirit of Catholic Christianity to contemporary man in such a way that he appears credible in himself and his historical development as well as in dialogue with the major forms of other interpretations of the world – and even feels confident in propos-ing the unique complete ('Catholic') solution to the riddle of existence' (*The Theology of Henri de Lubac: An Overview* [San Francisco: Ignatius Press, 1991], p. 24).

[40] Henri de Lubac, *Medieval Exegesis: The Four Senses of Scripture*, 3 vols. (trans. Mark Sebank and E.M. Macierowski; Grand Rapids: Eerdmans, 1998-2009).

interpretation in the medieval Church by examining prominent interpreters and their texts. Although the dominant practice of biblical
interpretation in the Church of the Latin Middle Ages has been criticized by modern biblical interpreters as naïvely precritical, de Lubac
argues that a thorough understanding of this early practice offers val-
uable insights for contemporary theological and biblical scholarship.

In a broad sense, de Lubac's spiritual exegesis recognizes the four
senses of Scripture: the literal, allegorical, tropological, and anagogical senses.[41] The senses are different ways of reading Scripture. Generally, the Christian tradition identifies the four senses in terms of
only two senses – the literal and the spiritual or 'pneumatic', which
includes the allegorical, tropological, and anagogical. The literal sense
simply refers to the plain historical sense of the text and pays attention only to the written letters of the text. For de Lubac, the literal
sense is synonymous with the *historia* of the text, since it shows the
historical event and the literary text provided in the words of Scripture with a meaning simply discovered from the letters.[42] In its literal
sense, Scripture delivers facts that are neither 'an exposition of an
abstract doctrine', nor 'a collection of myths', nor 'a manual of the
inner life'.[43] In his spiritual interpretation, de Lubac highlights the importance of the literal sense since it provides the essential historical
ground and serves as a foundation for the other senses of Scripture.
He emphasizes that all the other three senses belong to one and the
same spiritual sense for they are "'signified not through the letter but
through the spirit of the letter'".[44]

---

[41] A medieval couplet summarizes the significance of the four senses: *Lettera
gesta docet, quid credas allegoria, moralis quid agas, quo tendas* anagogia. 'The letter speaks
of deeds; allegory to faith; the moral how to act; anagogy our destiny'. The history
of exegesis indicates that there are varied ways of listing the senses of Scripture.
For instance, Origen and Jerome used a tripartite formula, mentioning only three
senses: historical, moral, and mystical senses. De Lubac followed the quadripartite
delineation used by Clement of Alexandria, John Cassian, and Augustine, which
lists the literal, the tropological, the allegorical, and the historical senses. This difference does not matter, since the quadripartite formula divides the allegorical (or
mystical) sense into two senses: the allegorical and the anagogical. See Susan K.
Wood, *Spiritual Exegesis and the Church in the Theology of Henri de Lubac* (Grand Rapids:
Eerdmans, 1998), pp. 27-30.

[42] De Lubac, *Medieval Exegesis*, II, p. 41.

[43] De Lubac, *Medieval Exegesis*, II, p. 44.

[44] De Lubac, *Medieval Exegesis*, II, p. 127.

The allegorical sense of Scripture perceives the historical facts of the literal sense in light of their mystical significance in Christ and the Church. It refers to the meaning hidden underneath the surface of the written letters in the text, which is the mystery (*mysterium*) of the text in the Christian sense of the word. The basic principle here is that the allegorical sense of Scripture is located not necessarily in the written text, but in the realities of which the text speaks. In other words, the allegory is found not in the history as narrative, but in the event narrated by the history.[45] Therefore, biblical allegory is fundamentally *allegoria facti et dicti*, allegory of deed and word. De Lubac explains the correlation between the events and their narration by saying that Scripture is doubly the word of God, since God speaks in words about what he has already spoken in deeds. He states, 'There are indeed symbols in the Bible, just as in other human books. But only the Bible in truth contains mysteries. It alone is to transmit the memory of allegorical deeds, whose reality is divinely guaranteed.'[46] In other words, de Lubac explains that in allegorical reading of Scripture one needs to read the Old Testament in light of its historical fulfillment in Christ to make sense of it. This reading is not arbitrarily imposed on the text; rather, it is a reading with the understanding of the historical facts concerning the incarnation of the Son of God.

The tropological sense refers to the application of the moral lessons that can be drawn from the biblical texts. Using the broadest sense of the word 'trope' as a figure of speech or 'a speech turned around', de Lubac understands *tropologia* to suggest a moral conversion. He insists on the importance of scrutinizing the Scriptures not only to extract the mystical sense, but also to draw out the moral sense out of them. Since it belongs to the spiritual understanding of Scripture, the exposition of the moral sense necessarily involves the mystical or allegorical reading of the Scriptures. Although the allegorical sense is related to faith and contributes to the development of dogma, the tropological sense contributes to Christian anthropology and morality. As an integral part and subjective aspect of the allegorical sense, the moral sense elaborates and completes the mystical reading of Scripture. The morality that develops out of the allegorical sense is not just any morality, but it is a morality perceived

---

[45] De Lubac, *Medieval Exegesis*, II, p. 86.
[46] De Lubac, *Medieval Exegesis*, II, p. 89.

through a Christian anthropological perspective. De Lubac states, 'If allegory, starting from the facts of history, envisions the mystical body in its head or in its totality, tropology envisions it in each of its members'.[47] In other words, the allegorical sense refers to the Church as a collective body of Christians and the tropological sense indicates the individual members in the body of the Church.

The fourth sense, anagogical, is concerned with the eschatological significance of the scriptural texts. This interpretation seeks to understand the texts of Scripture in light of the future consummation of everything in Christ at his final coming. To explain the anagogical sense, de Lubac relates all the senses of Scripture with the threefold advent of Christ. The first advent of Christ, as humble and hidden, is represented by the allegorical sense, since it interprets the literal historical event in reference to Christ and the Church. The tropological sense signifies the coming of Christ, the Second Advent, to the hearts of individuals. The final advent is represented by the anagogical sense, which refers to the final triumphant return of Christ in his glory. De Lubac observes that the anagogical sense has two types; one is objective and doctrinal the other one subjective and contemplative. The first is eschatological and defined by its object and the second one is mystical and explained in the way it understands the object. The significance of the two orientations of the anagogical sense is the identification of the Church in heaven with the Church on earth. In other words, the anagogical sense views realities and events and interprets Scripture in terms of their eternal significance in order that this eschatological sense facilitates the unity of de Lubac's doctrine of the four senses of Scripture.

Although the principle of the four senses of Scripture has been a longstanding patristic and medieval practice of the Church, de Lubac's presentation of it as a Roman Catholic interpretation intensifies it and provides a substantial contribution to the contemporary understanding of pneumatic interpretation of Scripture and the Spirit's interpretive role in scriptural reading. His spiritual exegesis suggests that reading Scripture involves following the guidance of the Spirit and listening to his voice through the texts more than merely attempting to understand the literal historical sense of the Bible. He states,

---

[47] De Lubac, *Medieval Exegesis*, II, p. 132.

One ought not to imagine the sacred text as harboring completely formed sequences of meaning more or less ready to allow themselves to be discovered. The Spirit communicates to it a virtuality without limits: hence it involves infinitely possible degrees of depth. No more than it is the case that the world is created once and for all, is this true of that other world, Scripture: the Spirit is still 'creating' it each day so to speak to the extent that he 'is working' it. By a marvelous and rigorous proportion, he 'expands' it to the measure that he expands the understanding of the one who receives it.[48]

As de Lubac suggests, both the literal and the spiritual senses, despite the successive acts involved in them, constitute one Christian exegetical practice. The Spirit, as the giver of Scripture and the one who makes it possible to grasp it, has a considerable part in de Lubac's theology of spiritual exegesis.

Lectio Divina: Divine Reading of Scripture
Another interpretive practice that characterizes pneumatic hermeneutics in Roman Catholicism is the traditional Benedictine practice, *Lectio Divina*. *Lectio Divina* or 'Divine Reading' is an ancient Christian custom identified as a sacred reading of Scripture. As an early patristic and monastic tradition, though not exclusive to the monks and the friars, *Lectio Divina* is a practice of reading Scripture either as an individual or at a communal level within the context of prayer and the liturgy of the Word. *Lectio Divina* is considered as a 'method-less method' for it is less controlled and structured and is more of a spontaneous dialogue between the written biblical word and life experience.[49] Although there are various ways and forms of performing *Lectio Divina*, the fundamental principle involved in the practice is that it is an encounter with God through the words of Scripture. Inspired by the basic principles of reading Scripture in the Jewish tradition, *Lectio Divina* is a practice that can be traced back to Origen in the third century, a practice that fosters deeper engagement with the

---

[48] De Lubac, *Medieval Exegesis*, II, p. 205.
[49] Thomas Keating, *The Better Part: Stages of Contemplative Living* (New York: Continuum, 2000), pp. 31-48. See also Thelma Hall, *Too Deep for Words: Rediscovering Lectio Divina* (New York: Paulist, 1988), pp. 9-10.

word of God so as to enter into God's presence and prepare a pathway for him into the hearts of the readers.[50]

Enzo Bianchi, a key voice in monastic and Christian spirituality, comments that *Lectio Divina* is not an intellectual or theological analysis of Scripture, although it involves study as part of the practice. More than a written document that seeks cognitive understanding, Scripture is regarded in this tradition as a living word that demands faith and obedience. The disposition of the readers in this practice is more of a communion with Christ, the living Word, through the written texts than an acquiring of academic information from the Bible as literal and historical manuscript. Bianchi writes, '*Lectio Divina,* whether by ourselves or in community, requires a context of faith and prayer. We start in silence, confessing our faith that the Lord is speaking to us today through the biblical page. We invoke the Holy Spirit and open ourselves in humility to his action, because insight into the text is a Spirit-led event, not an intellectual pursuit'.[51]

As an act of spiritual reading, *Lectio Divina* identifies invoking the Holy Spirit as a key posture or attitude in the liturgy. The assumption is that the Holy Spirit is the crucial hermeneutical key to interpret the words of Scripture in the way of encountering the living God through the practice of prayerful reading. Bianchi states,

> With its words and silences, Scripture wants to guide readers to a way of knowing Christ that is the Spirit's work and the fruit of spiritual interpretation … It is the gift of the Spirit that gives Jesus' disciples insight into the words he has spoken, and into scriptural words. The Spirit is also the interpreter of what Christ left unspoken, inspiring his disciples throughout history to be faithful to the Gospel in creative, not literal or legalistic, ways.[52]

---

[50] Pope Benedict XVI recognizes Origen (184/185 – 253/254) as the one who invented *Lectio Divina* in his *General Audience* in 2007, quoting Origen's letter to Gregory of Neocaesarea. He states, 'The "primordial role" played by Origen in the history of *Lectio Divina* instantly flashes before one's eyes'. Bishop Ambrose of Milan, who learned from Origen's works to interpret the Scriptures, later introduced them into the West to hand them on to Augustine and to the monastic tradition that followed (Benedict XVI, 'General Audience,' 2 May 2007, accessed 25 June 2015, http://w2.vatican.va/content/benedict-xvi/en/audiences/2007/documents/hf_ben-xvi_aud_20070502.html).

[51] Enzo Bianchi, *Lectio Divina: From God's Word to Our Lives* (London: SPCK, 2015), p. 90.

[52] Bianchi, *Lectio Divina*, pp. 7-8.

In this sense, invoking the Spirit at the very beginning of *Lectio Divina* is a way of cultivating the ability to listen deeply with the ears of the heart.

The actual practice of *Lectio Divina* involves four consecutive moments. The first step is *lectio*, which refers to an attentive 'reading' of the scriptural passage slowly, reverently, and gradually, several times, to achieve a reasonable understanding of the text. It is a careful reading of Scripture whereby the reader's attention is fully engaged. Although *Lectio Divina* is known as a reading practice and the first stage involves careful reading of texts, it is more a listening to the inner voice of the Holy Spirit through the Scripture than a mere reading. The reading of the text is followed by the second step, which is *meditatio* or 'meditation', a process by which the reader ponders and meditates on the scriptural passage. By meditation, the reader enters into the inner parts of the text through an imagination and identification with the characters and the movement in the passage. It is an innermost conversational reasoning process in which words and events are prayerfully pondered and reflected upon. *Oratio* or 'prayer' is the next step in *Lectio Divina*, and it flows spontaneously from *meditatio*. It is the heart's response and a returning to God inspired by the reflection of the scriptural reading that may include thanksgiving, repentance, need for reconciliation, confidence, love, intercession, etc. The final stage, *contemplatio* or 'contemplation', is tantamount to resting in God where the participant releases her own thoughts and ideas in order to listen to God from within at the deepest level of the heart. As Bianchi explains, 'Contemplation is when the mind is in some sort lifted up to God and held above itself, so that it tastes the joys of everlasting sweetness'.[53] With these four moments of divine reading,

---

[53] Bianchi, *Lectio Divina*, p. 90. The four stages of *Lectio Divina* are summarized by the medieval writer Guigo II the Carthusian in his *The Ladder of Monks*: 'Reading is the careful study of the Scriptures, concentrating all one's powers on it. Meditation is the busy application of the mind to seek with the help of one's own reason for knowledge of hidden truth. Prayer is the heart's devoted turning to God to drive away evil and obtain what is good. Contemplation is when the mind is in some sort lifted up to God and held above itself, so that it tastes the joys of everlasting sweetness ... Reading seeks for the sweetness of a blessed life, meditation perceives it, prayer asks for it, contemplation tastes it. Reading, as it were, puts food whole into the mouth, meditation chews it and breaks it up, prayer extracts its flavor, contemplation is the sweetness itself, which gladdens and refreshes. Reading works on the outside meditation on the pith: prayer asks for what we long for, contemplation gives us delight in the sweetness which we have found' (*The Ladder*

Lectio Divina provides an important exemplar of pneumatic interpretation of Scripture in the Roman Catholic tradition.

Summary

In this chapter, I have discussed pneumatic hermeneutical approaches within the Eastern Orthodox and Roman Catholic traditions. Both traditions have a distinct historical and theological background that shapes the way they perceive the Spirit's role in theological reflection and biblical interpretation. The prominently mystical approach in Eastern Orthodoxy deeply influences its understanding of spiritual reading of Scripture in a different way than the religious tradition of Roman Catholicism. However, the strong affirmation that Scripture is an original and authentic means of divine revelation that demands the Holy Spirit's interpretive guidance is a significant emphasis in both Christian traditions.

The strict pneumatological sensibility in the Eastern Orthodox tradition characterizes its biblical interpretation as a contemplative prayerful practice rather than a cognitive intellectual engagement. Reading the Bible in the Eastern tradition is a divine encounter that eventually leads to a profound inward transformation of the human spirit. The aspiration to perceive divine truth beyond the reality of this world orients the deep-seated pneumatic character of biblical interpretation within the Orthodox Christianity. Its theology strongly affirms the Church and tradition as the proper context within which the Spirit's interpretive guidance takes place. The Spirit provides illumination of Scripture through the Church's tradition and its liturgical setting, so it experiences and enjoys the divine truth and reality.

The Catholic approach also considers the Church to be the appropriate interpretive context, although it gives more interpretive authority to the Church than its Orthodox counterpart. Based on the dogmatic constitution of divine revelation, the Roman Catholic spiritual interpretation involves Christological, ecclesial, and theological elements. The Christological concern maintains that Christ is the unifying principle of the biblical canon and knowledge of him through Scripture is the ultimate goal of spiritual reading. The orally

---

of Monks: A Letter on the Contemplative Life and Twelve Meditations [trans. Edmund Colledge and James Walsh; Kalamazoo, MI: Cistercian Publications, 1981], pp. 68-69).

transmitted ecclesial tradition as reflected in the beliefs and worship of the Church is another key issue in the Church's spiritual exegesis. The 'rule of faith', in which the Spirit guides the Church's journey of faith seeking understanding through the sacred texts is also a significant theological concern in Roman Catholicism. There is a mutual influence between the Spirit's interpretive work and these three elements that maintains the principle of the Roman Catholic spiritual interpretation. As de Lubac's spiritual exegesis suggests, the Spirit guides the Church to listen to God's voice beyond reading the literal historical sense of Scripture. This is illustrated by the practice of Lectio Divina as listening to the Spirit through the reading of Scripture.

Clearly, the Spirit's interpretive role has real significance for both the Eastern Orthodox and the Roman Catholic interpretive traditions. Dealing with these ecclesial traditions not only provides a helpful contextual background to the Spirit's role in theological interpretation, but it also explains the fundamental importance of the issue and offers a practical demonstration within the context of Christian communities. Given the fact that these two traditions represent major streams of the Christian Church, the approaches within these communities directly or indirectly influence other Christian traditions, including the Pentecostal Churches.

4

SPIRIT AND SCRIPTURE IN THE PROTESTANT TRADITION

Given the historical and theological diversities within the Christian Churches identified as Protestant, a variety of appropriations exist concerning the doctrine of Scripture and the Spirit's work in interpretation and theological activities. In this chapter I will discuss selected Protestant perspectives on the interplay between the Spirit and interpretation of Scripture. Because of its historical and theological significance, the sixteenth century Reformation and subsequent developments in Western Christianity primarily characterize the Protestant tradition and its distinctive biblical interpretation. The persistent claim of *sola Scriptura* in the Reformation movement symbolizes the Reformers' high view of the Bible and its supreme authority in all matters of doctrine and practice in early Protestantism. The essence of this claim arose from the Reformers' deep conviction that Scripture does not require the teaching authority of the Church to make it meaningful and understandable because of its competence for self-interpretation. Based on their doctrine of the perspicuity or clarity of Scripture, the Reformers insist that the meaning of biblical texts can be clear to the ordinary reader without seeking the interpretive framework of church tradition. The crucial importance of the papacy and the magisterium for Roman Catholic interpretation of the sacred texts was strongly criticized by the Protestant Reformation owing to this insistence on the perspicuity and self-sufficiency of the Bible. Accordingly, the principle of *sola Scriptura* is a key issue that distinguishes Protestants from Roman Catholics – and even Eastern

Orthodox Christians, though by ancillary implication – who place a significant weight on church tradition as a rule of faith for understanding Scripture.

Protestantism, for the past five centuries, has passed through several stages of development that resulted in assorted denominational clusters in different parts of the world. Admittedly, the fragmentation among Christian groups considered Protestant makes it laborious, if not impossible, to deal with Protestantism as if it were a single denomination or ecclesial tradition. However, among other common features in Protestant denominations, the appeal to the Bible as the final authority and the emphasis on its sole significance for doctrine and Christian life, as well as the self-sufficiency of its interpretation, occupies a rather stable place at the heart of most Protestant hermeneutical approaches. As the only authoritative voice of God and the means through which God's will and purpose are disclosed, Scripture is central in the lives and doctrines of Protestant churches and believers. Although other authorities for Christian life and commitment are not denied, they are generally given a subordinate position to Scripture, for Scripture is believed to be the only rule of faith (*sola fidei regula*) according to the hermeneutical principles of Protestant traditions.

Insofar as Scripture is affirmed as the voice of God in Protestant theological traditions, Protestantism recognizes a correlation between the Spirit and the Word. The Protestant doctrine of inspiration strongly affirms the Spirit's providential guidance in the inscription, compilation, and determination of the biblical canon. Although it is not as extensively articulated and expounded as the doctrine of inspiration, there is a reasonable understanding in the Protestant churches that the Spirit has an important role in the interpretation of the biblical texts as well. Based on the biblical promises of the Spirit's role as guiding Jesus' followers into all truth (e.g. John 14, 16), Protestant traditions recognize that the Spirit has an ongoing role in revealing scriptural truth. The Westminster Confession of Faith, for instance, concludes its section on the Holy Scripture by affirming this ongoing work of the Holy Spirit: 'The supreme judge by which all controversies of religion are to be determined, and all decrees of councils, opinions of ancient writers, doctrines of men, and private spirits, are to be examined, and in whose sentence we are to rest, can be no other but the Holy Spirit speaking in the Scripture'.[1] This kind of recognition within the Protestant churches is grounded on the assertion that the same Spirit, who worked in the past to generate and preserve, as well as to provide the means for the universal transmission of the sacred texts, also works in the present to provide perpetual clarification and understanding of the same texts.

Since they are mainly characterized by the Reformation events and subsequent theological vision, one way to understand the Protestant approaches in relation to the Spirit's interpretive role is to take a closer look at the thoughts of prominent Reformation and later theologians whose ideas were shaped by the Reformation principle. Three Protestant theologians from the sixteen, seventeen, and eighteen centuries are selected for this project because of their relative emphasis on the Spirit's work in relation to biblical interpretation as well as the ongoing influence of their thought on subsequent generations of the Protestant tradition and beyond. John Calvin (1509-1564) is one of the major figures in theology and biblical interpretation in Christian tradition. He is recognized as a great theologian and biblical scholar with a well-established reputation even beyond the Reformed circle. Born half a century after Calvin's death, John Owen (1616-1683) also left a legacy as an influential theologian and a leading voice from the Puritan tradition. Both Calvin and Owen made significant theological contributions regarding the Spirit's interpretive role in understanding Scripture. By examining their approaches to the illuminative work of the Holy Spirit, we can better understand the way the Protestant tradition correlates Spirit and Scripture in theology and biblical interpretation.

John Wesley (1703-1791) is another Protestant theologian under consideration in this project, and he has special importance for our discussion in two ways. First, his thought and influence make a substantial contribution, like Calvin and Owen, to the topic of the Spirit and his role in the interpretation of Scripture both for the Wesleyan and the wider Protestant tradition. Second, since the Wesleyan-Holiness tradition is considered to be a primary root for Pentecostalism, Wesley's interpretive approach provides a contextual background for perspectives within the Pentecostal tradition. Understanding Wesley

---

[1] John Macpherson, *Westminster Confession of Faith*, 1.10. (Edinburgh: T&T Clark, 1907), p. 41.

and his successive tradition as background is helpful as a backdrop for a careful exploration of Pentecostal interpretive engagements. It is, therefore, crucial to deal with Wesley's pneumatology and his approach to the Spirit's role in theology and biblical interpretation. Before providing a brief survey of the approaches of the three selected Protestant theologians on the Spirit's role in theology and biblical interpretation, a few comments about the concepts of divine illumination and the internal testimony of the Spirit within the Protestant theological perspectives are in order.

Divine Illumination and Internal Testimony of the Spirit

In a general sense, divine illumination and internal testimony of the Spirit (*testimonium Spiritus Sancti internum*) are key doctrines that convey the Spirit's role in Protestant hermeneutical approaches. The key difference between the two doctrines can be described in terms of the emphasis illumination gives to the actual interpretation of Scripture and the focus of *testimonium* on the readers' certainty of it as the word of God. The doctrine of divine illumination denotes the special ministry of the Holy Spirit to enlighten readers to understand the spiritual meaning of the written word of God. For its part, the doctrine of internal testimony of the Spirit has two aspects that have more to do with the Spirit's internal witness that affirms the authority and reliability of the Bible as the word of God on the one hand and the assurance of faith and salvation of the believer on the other. In other words, the doctrine of illumination refers to the Holy Spirit's assistance in helping the reader to attain clarity in understanding the spiritual meaning of Scripture, whereas the *testimonium* focuses on the internal conviction that the Spirit provides for the trustworthiness of the Bible. Although the two doctrines are perceived as distinct doctrinal principles in the Protestant interpretive tradition, they overlap significantly in the way they are explained in relation to the reading of Scripture. Because of this overlap in the doctrines, they are commonly perceived as kin to each other, as two sides of a coin in doctrinal discussions within the Protestant hermeneutical framework.

The significance of the Spirit's role in illumination has not been given a thorough analysis in major textbooks on contemporary Protestant biblical interpretation. Nevertheless, the fact that it is mentioned at all illustrates an essential recognition of the Spirit's role in the Protestant hermeneutical approaches. For instance, in his *Protestant Biblical Interpretation*, Bernard Ramm acknowledged the Spirit's role in biblical illumination by simply stating, 'The function of the Spirit is not to communicate new truth or to instruct in *matters unknown*, but to illuminate what is revealed in Scripture'.[2] Grant R. Osborne also states, 'The "illumination" of the interpreter is one aspect of the larger ministry of the Holy Spirit in bringing people to regeneration and daily growth in their Christian life. It is that portion of the "internal testimony" that relates to understanding and applying God's revealed Word.'[3] However, it is surprising that contemporary Protestant biblical interpretations do not deal in more depth with the doctrine of illumination, typically mentioning its interpretive importance only in passing.

Despite this deficit, the doctrine of illumination remains important for our understanding of the relation of the Spirit and Scripture in the Protestant tradition. The notion underpinning this doctrine is the Augustinian teaching of total human depravity as a result of the Adamic fall, which made it impossible for human minds to understand divine things without external, special, and supernatural enlightenment. This means that divine illumination is not aimed in the Protestant interpretation to address a certain lack in the character of the biblical text; rather, it is due to the spiritual blindness of fallen humanity. The doctrine is significantly intertwined with the Spirit's work of regeneration that produces a fundamental spiritual change of heart and reorientation of mind that begins in faith and repentance. Illumination is the enlightenment of the mind and impartation of the Spirit to acquire spiritual knowledge and understanding. Clarifying the concept of divine illumination, J.I. Packer writes, 'It is not a giving of new revelation, but a work within us that enables us to grasp and to love the revelation that is there before us in the biblical text as heard and read, and as explained by teachers and writers'.[4] Fred H. Klooster also describes illumination in terms of its concern

---

[2] Bernard Ramm, *Protestant Biblical Interpretation: A Textbook of Hermeneutics for Conservative Protestants* (Grand Rapids: Baker, 1956), p. 18.

[3] Grant R. Osborne, *The Hermeneutical Spiral: A Comprehensive Introduction to Biblical Interpretation* (Downers Grove, IL: InterVarsity, 2006), p. 436.

[4] J.I. Packer, 'Illumination', in *Concise Theology: A Guide to Historic Christian Beliefs* (Wheaton, IL: Tyndale, 1993), p. 154.

with 'the correlation of Word and Spirit and the correlation of the Spirit's activity and human activity'.[5]

Klooster observes that illumination can be used in either broad or narrow senses.[6] He mentions that illumination should not necessarily be understood as an umbrella term for the work of the Spirit, including regeneration, conversion, faith, internal testimony, and sanctification, although it cannot be divorced from these activities of the Spirit since it includes aspects of these. He states, 'One should attempt to be as precise as possible, that is, as precise as the scriptural givens warrant, in describing the nature of illumination. At the same time one should avoid the danger of isolating illumination from the broader context of the Spirit's ministry to renewing the children of God.'[7] Having this in mind, without restricting the doctrine only to the context of reading the Bible, divine illumination in the Protestant interpretive approach is primarily understood in relation to the Spirit's work in the interpretation of Scripture. It is perceived as a crucial element for discerning the meaning of the Spirit-breathed Scripture.

Although it was not the primary influence on Protestant understandings of the doctrine as it was in the medieval thinkers, it is helpful to mention Augustine's illumination theory and his philosophy of knowledge in the discussion of the doctrine of divine illumination so as to understand the essence and usage of the term.[8] Augustine's epistemology profoundly involves divine illumination in human understanding of truth and is grounded in three premises: the nature of God as light and as the source of human illumination, the intelligibility of divine truth, and the possibility of human understanding of divine truth that is contingent on God's illumination. In his description of divine illumination, Augustine writes that '[the mind] needs to be enlightened by another light in order to be a partaker in

---

[5] Fred H. Klooster, 'The Role of the Holy Spirit in the Hermeneutic Process: The Relationship of the Spirit's Illumination to Biblical Interpretation', in Earl D. Radmacher and Robert D. Preus (eds.), *Hermeneutics, Inerrancy, and the Bible* (Grand Rapids: Zondervan, 1984), pp. 451-72.

[6] Klooster, 'The Role of the Holy Spirit', p. 451.

[7] Klooster, 'The Role of the Holy Spirit', p. 452.

[8] For a detailed treatment of Augustine's theory of illumination, see Ronald H. Nash, *The Light of the Mind: St. Augustine's Theory of Knowledge* (Lexington: University of Kentucky Press, 1969). See also Lydia Schumacher, *Divine Illumination: The History and Future of Augustine's Theory of Knowledge* (Chichester: Wiley-Blackwell, 2011).

the truth, since it is not itself the essence of truth'.[9] Thus, he shows the deep sense of his need for divine illumination: 'for you will light my lamp, O Lord my God, you will enlighten my darkness, and of your fullness we have all received'.[10] His version of illumination theory emphasizes divine insight in order to understand the truth of given information. Ronald Nash rightly observes that the function of illumination in Augustine's theory is to provide 'the quality of certainty and necessity to certain ideas' rather than to give a definite content of knowledge to the human mind.[11] Although Augustine clearly articulated the human need for divine illumination to understand truth, there is less clarity in his description of the way the illumination process takes place. This obscurity might permit ranges of potential interpretations on how the Spirit works to illuminate the readers of Scripture.

Despite the significance of Augustine's epistemology in discussions of illumination, it is important to highlight that it did not have a direct influence on the pre-Enlightenment Protestant understanding of the doctrine (as was surely the case in, for example, the doctrine of sin or divine grace).[12] Although the Reformation theologians were profoundly influenced by Augustinianism in many ways, they shied away from his philosophy of knowledge in their explanation of divine illumination. One could still argue, though, that Augustine's

---

[9] Augustine, *The Confessions of St. Augustine*, 4.15.25.

[10] Augustine, *The Confessions of St. Augustine*, 4.15.25.

[11] Nash, *The Light of the Mind*, p. 98. Nash provides three interpretations of Augustine's theory of illumination. The Thomistic interpretation identifies the divine light of God and the human intellect or the lesser light. This view associates divine illumination with intellectual cognition. The Franciscan interpretation differs in its ascription of God as the agent of illumination who generates, imparts, and imprints the divine forms on human mind. The third interpretation is the 'formal theory' of Etienne Gilson and Frederick Copleston, which understands illumination as providing quality of certainty and necessity to particular ideas. Although Nash does not seriously object to the Franciscan interpretation and rejects the Thomistic interpretation as the most unsatisfactory one, he argues that the formal theory is a correct interpretation of Augustine's theory of illumination, even though it fails to allow specific conceptual content to divine illumination (pp. 94-101). See also Carl R. Trueman, 'Illumination', in Kevin J. Vanhoozer (ed.), *Dictionary for the Theological Interpretation of the Bible* (Grand Rapids: Baker Academic, 2005), pp. 316-18.

[12] Richard A. Muller, 'Augustinianism in the Reformation', in Allan Fitzgerald and John C. Cavadin (eds.), *Augustine through the Ages: An Encyclopedia*, i (Grand Rapids: Eerdmans, 1999), pp. 705-707.

doctrine of human depravity, which made divine illumination indispensable for understanding truth, has had significant bearing on the Protestant understanding of the Spirit's illumination. Nevertheless, early Protestant theologians did not use much of Augustine in their discussion of the doctrine of illumination. Instead, they developed an approach that identifies divine illumination with the internal testimony of the Holy Spirit in which illumination is understood as a manner of knowing rather than a mere notional assent to divine truths. Therefore, as Carl R. Trueman indicates, 'though the sense of the Bible could be grasped by the application of the standard rules of linguistic interpretation, the mode by which these truths were themselves known was radically different in the believer and the unbeliever because of the action of the Holy Spirit'.[13] Because of the work of the Spirit, the truthfulness of Scripture is explained not only in the general sense, but also in the sense that it is true for those who are given the assurance of faith and the illumination of the Spirit.

Having the concept of divine illumination as a principal notion within the Protestant hermeneutical approaches, we will examine the Reformed, Puritan, and Wesleyan perspectives by way of studying Calvin, Owen, and Wesley to have a more nuanced understanding of the ways the Spirit's role in the interpretive process is appropriated in Protestant ecclesial traditions.

John Calvin's Interpretive Approach

The doctrine of divine illumination in the Protestant tradition began to develop formally as a theological concept during the Reformation era, in which John Calvin was a leading theologian and biblical exegete. During the same period, the doctrine of the internal testimony of the Holy Spirit also emerged in the Protestant hermeneutical tradition with a substantial overlap with the doctrine of divine illumination. Calvin is usually attributed with offering clear instruction on the witness of the Spirit as both the testimony in the heart to confirm that Scripture is the word of God and the giver of assurance to believers about their new status as children of God. He is also credited with being the first in the Protestant tradition to develop and promote the doctrine of divine illumination by providing a clear and

---

[13] Trueman, 'Illumination', p. 317.

extended articulation of it along with an understanding of the internal testimony of the Spirit.[14]

On the basis of the doctrine of total depravity, a result of the fall, Calvin underlines the indispensability of the Spirit's illuminative work in the interpretation of Scripture. For Calvin, the human soul consists of two parts: mind and heart or intellect and will. The fall has significantly affected both human faculties, giving the mind over to blindness and the heart to corruption.[15] The incapacity of the human mind to understand divine truth makes the illuminative work of the Holy Spirit absolutely necessary in the interpretation of Scripture. Calvin shows this in the *Geneva Catechism*, in a well-defined expression.

> Truly, our understandings are too weak to comprehend that spiritual knowledge of God, which is revealed to us by Faith; and our hearts have too strong a propensity to distrust God, and to put a perverse confidence in ourselves or the creatures, for us to submit to him of our own mere motion. But the Holy Spirit makes us capable, by his own illumination, of understanding those things, which would otherwise very far exceed our capacity, and forms in us a sure persuasion, by sealing in our hearts the promises of salvation.[16]

For Calvin, although the word of God is sufficient to produce faith, it has no significant effect unless our spiritually inactive mind is enlightened by the Holy Spirit. Scripture is like a closed book until the reader receives the Spirit's illumination and impartation of understanding. Reading Scripture deprived of the illumination of the Spirit is to remain 'utterly devoid of the light of truth', since 'the word is the instrument by which the illumination of the Spirit is dispensed'.[17] Affirming the illumination of the Spirit as the true source of understanding in the intellect, Calvin contends that the word has no effect without the illuminative work of the Holy Spirit. He writes,

---

[14] R.C. Sproul, 'The Internal Testimony of the Holy Spirit', in Norman L. Geisler (ed.), *Inerrancy* (Grand Rapids: Zondervan, 1980), pp. 337-54.

[15] John Calvin, *The Institutes of the Christian Religion*, 1.15.7.

[16] John Calvin. *The Catechism of the Church of Geneva* (trans. Elijah Waterman; Harford: Sheldon & Goodwin, 1815). Accessed 12 May 2015. Online: https://archive.org/details/catechismofchurc00calv

[17] Calvin, *Institutes*, 1.9.3.

A simple external manifestation of the word ought to be amply
sufficient to produce faith, did not our blindness and perverseness
prevent. But such is the proneness of our mind to vanity, that it
can never adhere to the truth of God, and such its dullness, that
it is always blind even in his light. Hence without the illumination
of the Spirit the word has no effect; and hence also it is obvious
that faith is something higher than human understanding. Nor
were it sufficient for the mind to be illumined by the Spirit of God
unless the heart also were strengthened and supported by his
power.[18]

Other than the Spirit's role in scriptural inspiration, Calvin consistently identifies the Spirit in relation to Scripture with his teaching
and interpretive activities through providing internal testimony and
illumination of the words of the biblical texts. The Spirit teaches believers by illuminating them with the knowledge and understanding
of truth without which they would remain blind. In his commentary
on Psalm 119, Calvin asserts that everyone is blind unless the Spirit
enlightens the eyes of inner understanding. 'God gives light to us by
his word', because 'we are blind amid the clearest light, until he re-
moves the veil from our eyes'.[19] Illumination, in this sense, is an in-
visible grace offered as a remedy for spiritual blindness and abiding
power imparted by the Holy Spirit to enlighten us to discern the true
meaning of Scripture. Calvin also considers illumination as a precondition to proper exegesis of the biblical texts, particularly in his understanding of Old Testament exegesis that has more to do with the
purpose of finding Christ through the enlightenment of the Spirit.

The interpretive role of the Spirit begins with his work of confirming Scripture and providing an internal testimony to its trustworthiness as the word of God. It is the divine act of the Spirit within
the believer that provides the conviction and assurance of Scripture
as the self-authenticated and reliable word of God, which demands
full attentiveness and obedience. 'The same Spirit, therefore, who has
spoken through the mouths of the prophets must penetrate into our
hearts to persuade us that they faithfully proclaimed what had been

---

[18] Calvin, *Institutes*, 3.2.33.

[19] John Calvin, 'Commentary on Psalm 119.17'. Accessed 12 May 2015. Online:
http://www.ccel.org/ccel/calvin/calcom11.xxvii.iii.html.

divinely commanded.'[20] Although the Spirit's testimony comes from within the heart, Calvin vehemently argues that the Spirit's assurance does not take place apart from the Word. There is a necessary correlation between the Spirit and the Word in that neither of them works without the other. Commenting on Acts, he clarifies this balanced approach of correlation between the Spirit and the Word.

> Scripture is the true touchstone whereby all doctrines must be tried. If any man say that this kind of trial is doubtful, forasmuch as the Scripture is oftentimes doubtful, and is interpreted diverse ways, I say, that we must also add judgment of the Spirit, who is, not without cause, called the Spirit of discretion, [discernment.] But the faithful must judge of every doctrine no otherwise then out of, and according to, the Scriptures, having the Spirit for their leader and guide.[21]

Calvin's explanation of the doctrine of divine illumination goes beyond intellectually understanding the meaning of the biblical texts. He argues that the Spirit's illumination provides not only a merely cognitive knowledge, but also a divine influence that generates obedience. He says that the Spirit teaches us 'by illuminating with sound knowledge', and then 'renders us docile by [his] secret influence'.[22] There is no purpose in reading or hearing Scripture unless the Spirit in his illumination 'effectually pierces into our hearts' and regulates our lives to make it possible 'to walk in that righteousness the law enjoins'.[23] In doing so, Calvin shows that the illumination of the Spirit aims ultimately to produce an obedient Christian life that 'discerns the light of life that God manifests by his word' and that 'humbles us to contemplate with admiration' and 'to convince us the more of our need of the grace of God, to comprehend the mysteries, which surpass our limited capacity'.[24] As the first theologian to develop a clear and outstanding presentation of the witness of the

---

[20] Calvin, *Institutes*, 1.9.4.

[21] John Calvin, 'Commentary on Acts 17.11'. http://www.ccel.org/ccel/calvin/ calcom37.v.iii.html

[22] John Calvin, 'Commentary on Psalm 119.125'. Accessed 12 May 2015. Online: http://www.ccel.org/ccel/calvin/calcom12.iii.i.html.

[23] John Calvin, 'Commentary on Psalm 119.133'. Accessed 12 May 2015. Online: http://www.ccel.org/ccel/calvin/calcom12.iii.ii.html.

[24] John Calvin, 'Commentary on Psalm 119.17'. Accessed 12 May 2015. Online: http://www.ccel.org/ccel/calvin/calcom11.xxviii.iii.html.

Spirit and divine illumination, Calvin's contribution in this discussion helps to pinpoint the Protestant understanding of the Spirit's role in biblical interpretation.

John Owen's Interpretive Approach

The Puritan Reformed pastor and theologian from the seventeenth century, John Owen is another important figure who represents the Protestant appropriation of the Spirit's role in scriptural interpretation.[25] Commenting on Owen's interpretive principles, K.M. Kapic writes, 'One cannot appreciate Owen's approach to Scripture and interpretation without focusing on his view of the Holy Spirit's activity in the formation of the Scriptures and in the reception of the Scriptures by their readers. This emphasis on the Spirit enabled Owen to maintain a path between what he regarded as the extremes of his day.'[26] His Puritan background influenced his conviction that only readers whose minds are enlightened by the Holy Spirit understand the true significance of the biblical texts.[27] Developing a hermeneutic that operates within the Reformation and post-Reformation Protestant scholastic tradition, Owen offered a detailed explanation of the Spirit's interpretive role in his voluminous treatises.[28]

Owen's doctrine of Scripture is grounded on two essential affirmations: a belief that the sacred Scriptures are the word of God and an understanding that the mind and purpose of God are revealed in them. He identifies these assertions as the 'two springs' of all

[25] Within the context of a distinctively Protestant framework, categorizing Owen's theology as either Puritan or Reformed is somewhat controversial. Although without a doubt Owen is a Puritan theologian, his thoughts better fit in the context of Reformed Orthodoxy. Carl R. Trueman raises this point, suggesting that it is appropriate to locate Owen in the context of both Puritan and Reformed theologies. See his discussion in *John Owen: Reformed Catholic Renaissance Man* (Aldershot: Ashgate, 2007), pp. 5-12. See also H.M. Knapp, *Understanding the Mind of God: John Owen and Seventeenth-Century Exegetical Methodology* (PhD thesis, Calvin Theological Seminary, 2002), pp. 40-93.

[26] 'John Owen (1616-1683)', in Donald K. McKim (ed.), *Dictionary of Major Biblical Interpreters* (Downers Grove, IL: IVP Academic, 2007), pp. 795-99.

[27] For a short summary of the Puritans' approach to divine illumination, see Stanley J. Grenz, *Renewing the Center: Evangelical Theology in a Post-Theological Era* (Grand Rapids: Baker, 2nd edn, 2006), pp. 68-72.

[28] John Owen's detailed discussion of the doctrine of illumination is mainly located in *Pneumatologia: A Discourse Concerning the Holy Spirit*, vols. 3-4 of *The Works of John Owen* (ed. William H. Goold; Edinburgh: T&T Clark, 1862).

Christian knowledge and understanding that needs to be 'neither stopped nor defiled'.[29] The backdrop of these assertions is his Protestant viewpoint that criticizes the perspective of Roman Catholicism about Scripture and its interpretation. The certainty that Scripture is divine revelation and is self-sufficient to be interpreted without the guardianship of the Roman Church are essential principles around which Owen centers his argument concerning the importance of the Spirit in biblical interpretation. Owen underlines the Spirit's role as the 'principal efficient cause of the due knowledge and understanding of the will of God in the Scripture' that assists believers to attain the right perception of the mind of God in the Scripture.[30] He writes,

> There is an especial work of the Spirit of God on the minds of men, communicating spiritual wisdom, light, and understanding unto them, necessary unto their discerning and apprehending aright the mind of God in his word, and the understanding of the mysteries of heavenly truth contained therein.[31]

Like Calvin, Owen explains the special work of the Holy Spirit in terms of supernatural illumination of the minds of the readers to understand God's will as revealed in Scripture. Although the extent of his definition of divine illumination goes beyond biblical exegesis, Owen provides a thorough discussion that allows understanding of the Spirit's illuminative work in the reading of Scripture. For him, divine illumination is the enlightening of the inner eyes of understanding through the removal of darkness of the mind and the gift of insight to understand the ways and purposes of God as displayed in the written texts of the word of God. It is a divine enablement to know the mind and will of God as supernaturally revealed in Scripture. No one can acquire this understanding without the special illumination of the Spirit of God. Owen explains,

> There is an efficacious work of the Spirit of God opening our eyes, enlightening our understandings or minds, to understand the things contained in the Scripture, distinct from the objective proposition of them in the Scripture itself; which the testimonies

---

[29] Owen, *Pneumatologia*, IV, p. 121.
[30] Owen, *Pneumatologia*, IV, p. 124.
[31] Owen, *Pneumatologia*, IV, pp. 124-25.

urged to fully confirm … It is expressed as a translation out of darkness into light. That in these and the like testimonies, the removal of the inward darkness of our minds, by the communication of spiritual light unto them, and not merely the objective revelation of truth in the Scripture.[32]

Since Owen's extended discussion of divine illumination was prompted by seventeenth-century theological debates, it is important to mention the context in which his teachings developed. Primarily, as a theologian of the Reformation, Owen disapproved of the Roman Catholic Church's dogma that claims the interpretation of Scripture is subject to the authority of the Church. He insists that there is no need to depend on the tradition of the Church to understand the mystery of God in Scripture. On a different level, however, Owen addressed two extreme teachings that arose among proponents of the Reformation on the veracity of biblical understanding: the teachings of the Quakers or 'enthusiasts' on the one hand, and such 'rationalists' as the Cambridge Platonists and the Socinians on the other.[33] Although the former claimed that the truth of Scripture could be discerned by the Spirit alone, the latter thought that reason was utterly sufficient for understanding Scripture. In his response to both sides of the debate, Owen renounced the fanaticism and supposed prophetical inspirations of the Quakers as well as the supremacy of reason as the sole means of understanding Scripture. Arguing that no one can understand Scripture without the effectual help of the Holy Spirit, Owen contends that divine illumination works through reason as our mind is enlightened and guided by the Spirit to the right spiritual and scriptural understanding.

Owen claims that divine revelation is the basis for divine illumination and that the Spirit of God provides immediate power for supernatural illumination to understand the supernatural revelation revealed in Scripture. Without excluding various ways of God's external revelation, he asserts that Scripture is the only repository of all divine supernatural revelation; therefore, it is the only external means of

---

[32] Owen, *Pneumatologia*, IV, pp. 162-63.

[33] Kapic, 'John Owen', p. 796. See also, David J. McKinley, 'John Owen's View of Illumination: An Alternative to the Fuller-Erickson Dialogue', *BSac* 154.613 (1997), pp. 103-105.

divine spiritual illumination.[34] In Owen's view, Scripture is a medium of divine illumination to understand the mind and will of God. Scripture in this sense is a channel for divine illumination through which God is known. In another sense, however, Scripture is perceived as an object of divine illumination that seeks the Spirit's illuminative work for its message to be understood properly. Although these two senses seem to conflict on a surface level, Owen attempts to articulate the function of divine illumination ultimately to make God and his purpose known to all human beings through his written Word.

Divine illumination, according to Owen, consists of two parts. The first has to do with the Spirit's work in enabling us to believe in the divine nature of Scripture as the word of God. This is the internal testimony and an affirmation that the Spirit provides about the divine status of the Bible. It is the Holy Spirit who generates faith, the assurance of the truth of the divine origin of the Bible. 'Indeed', Owen writes, 'that all which is properly called faith, with respect unto divine revelation, and is accepted with God as such, is the work of the Spirit of God in us, or is bestowed on us by him'.[35] The second part of divine illumination is the opening of the mind to understand the truth of the biblical texts. It is the actual work of the Spirit to illuminate the mind so it can be able to see what God reveals in his written text. Owen identifies this with a 'supernatural light' that enlightens and renews the mind to understand divine truth in the Scripture. He argues that no one can discern the heavenly excellence of God revealed in Scripture without the effectual communication of the supernatural illumination. He writes,

> The Holy Spirit irradiates the mind with a spiritual light, whereby it is enabled to discern the glory of spiritual things ... Those who are under the power of their natural darkness and blindness, especially when there are in them also superadded prejudices, begotten and increased by the craft of Satan, as there are in the whole world of unbelievers, cannot see or discern that divine excellency in the Scripture, without an apprehension whereof no man believe it aright to be the word of God. Such persons may assent unto the truth of the Scripture and its divine original upon external

---

[34] Owen, *Pneumatologia*, IV, p. 8.
[35] Owen, *Pneumatologia*, IV, p. 56.

arguments and rational motives, but believe it with faith divine and supernatural, on those arguments and motives only, they cannot.[36]

In his discussion on spiritual understanding of Scripture, Owen highlights three important elements that help a Christian to experience the Spirit's illumination in reading Scripture. The first is spiritual, which involves prayer, readiness to receive divine truth, and practical obedience in the Christian walk. He maintains that Scripture needs to be read in an atmosphere of ardent and earnest prayer with a willing and obedient heart in order that the Spirit may enlighten the mind and lead the reader into the knowledge of divine truth. He emphasizes the significance of prayer in the reading of Scripture, stating that 'constant and fervent prayer for the divine assistance of the Holy Spirit is such an indispensable means for the attaining the knowledge of the mind of God in the Scripture as that without it all others will not be available'.[37]

Disciplinary growth is the second element that Owen underlines as a means to achieve spiritual understanding of Scripture. This discipline involves diligent study of the original languages of Scripture, knowledge of its historical and geographical background, and skill in ways and methods of reasoning. Although spiritual enlightenment is given much attention in Owen's hermeneutical approach, he does not downplay the importance of diligent study in the understanding of Scripture. In fact, as Kapic argues, Owen had a genuine appreciation and profound expertise in certain kinds of textual criticism that involved dealing with the original Greek and Hebrew languages as well as ancient texts, such as Syriac translations and Talmudic literature, in his study of Scripture.[38] However, he is consistent in arguing that the practice of discipline itself does not produce spiritual understanding without the illumination of the Holy Spirit.

Finally, Owen affirms the role of the ecclesial tradition in attaining spiritual understanding of the biblical texts. As a Reformer, he is clear in his view against the Roman Church's conclusive authority in the interpretation of Scripture. However, he is also unambiguous in his involving the universal tradition of the Analogy of Faith along with the teachings of the early Church fathers, and those who have gone

---

[36] Owen, *Pneumatologia*, IV, pp. 57-58.

[37] Owen, *Pneumatologia*, IV, p. 203.

[38] Kapic, 'John Owen', p. 798.

before, in receiving light, knowledge, and understanding concerning the interpretation of Scripture. Owen's theological understanding of divine illumination is thus illustrative to those who want to appreciate the Protestant tradition's recognition of the Spirit's role in the interpretation of Scripture.

John Wesley's Interpretive Approach

John Wesley, a prominent pastoral theologian and biblical interpreter from the eighteenth century, is an important figure in our discussion of the Spirit's role in the interpretation of Scripture. Wesley was an Anglican priest and evangelist who played a substantial role in the revival within the Church of England. As one of the significant leaders of the evangelical movement in Great Britain in the eighteenth century, Wesley has had considerable influence on Methodism and the Holiness Movement, which eventually had a major impact on the development of Pentecostal Christianity. Donald Dayton highlights the Methodist roots of Pentecostalism by pointing out Wesley's concern for a thorough restoration of the practices of the early Church, like that of Classical Pentecostalism, and his emphasis on the works of the Spirit; some would claim that he was a 'theologian of the Spirit'.[39] In fact, commenting on the reciprocity of Pentecostalism and Methodism, Dayton claims, 'Pentecostalism cannot be understood apart from its deep roots in the Methodism experience. And Methodism similarly cannot be understood entirely without acknowledgment of this paternity – though for sociological and theological reasons, this relationship has often been suppressed in official historiography'.[40] It makes sense to deal with the Wesleyan approach of the Spirit's work in theology and biblical interpretation in this study

---

[39] See Dayton's chapter on 'Methodist Roots of Pentecostalism', in Donald W. Dayton, *Theological Roots of Pentecostalism* (Grand Rapids: Baker, 1987), pp. 35-60. Dayton also analyzes Wesley's influence on the global Holiness Movement, which paved the way for the development of Pentecostalism in his 'Methodism and Pentecostalism', in William J. Abraham and James E. Kirby (eds.), *The Oxford Handbook of Methodist Studies* (New York: Oxford University Press, 2009), pp. 171-87.

[40] Dayton, 'Methodism and Pentecostalism', p. 171. Randall J. Stephens also recognizes that Pentecostalism is the product of an open Methodist tradition and its movement has the imprint of John Wesley's theology of Spirit. See his essay, 'The Holiness/Pentecostal/Charismatic Extension of the Wesleyan Tradition', in Randy L. Maddox and Jason E. Vickers (eds.), *The Cambridge Companion to John Wesley* (Cambridge: Cambridge University Press, 2009), pp. 262-81.

for at least two reasons. First, the theological interpretive approach employed by Wesley offers a substantial contribution to contemporary dialogue concerning the Spirit's role in theological interpretation of Scripture. Second, Wesley's influence in the development of Pentecostalism and its hermeneutics is eminent.

Most agree that diverse theological currents contributed to Wesley's thought and practices. Although, as the founder and leader of the movement, Wesley is mainly identified with the Methodist Christian tradition, his affiliation within the Anglican Church was maintained throughout his ministry and life. Despite the fact that Methodism became progressively separated from the High Church Anglican tradition, Wesley considered himself and his movement as part of the Church of England until he died in 1791.[41] Given the nature of Anglicanism as a middle way (*via media*) between Reformed Protestantism and Roman Catholicism, Wesley's Anglican background allowed him to develop doctrinal convictions that, in some sense, accommodated the blend of Catholic and Protestant influences. Whereas a strong emphasis on justification by faith as the basic doctrine establishes his Protestant side, the importance he gave to active human participation in salvation, his assumption of the necessity of growth in Christian holiness, and his emphasis on sacramental theology signal Catholic influence in his teachings. The influences of Luther and Calvin are present in Wesley's doctrine, but English Reformed Puritanism and Arminianism also inspired his theology and worship practices.[42] His keen interest in the theology and practices of the early Church and his appreciation of Eastern Orthodoxy prove further the influences of diverse traditions in his doctrinal formation. These complex and distinctive combinations of various doctrinal positions locate Wesley in a place where he provides a unique theological contribution.

Although Wesley is a major figure in the history of Christianity and Christian theology, modern theologians have not tended to consider his approach as worthy of study. His writings are characterized by their occasional nature, which marks them as unsystematic and

---

[41] See Dennis M. Campbell, 'Ministry and Itinerancy in Methodism', in William J. Abraham and James E. Kirby (eds.), *The Oxford Handbook of Methodist Studies* (New York: Oxford University Press, 2009), pp. 262-79.

[42] Randy L. Maddox, 'Reading Wesley as a Theologian', *WesTJ* 30.1 (1995), pp. 7-54.

uncritical for the modern critical enterprise. Paul Johnson construes the form of Wesley's Christianity as mere ethical and emotional commitment almost totally devoid of intellectual content and doctrinal insight.[43] Duncan S. Ferguson also charges Wesley for his non-historical understanding and failure to have a critical approach to study the Bible.[44] However, Wesleyan scholars like Albert Outler consider Wesley as a 'folk theologian' without relegating the significance of his theology.[45]

It is obvious that John Wesley was not a systematic theologian or a biblical scholar with an approach molded by the post-enlightenment historical-critical assumptions known to modern scholarship. But it is not fair to label him as uncritical in light of nineteenth and twentieth-century biblical criticism. His theological and hermeneutical approach cannot be evaluated simply through the lens of modern historical critical procedures and analytical presuppositions. Joel B. Green partially dismisses the charge against Wesley for being uncritical and for the absence of historical consciousness in his reading of Scripture by pointing out the charge's anachronism and by showing that Wesley's historical interests were appropriate in their own right to mid-eighteenth-century biblical interpretation.[46] J.B. Green argues that Wesley's hermeneutical approach, on the one hand, can be labeled as premodern – rather than uncritical or precritical – in the sense that it did not strictly follow modern historical-critical concerns. On the other hand, Wesley's involvement in the advent of modern biblical studies, particularly his emphasis on reason as an important factor in biblical interpretation and theological reflection, locates him somewhere between premodern and modern eras.[47]

Christian doctrine for Wesley has more to do with the practical matter of salvation than with a more speculative, philosophical

---

[43] Paul Johnson, *A History of Christianity* (New York: Atheneum, 1976), p. 365.

[44] Duncan S. Ferguson, 'John Wesley on Scripture: The Hermeneutics of Pietism', *MH* 22 (1984), pp. 234-45.

[45] Albert C. Outler, 'Towards a Re-Appraisal of John Wesley as a Theologian', in Thomas C. Oden and Leicester R. Longden (eds.), *The Wesleyan Theological Heritage: Essays of Albert C. Outler* (Grand Rapids: Zondervan, 1991), pp. 39-54.

[46] Joel B. Green, 'Wesley as Interpreter of Scripture and the Emergence of "History" in Biblical Interpretation', in Joel B. Green and David F. Watson (eds.), *Wesley, Wesleyans, and Reading the Bible as Scripture* (Waco, TX: Baylor University Press, 2012), pp. 47-62.

[47] Green, 'Wesley as Interpreter of Scripture', p. 51.

theology. Kenneth J. Collins suggests that Wesley's theological method should not be characterized by a grand systematic principle comparable to, for example, Paul Tillich's method of correlation or Emil Brunner's paradigm of divine-human correspondence.[48] Rather, his theological perspectives are formed and driven by his ongoing practical and soteriological concerns. Collins argues that Wesley's theology is shaped by his practical approach, organized around the *Ordo Salutis* – that is, the 'order of salvation' that outlines God's working in the process of salvation to liberate humans from sin.[49] Wesley's participation in the evangelical revival in eighteenth-century England and his preaching against nominal Christianity partly explain the practical sense of his understanding of the ultimate goal of engaging in Christian theology.

It is important to recognize Wesley as a practical theologian to understand his theology and interpretive engagements. His understanding of Scripture as well as his perception of the person and work of the Holy Spirit is significantly shaped by his practical theology and soteriological vision of Christian doctrine. Randy L. Maddox argues that Wesley's theological reflection could only be adequately understood in terms of practical theology (*scientia practica*) characterized by pre-university Christian reflection, which continued to be dominant in eighteenth-century Anglicanism. According to Maddox, Wesley's 'practical theology' should be understood in terms of the multilayered theological activities – spiritual, devotional, moral, and pastoral in nature – of the early Christians rather than its modern classification as a supplementary application discipline for systematic theology. The practical-theological activities disclosed in Wesley's written materials (i.e. his sermons, notes, letters, essays, treatises, dialogues, and journals) demonstrate the priority he gave to therapeutic, occasional, and contextual concerns rather than to abstract theoretical analysis.[50]

---

[48] Kenneth J. Collins, *The Theology of John Wesley: Holy Love and the Shape of Grace* (Nashville: Abingdon, 2007), p. 3; cf. Paul Tillich, *Systematic Theology* (3 vols.; Chicago: Chicago University Press, 1963); Emil Brunner, *Truth as Encounter* (Philadelphia: Westminster, 1943).

[49] Collins, *The Theology of John Wesley*, p. 15.

[50] Randy L. Maddox, *Responsible Grace: John Wesley's Practical Theology* (Nashville: Kingswood, 1994); *idem*, 'John Wesley: Practical Theologian?' *WesTJ* 23 (1988), pp. 122-47.

As with his other theological perspectives, Wesley's pneumatology is formed and informed by his practical approach. Rather than working on abstract formulations and speculations of the Spirit's nature, personality, procession, and place within the Trinity, Wesley's doctrine of the Holy Spirit tends to focus on the soteriological and practical aspects of the person and work of the Spirit in the context of vital religious experience. The significance of this doctrine, within his consistent trinitarian approach, lies in the practical emphasis he gave to the Spirit as the agent of redemption initiated by the Father and effected by the Son.[51] Of course, Wesley's biblical understanding of salvation is primarily expressed in christological terms, rather than pneumatological ones. His principal focus was on Jesus Christ and he stressed the Holy Spirit's role mainly in testifying about and making him real in present experience. Nevertheless, having a central place in his understanding of Christian life and experience, the Spirit is key to Wesley's soteriology. His pneumatological viewpoint is integrated into the divine initiative in restoring the fallen humanity into relationship with God as originally intended. In this soteriological scheme, the Holy Spirit is involved in drawing humans to the salvation provided by God, convicting them of their sins, and sanctifying them toward the life of holiness and love – God's own divine character.

In his sermon 'On the Holy Spirit', Wesley identifies the Holy Spirit as the restored presence of God in this world. Adam and Eve enjoyed the presence of God before the fall and that lost relationship was restored back through the person and work of Christ that made possible the coming of the Holy Spirit to the hearts of sinners. The life-giving Spirit, who is always intimately related to Christ in Wesley's doctrine based on Paul's statement in 2 Cor. 3.17, restores the gracious empowering presence of God to humanity as the fullness of God at work in our broken world. The Spirit is given to bestow life and mend sin-ruined souls; therefore, 'the incarnation, preaching, and death of Jesus Christ were designed to represent, proclaim, and purchase for us this gift of the Spirit'.[52]

---

[51] Lycurgus M. Starkey, *The Work of the Holy Spirit: A Study in Wesleyan Theology* (New York: Abingdon, 1962), p. 26.

[52] John Wesley, 'On the Holy Spirit', Sermon. Accessed on 15 April 2016. Online: http://www.umcmission.org/Find-Resources/John-Wesley-Sermons/Sermon-141-On-the-Holy-Spirit.

Wesley had a strong conviction on the divinity and personality of the Holy Spirit. Obviously, he did not have a sophisticated argument on these important beliefs, except assuming and implying, mostly in passing, as they were taken-for-granted doctrines.[53] Although he often spoke of the Spirit in terms of the power of God, he never equated the Spirit with some impersonal influence or energy, or as an attribute of God. His comment on Jn 15.26 explicitly shows his understanding of the Spirit as a divine person: 'The Spirit's coming, and being sent by our Lord from the Father, to testify of him, are personal characters, and plainly distinguish him from the Father and the Son; and his title as the Spirit of truth, together with his proceeding from the Father can agree to none but a Divine person'.[54] Wesley emphasizes the person of the Holy Spirit not only in relation to the Father and to the Son, but also in relation to humanity. In fact, as Rob L. Staples suggests, Wesley frequently uses personal pronouns and images mainly as he describes the Spirit's relationship to human beings.[55] Lycurgus M. Starkey also writes that Wesley perceived the Holy Spirit as 'a living, active, "personal" presence who enters into an intimate, interpersonal fellowship with man, and is addressed as a recipient of prayer, praise, and worship'.[56]

Wesley's emphasis on the personal presence of the Spirit resonates with the notion of Eastern Orthodox theology that stresses the gift of God's grace as the personal presence of the Holy Spirit.[57] Maddox suggests that Wesley shared Eastern concerns regarding the personality and work of the Holy Spirit, although he retained the position of the Church in the West about the *filioque* controversies. According to Maddox, Wesley maintained a balanced view on the work of the Spirit, that it does not supersede or contradict the work of Christ, but at the same time is not unduly subordinated to that of Christ. He states, 'Wesley's ascription to the *filioque* was simply routine, reflecting

---

[53] See, for instance, his assumption of the deity of the Holy Spirit in his comments on Acts 5.4 and 1 Cor. 2.11, as well as his use of personal pronouns in reference to the Spirit when commenting on Eph. 4.30 in John Wesley, *Explanatory Notes upon the New Testament*, I (London: Bowyer, 1755; reprint edn, Peabody, MA: Hendrickson, 1986).

[54] Wesley, John 15.26, *Explanatory Notes upon the New Testament*.

[55] Rob L. Staples, 'John Wesley's Doctrine of the Holy Spirit', *WesTJ* 21.2 (1986), pp. 91-115 (92).

[56] Starkey, *The Work of the Holy Spirit*, p. 26.

[57] Maddox, *Responsible Grace*, p. 120.

the limited contact (and debate) between East and West in his day. Indeed, a very plausible case could be made that Wesley's deepest sympathies would lie with those who are seeking an alternative to the *filioque* in current debates.[58]

Wesley believed that the Holy Spirit, as the gift of God's grace and his personal presence, is given to every believer for salvation and sanctification. His view incorporates these two aspects of grace – grace as pardon and grace as enabling power. He clearly expresses this in one of his sermons:

> By 'the grace of God' is sometimes to be understood that free love, that unmerited mercy, by which I, a sinner, through the merits of Christ, am now reconciled to God. But in this place it rather means that power of God the Holy Ghost, which 'worketh in us both to will and to do of his good pleasure'. As soon as ever the grace of God in the former sense, his pardoning love, is manifested to our souls, the grace of God in the latter sense, the power of his Spirit, takes place therein. And now we can perform, through God, what to man was impossible.[59]

Without lessening the importance of the aspect of grace as forgiveness of sins, Wesley tends to define grace largely in terms of the power of the Holy Spirit who enables sinners to experience a life of sanctification. This empowering presence of the Holy Spirit that enables us to love God, serve him, and become holy in the sense that God primordially intended for human beings is Wesley's definitive pneumatology. Therefore, the Holy Spirit, for him, is primarily 'the immediate cause' of all holiness in Christians that enlightens understanding, rectify wills and affections, and sanctify souls and bodies to a complete eternal enjoyment of God.[60]

The empowering presence of the Holy Spirit in Wesley's pneumatology has more to do with the fruit of the Spirit than the extraordinary gifts of the Spirit. Wesley never emphasized spiritual gifts in the sense of the heightened concern that would characterize the later Charismatic and Pentecostal movements. However, he did not downplay the importance of the gifts of the Spirit and Christian

---

[58] Maddox, *Responsible Grace*, p. 137.

[59] Sermon 12, 'The Witness of Our Spirit', §15, *Works*, I, p. 309. Bicentennial edition.

[60] *A Letter to a Roman Catholic*, §8. Bicentennial edition.

charismatic experiences. In fact, Howard Snyder claims that Wesley, with his distinctly and fundamentally charismatic theology, was charismatic in the true biblical sense of the term.[61] Similarly, Maddox asserts Wesley's openness to the extraordinary manifestations of the Spirit, despite his robust distinctive concern on the fruits of the Spirit, which are the primary embodiments of the Holy Spirit as the empowering presence of God.[62]

Wesley's practical soteriological framework also shapes his hermeneutical approach and his view of the Spirit's work in the interpretation of Scripture, which is part of the Spirit's role of sanctifying the believer. His theological activities were primarily established on the affirmation of divine inspiration and authority of Scripture. As the authoritative word of God, the Bible, to which he commonly refers as 'the oracles of God', should be the basic norm for Christian faith and practice. It is a written divine revelation that communicates the message of God spoken through the prophets, evangelists, and apostles. In the preface of his *Explanatory Notes upon the New Testament*, Wesley clearly states his view of Scripture:

> Concerning the Scriptures, in general, it may be observed, the word of the living God, which directed the first Patriarchs also, was, in the time of Moses, committed to writing. To this were added, in several succeeding generations, the inspired writings of the other Prophets. Afterwards, what the Son of God preached, and the Holy Ghost spake by the Apostles, the Apostles and Evangelists wrote ... The Scripture, therefore, of the Old and New Testament is a most solid and precious system of divine truth. Every part thereof is worthy of God; and all together are one entire body, wherein is no defect, no excess. It is the fountain of heavenly wisdom, which they who are able to taste, prefer to all writings of men, however, wise, or learned, or holy.[63]

---

[61] See Howard A. Snyder (with Daniel V. Runyon), *The Divided Flame: Wesleyans and the Charismatic Renewal* (Grand Rapids: Zondervan, 1986), pp. 54-67. Snyder recognized four broader areas of correlation between Wesley's theology and present Pentecostal and Charismatic movements: 1) their stress on God's grace in the life and experience of the Church, 2) the higher importance of the Spirit's role in their theologies, 3) their emphasis on the Church as community, and 4) the tension in their theology of the Church and its institutional expressions.

[62] Maddox, *Responsible Grace*, pp. 133-34.

[63] Wesley, *Explanatory Notes upon the New Testament*, Preface §10.

Wesley never had a written doctrine of Scripture; nor did he have any printed document that systematically outlines his practice of biblical interpretation because of his assumption of the widely accepted understanding of Scripture as God's revelation to humankind. However, he frequently refers to himself as a man of one book (*homo unius libri*) to emphasize the priority he gives to Scripture.[64] He was dogmatic about his position concerning the supremacy of the Bible. A journal entry states, 'My ground is the bible. Yea, I am a bible-bigot. I follow it in all those things, both great and small'.[65] This claim, as it may suggest, neither implies that Wesley was a naïve biblicist who never read other books, nor that his doctrines were formulated exclusively on the Bible.[66] It has more to do with his understanding of Scripture as the ultimate standard that transcends all other authorities that contribute to his theology. Scott J. Jones explains Wesley's reliance on the Bible alone in terms of his understanding that 'it is Scripture *alone* that carries such weight and that no other authorities are necessary to prove a point'.[67] Maddox clarifies Wesley's claim to be a man of one book as an affirmation of the primacy of authority of Scripture without setting aside other books. He explains Wesley's practice of reading the one book – the Bible – comparatively with various translations, scholarly tools, and the books within itself as well as in light of God's central purpose on the one hand and in conference with the Holy Spirit, other readers of the Bible, Christian tradition, and the book of nature on the other.[68]

---

[64] R. Larry Shelton suggests that *homo unius libri* was a watchword for Wesley in the same sense *sola scriptura* was for Luther ('The Trajectory of Wesleyan Theology', *WesTJ* 21.2 [1986], p. 160).

[65] John Wesley, June 5, 1766, *Journals and Diaries V (1765-75)*, vol. 22 of W. Reginald Ward and Richard P. Heitzenrater (eds.), *The Bicentennial Edition of the Works of John Wesley* (Nashville: Abingdon, 1976), p. 42.c.

[66] According to Robert W. Wall, Wesley 'was an Oxford-educated man of many books, who assembled, edited, and then published a well-stocked *Christian Library* for ministers of the Methodist movement' ('Wesley as Biblical Interpreter', in Randy L. Maddox and Jason E. Vickers [eds.], *The Cambridge Companion to John Wesley* [Cambridge: Cambridge University Press, 2009], pp. 113-28 [113]).

[67] Scott J. Jones, *John Wesley's Conception and Use of Scripture* (Nashville: Kingswood, 1995), p. 35.

[68] Randy L. Maddox, 'John Wesley – "A Man of One Book",' in Joel B. Green and David F. Watson (eds.), *Wesley, Wesleyans, and Reading the Bible as Scripture* (Waco, TX: Baylor, 2012), pp. 3-18.

In Wesley's understanding, Scripture serves as a means of grace, and the purpose of its interpretation is completely tied with his soteriological vision. He strongly affirms that God revealed the way to heaven through Scripture and it is the one book that will lead us there. As a means of grace, Scripture points to the way to heaven by prompting faith and wisdom in Christian life toward the goal of salvation for souls. He writes,

> I want to know one thing, the way to heaven – how to land safe on that happy shore. God himself has condescended to teach the way: for this very end he came from heaven. He hath written it down in a book. O give me that book! At any price give me the Book of God! I have it. Here is knowledge enough for me. Let me be *homo unius libri*. Here then I am, far from the busy ways of men. I sit down alone: only God is here. In his presence I open, I read his Book; for this end, to find the way to heaven.[69]

Wesley's theological understanding of heaven embraces the earthly life of sanctification rather than merely a place where believers go after this life. He defines Christianity as a practical way of life, not in terms of creeds or a system of doctrines. Clarifying this concept in one of his sermons Wesley states, 'The salvation which is here spoken of is not what is frequently understood by that word, the going to heaven, eternal happiness ... it is a present thing ... [it] might be extended to the entire work of God, from the first dawning of grace in the soul, till it is consummated in glory'.[70] Scripture plays a significant role in this way of life as a means of grace in leading Christians – through their reading, hearing and meditation of it – to a life of sanctification and transformation.[71] In other words, for Wesley, Christian formation through the knowledge and love of God is the fundamental goal of biblical interpretation. Commenting on Wesley's appropriation of Scripture as an important means of grace, Collins writes, 'In his own day, Wesley recognized the uncanny, God-breathed nature of the Bible as a key means of grace that reading this

---

[69] John Wesley, 'Preface', in *Sermons on Several Occasions*, §5, *Works*, I, pp. 105-106. Bicentennial edition.

[70] John Wesley, 'The Scripture Way of Salvation', §I.1, *Works*, II, p. 156. Bicentennial edition.

[71] John Wesley, 'The Means of Grace', §I.1, *Works*, I, p. 381. Bicentennial edition.

book repeatedly resulted in the transformation of lives in a way that no other writings, however celebrated, could ever accomplish'.[72]

Wesley's view of the Spirit's role in biblical interpretation is significantly intertwined with his practical theological approach and his doctrine of the work of the Spirit in sanctification. Like the Protestant Reformers before him, the Spirit's work in his hermeneutic is explained in terms of *testimonium Spiritus Sancti internum* – 'the inner witness of the Holy Spirit' to the truth of the Word on one hand and the doctrine of assurance – the 'witness of the Spirit' to our adoption and sanctification on an another.[73] Having a soteriological, practical, and experiential doctrine of the Holy Spirit, Wesley frequently uses the expression of 'heart-warming' experience to explain the Spirit's work of inspiration. He uses the word 'inspiration' broadly to describe the role of the Spirit in the life of a Christian, which indicates the entire work of sanctification as spiritual breathing and an 'inward assistance of the Holy Ghost'.[74] As part of this broader sense, inspiration in relation to Scripture is an ongoing activity of the Holy Spirit in which the Spirit continues to inspire or illuminate the readers as he inspired the human writers of the Bible. Wesley strongly affirms that the Holy Spirit plays a key role in our understanding of Scripture: 'I do firmly believe (and what serious man does not) – *omnis scriptura legi debet eo spiritu quo scripta est*: we need the same Spirit to *understand* the Scripture which enabled the holy men of old to *write* it'.[75]

Along with the Protestant interpreters in the eighteenth century and those who came before him, Wesley insisted on a hermeneutical approach that gave priority to the literal meaning of Scripture over the spiritual senses. He rejected the three other senses of biblical reading – allegorical, tropological (or moral), and anagogical – commonly used by medieval readers in favor of the plain, literal meaning of Scripture. The literal sense, for him, was equivalent to the obvious natural meaning of the biblical text. In one of his letters Wesley writes,

---

[72] Collins, 'Scripture as a Means of Grace', p. 22.

[73] Staples, 'John Wesley's Doctrine of the Holy Spirit', p. 97.

[74] John Wesley, *The Letters of Rev. John Wesley* (ed. John Telford; London: Epworth, 1931), I, p. 39.

[75] John Wesley, 'A Letter to the Right Reverend The Lord Bishop of Gloucester', §II.10, *Works*, XI, p. 509. Bicentennial edition.

To anyone who asketh me concerning myself or these whom I rejoice to call my brethren, what our principles are, I answer clearly, we have no principles but those revealed in the Word of God. In the interpretation whereof we always judge the most literal sense to be the best, unless where the literal sense of one contradicts some other Scripture.[76]

Wesley's – and of course all the Protestant Reformers' – understanding of the literal sense was far different from the term's usage in modern biblical criticism, which equates the literal sense with the intentions of human authors. The literal sense in Wesley's understanding goes beyond the human authors' intention and is grounded in the intent of the Holy Spirit, the divine author of Scripture. It is a Christian reading of Scripture that is in complete agreement with the analogy of faith and the general tenor of Scripture.[77]

Steven J. Koskie has sketched the literal sense in Wesley's hermeneutics.[78] According to Koskie, the literal sense of Scripture in Wesley's reading is the same as its soteriological sense. Based on the assumption of the divine purpose that intends to bring salvation for the fallen humanity, the Scripture's literal sense is a means by which God reveals himself and his way of salvation. Although Wesley was strict on the literal reading of the biblical texts, Koskie suggests that the literal sense in his reading was not merely descriptive. When apparent tensions exist that demand interpretation beyond the literal sense, Wesley would moderately allow allegorical or spiritual reading, which Koskie identifies as 'the literal-moral sense' of Scripture.[79] Wesley's literal reading was firmly grounded on the verbal sense of the final form of the biblical text. Although his literal reading concerns the verbal sense, Wesley never took the Bible as an object to which his interpretive aim focused on its linguistic analysis. He rather understood the literal sense of Scripture as the very words of the Spirit of God, although he recognized the spiritual sense of the readers rather than spiritual sense of Scripture. Thus, he insisted on the

---

[76] John Wesley, 'A Letter to Lady Cox', *Works*, III, p. 50. Bicentennial edition.

[77] John Wesley, *Explanatory Notes upon the Old Testament*, Preface §3 (Salem, OH: Schmul, 1975).

[78] Steven J. Koskie, *Reading the Way to Heaven: A Wesleyan Theological Hermeneutic of Scripture* (JTISup 8; Winona Lake, IN: Eisenbrauns, 2014), pp. 91-96.

[79] Koskie, *Reading the Way to Heaven*, p. 93.

need for awakening of the spiritual sense of the readers to understand the plain, literal sense of Scripture. In this sense, the literal and the spiritual senses were somehow conflated in Wesley's understanding.

Wesley emphasizes the significance of prayer as a means to facilitate the inspiration of the reader for a faithful hearing of God's Word in his understanding of the Spirit's role in biblical interpretation. The Spirit awakens and inspires the reader of Scripture through a prayerful reading and response to the guidance of the Spirit through the words of Scripture. Prayer allows the Holy Spirit to be active in the work of the biblical interpreter and in the entire sanctification experience of the Church as an interpretive community. Insisting on the connection of the Spirit's initial and ongoing inspiration as well as the importance of prayerful reading to have this heart-warming experience of inspiration, Wesley writes,

> All Scripture is inspired of God – The Spirit of God not only once inspired those who wrote it but continually inspires, supernaturally assists, those who read it with earnest prayer. Hence it is so profitable for doctrine, for instruction of the ignorant, for the reproof or conviction of them that are in error or sin, for the correction or amendment of whatever is amiss, and for instructing or training up the children of God in all righteousness.[80]

Although Wesley strongly affirms the continual inspiration or illumination of the Holy Spirit to provide guidance and assistance in the Christian life, he frequently insists that Scripture is reliable as the source of God's self-revelation. He makes a distinction between Scripture as a 'rule' and the Spirit as a 'guide' in our lives.

> For though the Spirit is our principal leader, yet He is not our rule at all; the Scripture are the rule whereby He leads us into all truth … the Spirit our 'guide', which signifies an intelligent being, and the Scripture our 'rule', which signifies something used by an intelligent being.[81]

In doing so, Wesley shows caution, introducing a significant restriction on the understanding of the Spirit's influence on

---

[80] John Wesley, 2 Timothy 3.16, *Explanatory Notes upon the New Testament*.

[81] John Wesley, *The Letters of Rev. John Wesley* (ed. John Telford; London: Epworth, 1931), II, p. 117.

interpretation so as to prevent the danger of 'enthusiasm', which he describes as 'a religious madness arising from some falsely imagined influence or inspiration of God'.[82] This provides a helpful guideline and limitation to the way one appropriates the Spirit in the interpretation of Scripture.

Summary

In this chapter, I have discussed a few landmarks from within the Protestant tradition pertaining to the interplay between the Spirit and Scripture by dealing with three selected Protestant theologians: Calvin, Owen, and Wesley. Generally, the Spirit's interpretive role in the Protestant tradition is perceived through the understanding of the internal testimony of the Spirit and divine illumination. The basic assumption within the Protestant hermeneutical framework that Scripture is a means of God's revelation as well as the supreme authority in all matters of doctrine and practice shapes the guiding interpretive principle. The perspective on the correlation between the Spirit and Scripture flows out of the affirmation that Scripture is the voice through which God speaks and the assumption that the same Spirit who inspired the texts of the Bible illuminates readers to understand their message. The doctrine of divine illumination ascribes to the Spirit the role of addressing the spiritual blindness of fallen humanity rather than supplementing a lack in the texts of the Bible. Thus, the Spirit's ongoing work in the interpretation of Scripture has mainly to do with the internal conviction that Scripture, as the word of God, is the authoritative and reliable source of truth and the illumination of the mind to attain clarity in discerning and understanding the meaning of Spirit-breathed Scripture.

A common feature among the Protestant theologians concerning the doctrine of illumination is that the Spirit's interpretive work does not have to do only with accurately understanding the scriptural text. Based on their strong conviction that the text is a medium through which God speaks and the reader gains spiritual knowledge and understanding of him, the Spirit's illuminative role has more to do with providing insight into the spiritual things through the reading of

---

[82] John Wesley, 'The Nature of Enthusiasm', §12, *Works*, II, p. 50. Bicentennial edition.

Scripture. With the similarities of emphasis they give to the Spirit's work beyond the cognitive understanding of the text, though, there are subtle differences in their approaches. In Calvin's doctrine of illumination, the Spirit's interpretive role is explained in terms of the ability the Spirit gives both to understand the text and to obey what it says. Here the focus seems to be the divine influence for obedience that the Spirit generates through the reading of Scripture. Owen's doctrine of illumination gives emphasis to the divine enablement to know and discern the mind and will of God, which ultimately leads to experience his glory. Wesley's understanding of divine illumination in terms of an ongoing inspiration allows him to see the guidance and assistance of the Spirit that makes the life of sanctification possible. As much as they are significantly textual in their hermeneutical approaches, their understanding of the Spirit's interpretive role goes beyond understanding of the text.

Given the dynamic nature of the Protestant tradition, the assessment of theologians discussed in this chapter is not global. However, because of the ongoing influence of these theologians, they can provide a basis for understanding Protestant perspectives on the Spirit's role in theological interpretation of Scripture. They also provide a helpful contextual background to the Pentecostal tradition's perspectives on these questions.

5

SPIRIT AND SCRIPTURE IN THE PENTECOSTAL TRADITION

The preceding two chapters explored the Spirit's interpretive role from within major streams of Christian tradition with the purpose of establishing a basis for examining Pentecostal hermeneutical practices and reflections on the issue. Insights from Eastern Orthodox, Roman Catholic, and Protestant ecclesial traditions provide useful resources for understanding and analyzing the hermeneutical contributions from the Pentecostal tradition pertaining to the Spirit's interpretive role. On the one hand, at least three general, common assumptions can be drawn from our study of the perspectives in these Christian traditions. First, there is a conventional affirmation regarding the nature of Scripture as the word of God or as God's means of communication. Based on the fundamental Christian presupposition of God's revelation, the understanding of Scripture as divinely inspired means of God's revelation is a common feature within all these traditions. Second, it is recognized that the purpose of biblical texts is for the instruction and edification of believers towards individual and communal transformation. Finally, there is a common notion in their doctrine of Scripture with regard to human limitations of understanding divine things through Scripture without the assistance of the Spirit of God.

On the other hand, each tradition has its own way of appropriating the Spirit's activity in the interpretation of Scripture. Eastern Orthodoxy, with its Spirit-sensitive theology, emphasizes a mystical participation of reading Scripture. The dynamic work of the Spirit in biblical interpretation is realized through its tradition of worship and prayerful reading. The Roman Catholic Church, as represented by its Dogmatic Constitution on Divine Revelation, *Dei Verbum*, the spiritual exegesis as examined in de Lubac's work, and the spiritual reading practice, *Lectio Divina*, provides a rich and dynamic perspective on the Spirit's interpretive role in reading Scripture. Protestantism, as observed in the doctrines of Calvin, Owen, and Wesley, primarily gives emphasis to the illumination of the Spirit towards the understanding of God's message through the biblical texts.

In this chapter, I will deal with perspectives within the Pentecostal Christian tradition in order to examine the approaches in relation to the Spirit's interpretive role. Dealing with Pentecostal viewpoints on pneumatic biblical hermeneutics will help to address the lacuna in discussions of the topic from contemporary proponents of theological interpretation of Scripture and will contribute to the collective understanding of the Spirit's work in theological reading of the biblical texts. I will analyze Pentecostal pneumatic hermeneutics in the chapter by exploring the works of three contemporary Pentecostal theologians: Kenneth J. Archer, Amos Yong, and L. William Oliverio. First, though, I will provide a general introduction to Pentecostalism, including its place in the wider landscape of the present-day Christian movement as well as its general approach toward pneumatic hermeneutics.

Pentecostalism and Pneumatic Hermeneutics

In his comprehensive survey of Christianity, *The World's Christians*, Douglas Jacobsen recognizes Pentecostalism as one of the four major Christian traditions, alongside Eastern Orthodoxy, Roman Catholicism, and Protestantism.[1] Despite the fact that it is an emerging tradition, it is appropriate to recognize Pentecostalism as one of the mainstream Christian traditions considering its phenomenal and rapid growth as well as the vigorous impact it is making in global Christendom.[2] Certainly, as a movement that mainly came out of

---

[1] Jacobsen, *The World's Christians*, pp. 50-62.

[2] Based on Jacobsen's study, almost a fifth of the world's Christian population belongs to the Pentecostal tradition, which began only a century ago. Insiders to the movement ascribe this remarkable explosion to the Holy Spirit and his work, although, as Jacobsen notes, there are diverse social factors as well that explain this

Protestantism, particularly the Wesleyan Holiness tradition, and because of its several overlapping points with the Protestant core beliefs, with the exception of the Apostolic Church's oneness Pentecostalism, some would suggest that it makes sense to locate Pentecostalism within the Protestant tradition. For instance, W. David Buschart treats the Pentecostal tradition as one of eight Protestant ecclesial traditions in his grand study of the Protestant churches.[3] Given its emphasis on the individual's relationship with God and its high view of Scripture, some contend that the Pentecostal movement is a new form of Protestantism.[4]

In response, Jacobsen argues that it is not helpful to conflate Pentecostalism with Protestantism, although they both share some common concerns. He identifies their relationship as somewhat similar to the relationship between Catholicism and Orthodoxy, which displays significant overlap, though also distinct spiritualties. Despite their significant intersections, Protestantism and Pentecostalism ought to be considered as two separate Christian traditions. Others also share this view, including, for example, Nimi Wariboko, who argues in a recent work on 'the Pentecostal Principle' that Pentecostalism is different from Protestantism even though they may share a number of common characteristics. Building his argument for a Pentecostal principle on Paul Tillich's work on a Protestant principle, Wariboko claims:

> The Pentecostal principle is Protestantism but something different from it in kind. Church, the communion that possesses Pentecostalism, must also be Protestant, for Pentecostalism presupposes Protestantism, just as Protestantism presupposes in its possessor the Catholic substance and Catholic substances social practices. Though Pentecostalism must be Protestant in the same way as it must be Catholic and socially relational, its nature is not

---

growth, including Pentecostalism's attentiveness to the needs of the poor, its emphasis on a personal emotional experience of God, and the lack of expense required to plant a church when compared with other Christian traditions. See Jacobsen, *The World's Christians*, p. 50.

[3] W. David Buschart, *Exploring Protestant Traditions: An Invitation to Theological Hospitality* (Downers Grove, IL: IVP Academic, 2006).

[4] Jacobsen, *The World's Christians*, p. 52.

Protestant. Pentecostalism is something new and while it is also Protestant, it is not merely Protestant.[5]

One of the primary characteristics that distinguish Pentecostalism from Protestantism is its vigorous enthusiasm for an experientially oriented spirituality. Despite their differences on categorizing the Pentecostal tradition, both Jacobsen and Buschart agree that the Holy Spirit and charismatic faith experience play a crucial role in the Pentecostal spirituality and theology.[6] Jacobsen observes that the attention given in the Protestant tradition to doctrinal articulation contrasts with the way the Pentecostal tradition emphasizes the importance of practical experiences for understanding God. For him, the distinctiveness of Pentecostalism is more of an 'emphasis' rather than a 'different set of beliefs'.[7] He writes:

> Protestantism's focus on understanding – on describing faith in words, concepts, and clearly formulated doctrines is very different from the Pentecostal/ Charismatic tradition's focus on experiencing God beyond or outside the realm of words. Pentecostal/Charismatic faith is about being enveloped in the love of God; it is about being healed emotionally and physically by God's presence … Self-control is a Protestant virtue, but it is precisely the willingness to sometimes lose control, even of one's own body, that allows Pentecostal/Charismatic Christians to experience God in the way they do.[8]

Establishing the particular characteristics of the Pentecostal tradition is helpful to understand better its distinctive features and approaches to the correlation of Spirit and Scripture. Scholars from within and outside the movement share the view that the Pentecostal tradition's hermeneutical understanding is primarily centered around its emphasis on the shared and individual pneumatic experiences of the believers. From his evangelical perspective, Robert K. Johnston, for instance, describes Pentecostal hermeneutics as experientially based and biblically authorized with its development towards more

---

[5] Nimi Wariboko, *The Pentecostal Principle: Ethical Methodology in New Spirit* (Grand Rapids: Eerdmans, 2012), pp. 16-17; cf. Paul Tillich, *The Protestant Era* (Chicago: University of Chicago Press, 1948).

[6] Buschart, *Exploring Protestant Traditions*, p. 242.

[7] Jacobsen, *The World's Christians*, p. 10.

[8] Jacobsen, *The World's Christians*, p. 52.

theological responsibility. The fact that it is primarily an experience-oriented hermeneutical approach provides Pentecostalism with a unique stance in its theology of Scripture. Since experience grants an exceptional ability to connect with reality in a far better way than abstract theoretical knowledge does, Johnston argues that the Pentecostal emphasis on pneumatic experience as an encounter with the Holy Spirit has a strategic hermeneutical advantage.[9] As he acknowledges, Pentecostalism's experiential orientation contributes a fresh understanding to the broader Christian view of the power of the Spirit that actively works in the Church as a life-movement.[10] This experiential-practical orientation shapes Pentecostal hermeneutics by positioning the Holy Spirit at the center of biblical interpretation and theological engagement.

The Holy Spirit's supreme interpretive role is a guiding presupposition in the Pentecostal theology and biblical interpretation. French L. Arrington uses the biblical model of Scripture as the sword of the Spirit to describe the Pentecostal understanding of the Spirit in scriptural interpretation. Pentecostals, he claims, 'believe that only through the Spirit can the heart of biblical message be penetrated. By the work of the Holy Spirit in our hearts and minds, the truth spoken by the prophets and apostles can be personally understood and appropriated'.[11] He states that biblical reading involves the interplay between the understanding of the truth and an earnest response to the transforming call of the Spirit through the word. Thus, personal experience has a significant interpretive role in the Pentecostal hermeneutical tradition.[12]

It has become clear in recent decades that a Pentecostal hermeneutic has been emerging with its own distinguishing features – as opposed to earlier attempts marked more by accommodation to and adaptation of dominant interpretive paradigms found in evangelical biblical scholarship. Unlike earlier attempts to incorporate evangelical interpretive assumptions, recent Pentecostal hermeneutical engagements demonstrate a growing concern with developing a distinctively

[9] Robert K. Johnston, 'Pentecostalism and Theological Hermeneutics: Evangelical Options', *Pneuma* 6.1 (1984), pp. 51-66.

[10] Johnston, 'Pentecostalism and Theological Hermeneutics', p. 52.

[11] French L. Arrington, *Christian Doctrine: A Pentecostal Perspective* (3 vols.; Cleveland, TN: Pathway, 1992), I, p. 73.

[12] Arrington, *Christian Doctrine*, I, pp. 82-83.

Pentecostal approach. This recent initiative is a 'liberation' of Pentecostal hermeneutics, as Cheryl Bridges Johns describes it, from the standard fundamentalist reading of biblical texts after diversified internal and external struggles within Pentecostalism.[13] Lee Roy Martin, for his part, claims that distinctive hermeneutical approaches were present from the beginning of the Pentecostal movement, although it is only recently that Pentecostal scholars involved themselves in critical reflection on those interpretive experiences.[14] These hermeneutical approaches contributed to the development of a typically 'Pentecostal' way of reading of Scripture and doing theology, although it is not strictly unique to Pentecostals, since it is shared among some within the Holiness tradition and Third Wave non-charismatic mainline church renewal movements.

By analyzing the works of Archer, Yong, and Oliverio, we will explore the nature of these Pentecostal approaches to theological interpretation of Scripture and the Spirit's interpretive role. Archer's work is more focused on scriptural interpretation, whereas the works of Yong and Oliverio have a broader scope, dealing with wide-ranging hermeneutical issues that extend beyond the theological interpretation of biblical texts. Exploring the works of these thinkers not only introduces their contributions to the conversation, but also assists us with our concern to close the scholarly gap between contemporary discussions in theological interpretation of Scripture and the Spirit's interpretive role in the practice.

Tridactic Negotiation of Theological Meaning: Kenneth J. Archer

Recognizing a Pentecostal hermeneutical approach is an important strategic venture in dealing with the Spirit's role in theological

---

[13] Cheryl Bridges Johns, 'Grieving, Brooding, and Transforming: The Spirit, the Bible, and Gender', *JPT* 23.2 (2014), pp. 142-43. Johns argues that this liberated Pentecostal hermeneutics has a pneumatic grounding that frees biblical texts from the boundaries of history and provides an ontological category of the biblical texts as 'Spirit-Word'. She uses the marital relationship as a metaphor to explain the Pentecostal understanding of the correlation between the Word and the Spirit. She also argues that the triune life of God is the foundation for this 'marriage' between the Bible and the work of the Spirit.

[14] Lee Roy Martin, 'Introduction to Pentecostal Hermeneutics', in Lee Roy Martin (ed.), *Pentecostal Hermeneutics: A Reader* (Leiden: Brill, 2003), pp. 1-11.

interpretation of Scripture. As a leading voice in the study of Pentecostal hermeneutics, Kenneth J. Archer examines the hermeneutical context of early Pentecostalism to document its contribution to the hermeneutical practices of the Church in the twenty-first century. Archer contends that the Pentecostals' continuation of the Wesleyan Holiness tradition in its confrontation with fundamentalism in the Fundamentalism versus Liberalism controversy marked the emergence of a Pentecostal hermeneutic. He asserts that the Pentecostals' response to this paradigm shift carved out a third or alternative path, one that is neither fundamentalist nor liberal in its approach to scriptural interpretation. Archer indicates that the first generation of Pentecostals used a premodern 'Bible Reading Method' in a way that was similar to those of the Wesleyan and Keswickian Holiness movements. As a modified 'proof-texting system', the Bible Reading Method depends on inductive and deductive skills to analyze biblical data on a specific topic with the help of a Bible concordance, and then to synthesize that data to establish a doctrinal statement.[15] Further elucidating early Pentecostalism as a countercultural paramodern approach, Archer comments:

> The Pentecostals were not full-fledged citizens of modernity. They were like the traveling circus sideshows, living on the margins of society and presenting to those who ventured into their tents an electrifying vision of Pentecost revisited. The truthfulness of Scripture was discovered relationally, personally and experientially more so than 'scientifically'. They attempted to use the language and arguments of modernity, yet they always had a distinguishable accent that was neither premodern nor postmodern. They were a paramodern Christian community that attempted to deconstruct those elements of modernity and non-Pentecostal Christianity that they viewed as hostile. Pentecostal faith and interpretive practices cannot embrace the enlightened mind; 'like oil and water, they don't mix'. A contemporary and critical Pentecostal reading that desires to embody the interpretation as well as

---

[15] Archer reviews how early Pentecostals used the Bible Reading Method to cultivate two unique doctrines within Pentecostalism: 1) Spirit baptism with physical evidence of speaking in tongues, a teaching accepted by all mainline Pentecostals; and 2) baptism in the name of Jesus only, which led to the formation of Oneness Pentecostalism, a teaching not supported by all Pentecostals. See Archer, *A Pentecostal Hermeneutic*, p. 102.

explain it meaningfully should find a postmodern or post-critical approach more conducive to Pentecostal identity than the historical critical methods of enlightened modernity.[16]

Having this viewpoint, early Pentecostals resisted conventional, modernist exegetical practices fashioned by historical criticism. Rather than constructing a systematic theology or exegetical commentary, early Pentecostals' main hermeneutical agenda was regulated by concerns to live the Christian life and defend their understanding of the apostolic faith. For Archer, the primary conviction of Pentecostalism was centered on Jesus as the giver of salvation, sanctification, healing, and Spirit baptism. As a form of Christianity marked by its 'praxis-driven Jesus-centrism', Pentecostal interpretation was highly influenced by the conviction that Jesus empowers Christians to live a holy and productive life through the Holy Spirit.[17] Using the Bible Reading Method as a prominent interpretive strategy, the Pentecostals emphasized interpreting Scripture under the illumination of the Holy Spirit. Early Pentecostals strongly believed that the Holy Spirit, as the primary originator of Scripture, is fully present in scriptural interpretation.

Although the importance of historical and grammatical contexts to understand the biblical texts was recognized, recovering the biblical meaning using the scientific historical-critical method was not a primary factor in early Pentecostal interpretation. Rather, early Pentecostal interpretation comprised a precritical, popularist, text-centered approach to interpreting the Bible for practical purposes. Archer comments, citing the early Pentecostals David Wesley Myland and G.F. Taylor, that early Pentecostals were 'simply following the standard procedure that every scripture must be interpreted by scripture, under the illumination of the Holy Spirit. In order to achieve this, one had to have "an open heart" before God and "ask God to help [them] to harmonize and understand the Scriptures." In other words, they used the Bible Reading Method with a desire both to believe and obey.'[18]

Archer's aim is to construct a contemporary Pentecostal hermeneutical strategy by retrieving and critically reappropriating the values

---

[16] Archer, *A Pentecostal Hermeneutic*, p. 97.

[17] Archer, *A Pentecostal Hermeneutic*, p. 75.

[18] Archer, *A Pentecostal Hermeneutic*, p. 127.

and beliefs of early Pentecostal interpretation. In doing so, he establishes the identity and essential themes of the Pentecostal community
informed by the first-generation hermeneutical approach. As he observes both here and in a later article, 'The Spirit and Theological
Interpretation: A Pentecostal Strategy', this strategy for theological
interpretation is neither necessarily unique to Pentecostals nor beneficial only to Pentecostalism; it can also be useful in other Christian
traditions as well.[19]

At some point, Pentecostal hermeneutical debates were focused
primarily on methodological issues regarding exegesis and redaction
criticism. On the one hand, some of those involved in Pentecostal
scholarship tended to understand Pentecostal hermeneutics as a subcategory of evangelical scholarship. This understanding led some
Pentecostal scholars to become more modern and to employ so-
called objective, neutral, and scientific hermeneutical methods in
their interpretation, with the intention of discovering the author's intended meaning.[20] This hermeneutical procedure is deeply entrenched in the sophistication of modernism, which leaves little
room for experience and the Spirit's role in biblical interpretation. On
the other hand, aligning himself with the minority voice, Archer argues that Pentecostalism has its unique identity and distinctive hermeneutical approach, which gives more emphasis to the text and
readers than to authorial intention. This position recognizes Pentecostalism 'as an authentic Christian movement whose identity cannot
be submerged into Evangelicalism without losing important aspects
of Pentecostal identity'.[21] In fact, Archer takes seriously that this accommodation to evangelicalism, the roots of which are modernistic,
has had a devastating effect on genuine Pentecostal identity and doctrine. In short, Archer calls attention to a third category of narrative-
based Pentecostal hermeneutics – which, on the one hand, refutes
the modernistic accommodation of Pentecostal hermeneutic

[19] Kenneth J. Archer, 'The Spirit and Theological Interpretation: A Pentecostal
Strategy', in *The Gospel Revisited: Towards a Pentecostal Theology of Worship* (Eugene,
OR: Pickwick, 2011), pp. 118-37.

[20] Gordon L. Anderson, Russell P. Spittler, and Gordon D. Fee are important
voices in this author-centered evangelical Pentecostal hermeneutic. Craig S. Keener
demonstrates that he follows this interpretive trend in his recent work *Spirit Hermeneutics: Reading Scripture in Light of Pentecost* (Grand Rapids: Eerdmans, 2016).

[21] Archer, *A Pentecostal Hermeneutic*, p. 6.

approach, and, on the other, embraces early Pentecostal interpretation with some modification.

In discussing the Pentecostal story as a hermeneutical filter that shapes Pentecostal interpretation, Archer identifies the Latter Rain motif as the controlling narrative that provides the primary theological concept and organizational structure for early Pentecostalism. He refers to narrative both as an overarching theological category as well as a method for biblical interpretation.[22] The Latter Rain motif is the narrative that distinguishes Pentecostal Bible Reading Method from that of the Holiness tradition. This motif is built on the standard weather cycle in Palestine and the scriptural promise in the Old Testament that God would provide the former and latter rains necessary for the harvest as a consequence of Israel's covenantal faithfulness. Early Pentecostals used the Latter Rain motif as an apologetic explanation for the outpouring of the Holy Spirit at the turn of the twentieth century in a way reminiscent of the former outpouring of the Spirit on the day of Pentecost in Acts 2. The latter outpouring of the Holy Spirit was intended to empower Christians to be witnesses and to bring the Church to perfection and unity in these last days. The 'full gospel', or the 'fivefold gospel' – that is, the proclamation of Jesus as savior, sanctifier, Spirit baptizer, healer, and coming king – better explains this Pentecostal narrative.[23] Early Pentecostals had a strong conviction that the Latter Rain motif enabled them to return to primitive Christianity, crossing all the historical gaps separating the present and the early Church, and to restore the fivefold or full gospel. This central narrative conviction of the Latter Rain motif provides the hermeneutical lens for the reading of Scripture.

Given the strong affirmation within the community that extraordinary, supernatural experiences in the Bible are possible for

---

[22] Archer, 'The Spirit', p. 120.

[23] Some Pentecostal traditions opt to use the 'fourfold' Gospel instead of 'fivefold', following A.B. Simpson, the founder of the Christian and Missionary Alliance in the late nineteenth century, who conflates the roles of Spirit baptizer and Sanctifier. The two gospel patterns became competing claims, although the fivefold pattern is historically prior and the fourfold pattern rose to prominence mainly following the global expansion of Pentecostalism. Donald W. Dayton argues that the fourfold pattern better expresses the logic within Pentecostal theology: 'It is contained within the more complex pattern and thus has a certain claim to be at least logically, if not historically, prior to the fivefold pattern'. For more discussion, see Dayton, *Theological Roots of Pentecostalism* (Grand Rapids: Baker, 1987), pp. 17-23 (21).

contemporary believers, Pentecostals allow biblical stories to directly challenge and reshape their tradition as well as their present experiences to inform their understanding of Scripture. This explains what Archer calls a dialogical process between experience and Scripture. According to him, the Pentecostal narrative hermeneutical strategy moves the emphasis of biblical interpretation away from applying correct interpretive methods in order to understand the meaning of a text to the Christian community as a spiritual context in which interpretation takes place. It is a hermeneutical strategy that seeks to have a strong tie with the first generation of the Pentecostal movement by giving considerable attention to the challenge that 'meaning exists in the social-linguistic-cultural location in which a community reads'.[24] Archer continues:

> There is a dialectical interdependent relationship between the written text and the community of readers. Thus, there exists an actual communication event that takes place as the text is read. The text, which in this case is a biblical passage, desires to be understood by the readers in a Christian community. The biblical passage is at the mercy of the community. However, a Pentecostal Christian community will want to give the biblical passage the opportunity to interact with the readers in such a way that the passage fulfills its dialogical role in the communicative event.[25]

The Pentecostal hermeneutical strategy that Archer proposes incorporates the Holy Spirit within its interpretive matrix. In fact, he identifies the Holy Spirit as the most important person in the conversation. He claims that this strategy is self-consciously a narrative strategy that embraces a tridactic negotiation between sacred Scripture, the ecclesial community, and the Holy Spirit.[26] Therefore, as a text-centered and reader-oriented interpretive method, the Pentecostal hermeneutic puts significant emphasis on the Spirit's interpretive role in understanding biblical texts. This interdependent tridactic dialogical relationship between Scripture, the Spirit, and the community produces a negotiated theological meaning of a text that is genuine

---

[24] Archer, *A Pentecostal Hermeneutic*, p. 206.

[25] Archer, *A Pentecostal Hermeneutic*, p. 214.

[26] Archer builds on Thomas, 'Women, Pentecostals, and the Bible', who first proposed the hermeneutical paradigm of Scripture, the Spirit, and the community.

and practical. Archer argues that the study of semiotics,[27] which involves understanding the signs and significance of the texts of Scripture, and the narrative approach of the Christian community – particularly the Pentecostal community's understanding of the Bible as a grand story or metanarrative and the testimony of personal experiences – combined with the willingness to hear and discern the voice of the Holy Spirit, creates a meaningful theological interpretation of Scripture.[28]

Despite the overarching emphasis displayed in the Pentecostal hermeneutical strategy on the contribution of the Spirit in theological interpretation, the challenge of speaking of the Spirit's role is noticeable in Archer's analysis. The difficulty arises from the fact that the Spirit's interpretive role is still explained in terms of the discernment abilities of the community and the clarity of the scriptural text. This requires careful attentiveness and harmonization between the human and divine elements of interpretation; in other words, it is important to find a balance between reader-response criticism and attuning to the divine voice and guidance. In describing how the Spirit's voice is discerned through the texts of the Bible and the Christian community, Archer comments:

> The Holy Spirit's voice is heard in and through the individuals in community as well as in and through Scripture (which may be words of correction, reproof, or even a word of resistance to a certain biblical statement). The Spirit's voice is not reduced to or simply equated with the biblical text or the community, but is connected to an interdependent upon these as a necessary means for expressing the past-present-future concerns of the Social Trinity. The Holy Spirit has more to say than Scripture, yet it will be scripturally based. The community must read and discern the signs and

---

[27] In his discussion of semiotics, Archer draws on the work of Umberto Eco in Eco, with Richard Rorty, Jonathan Culler, and Christine Brooke-Rose, *Interpretation and Overinterpretation* (ed. Stefan Collini; New York: Cambridge University Press, 1992).

[28] Archer also follows Alasdair MacIntyre, who argues for a particular narrative tradition as a basis for the version of reality in different communities. Archer, *A Pentecostal Hermeneutic*, p. 164. For his discussion of MacIntyre, see pp. 96-98. See also Alasdair MacIntyre, *After Virtue: A Study in Moral Theory* (Notre Dame, IN: University of Notre Dame Press, 1984); *idem, Whose Justice? Which Rationality?* (Notre Dame, IN: University of Notre Dame Press, 1988).

the sound of the Spirit amongst the community in dialogical relationship with the Scriptures.[29]

Archer notes that the role of the Holy Spirit in biblical interpretation is an extension of the ministry of Christ who is incarnate, crucified, ascended, and glorified. As a continuation of Christ's presence after he has physically departed, the Spirit's primary role is to guide and direct the believing community in understanding the meaning of Scripture in the present life. For Archer, the modernist hermeneutical attempt to reconstruct the history behind the text and discover the author's intended meaning through historical-critical strategies does not necessarily provide the warrant necessary to bridge the gap between the biblical texts and the reader. Rather, giving emphasis to the pneumatic and experiential dimensions of interpretation, he argues that the Holy Spirit enables the reader to understand Scripture by spanning the historical divide between the ancient writers of Scripture and present-day readers. Archer bases his argument on Arrington's pneumatic and experiential dimension of interpretation, in which he suggests four ways that biblical readers depend on the Spirit: 1) submission of the mind to God so that the critical and analytical abilities are exercised under the guidance of the Holy Spirit; 2) genuine openness to the witness of the Spirit as the text is examined; 3) the personal experience of faith as part of the entire interpretive process; and 4) response to the transforming call of God's word.[30]

Since early Pentecostalism was identified as a paramodern movement and a protest against modernism, the hermeneutical strategy proposed here militates against the essence of a modernist interpretive approach. The fact that the predominant mode of transmission of biblical and theological teachings in early Pentecostal communities was oral, according to Archer, does not necessarily suggest the insignificance of academic study of Scripture. Rather, it shows that all doctrinal reflection and articulation should focus primarily on the experiential knowledge of God and his redemptive acts. This experiential knowledge must be *revealed* by the Holy Spirit, *validated* by

---

[29] Archer, 'The Spirit', p. 132.

[30] French L. Arrington, 'The Use of the Bible by Pentecostals', *Pneuma* 16.1 (1994), pp. 101-107.

Scripture, and *confirmed* by the community'.[31] Thus, the hermeneutical strategy proposed by Archer involves an interdependent tridactic dialogue between Scripture, community, and the Spirit, engaging their contributions toward exchanging a meaningful understanding of Scripture with the purpose of hearing God's voice to do his will in the present.

Hermeneutical Trialectic of Spirit, Word, and Community: Amos Yong

As another important voice in the Pentecostal engagement on the Spirit's interpretive role, Amos Yong's approach is a trinitarian-based pneumatological theological hermeneutics. Located in a pneumatological framework, the central argument Yong forwards is that theological hermeneutics occurs in a 'trialectic' of Spirit, word, and community.[32] Critical of the predominantly textual focus of theological hermeneutics in, for example, Francis Watson's suggestion that biblical theology is the primary sphere for theological hermeneutics or Charles Wood's definition of theological interpretation as Christian understanding of Scripture, Yong's holistic vision of theological hermeneutics focuses on a dynamic interpretive process that connects life and reality by theologically understanding God, self, and the world. He insists, 'A hermeneutics of the divine that fails to properly account for the interpretation of the extra-scriptural world will ultimately sabotage the theological task regardless of how polished one's biblical or canonical hermeneutics'.[33] Despite his agreement with the significance of biblical and canonical hermeneutics as two major aspects of theological interpretation, although he goes so far as to suggest that they are not the most important ones, his model of theological hermeneutics goes beyond scriptural exegesis. He argues for a broadened understanding of theological hermeneutics as a hermeneutic that 'aims at interpreting the totality of human experience – and that includes God and God's relationship with human selves and the world as a whole – from a perspective that is specifically and

---

[31] Archer, *A Pentecostal Hermeneutic*, pp. 144-45.

[32] As stated above, the paradigm of Spirit, word, and community was first proposed by Thomas, 'Women, Pentecostals, and the Bible', and developed further by Archer, *A Pentecostal Hermeneutic*.

[33] Yong, *Spirit-Word-Community*, p. 4.

explicitly informed by faith'.[34] In this way, he envisions a philosophically informed approach to theological interpretation that incorporates epistemology, metaphysics, and anthropology.

The pneumatological starting point in Yong's proposal controls the flow of the overall argument in his account and sustains his understanding of human undertakings in interpretation. Because of his theological background as a Pentecostal believer, he opts to begin with pneumatology for pedagogical purposes, as he prefers to argue from concrete to abstract.[35] Based on his understanding of how pneumatology informs theological knowledge, Yong states that ongoing firsthand pneumatic experiences function as the basis for second-order theological reflection and discourse toward developing an all-inclusive vision of theological interpretation. He makes a clear distinction between 'pneumatic' and 'pneumatological', in the sense that the former is the experience of the spiritual, while the latter is its second-order reflection. Perceiving the lacuna of pneumatological concerns in the theological visions of recent discussions regarding theological hermeneutic and theological method as observed in, for example, Kevin Vanhoozer's *Is There a Meaning in This Text?* (1998) and Stanley Grenz and John Franke's *Beyond Foundationalism* (2001), Yong attempts to bridge the gap by introducing pneumatological emphases into the conversations. This emphasis on the dynamic of the Spirit generates a pneumatological framework by which the world is to be interpreted. As Yong clarifies, this pneumatological structure

---

[34] Yong, *Spirit-Word-Community*, p. 6.

[35] In his argument about the pneumatological imagination and truthful discernment, Yong takes up the question of traditional notions of truth as pragmatic, truth as correspondence, and truth as coherence. His conclusion is that

a robust theory of truth that includes a pneumatological component whereby truth is not an abstract relation between a proposition and certain facts or states of affairs, but is a personal, affective, existential and embodied relation whereby to know the truth both implicitly and explicitly demands and, in some sense, brings about conformity of life to it. The Spirit of Truth is not just a demonstrated theological definition but is the one who brings about correction of error, healing of brokenness, reconciliation of fractured relationships, in short, who orients human selves wholly – affectionately, spiritually, and materially – to truthful living. As personal rather than abstract and ethical rather than totalistic, truth is that which is transformative and directive toward eschatological fulfillment. It therefore has to be a thoroughly relational affair that involves communities of knowers in the knowing process (Yong, *Spirit-Word-Community*, p. 175).

opens up and demands a trinitarian theology, since he envisions that 'pneumatology is central to a robustly trinitarian vision of God'.[36]

Yong explains the trinitarian vision of God as central to pneumatological approach using the Irenaean metaphor of Spirit and Word as the 'two hands of the Father' and the Augustinian metaphor of the Spirit as the 'mutual love between the Father and the Son'.[37] Based on these insights, the Spirit, as the bond of mutual love, is the key person in the relational and social aspects of the Triune God. Yong argues that a trinitarian hermeneutical vision is significantly shaped by this fully relational trinitarian theology. He writes, 'The Spirit is not only the relational key to the triune life as the mutual love between the Father and the Son, but is also the relational presupposition to our encountering and accessing that life personally as the gift of God to the world'.[38] Therefore, the work of the Spirit is the starting point for all theological understanding as the Spirit is 'the divine person who we encounter first, and through whom we experience the salvific work of God through Christ'.[39] Agreeing with the *Ressourcement* theologian Hans Urs von Balthasar, he states, 'The Spirit is the transcendental condition of the human experience of God'.[40] On this basis, Yong attempts to demonstrate how pneumatological categories illuminate Christian understanding and a hermeneutical trialectic that is driven and informed by pneumatological imagination. Further exploring the pneumatological imagination he writes:

> There is a pneumatological dimension to knowing without which rationality is itself undermined. Such an imagination is thereby at once theological and philosophical – at once pneumatic and trinitarian. It is pneumatic in terms of the experiences of the Spirit and the categories drawn from foundational pneumatology. It is trinitarian in the way it structures the processes of knowing itself, of truth and error, and of normative living. This means that pneumatology provides the proper interpretive key to understanding both the structures and processes of knowledge and the failure

---

[36] Yong, *Spirit-Word-Community*, p. 49.

[37] By deliberately reversing the order from 'Word and Spirit' to 'Spirit and Word', Yong calls attention to pneumatological emphasis developed in the book.

[38] Yong, *Spirit-Word-Community*, p. 63.

[39] Yong, *Spirit-Word-Community*, p. 61.

[40] Yong, *Spirit-Word-Community*, p. 228.

of the knowing process to adequately and correctly grasp its object … I suggest that a pneumatological imagination is capable of negotiating this trialectical interplay so as to provide for an epistemology adequate not only for the human engagement with the world in general and with others in particular, but also for the human quest for theological understanding more specifically.[41]

Trinitarian epistemology and the pneumatological imagination have significant bearing on Yong's constructive proposal toward method in theology and theological hermeneutics. For him, 'theology begins with the Spirit, which is always informed in some respect by Word and Community, and moves through, not necessarily in sequential order, the moment of Word, which is also never entirely bereft of either Spirit or Community, and the moment of Community, which is also never entirely disconnected, from Spirit and Word'.[42] In a similar way, he understands theological interpretation as a trialectical movement of Spirit, word, and community because it involves the continuous interplay between all the three elements at any given point in the interpretation process. There is a strong correlation between Spirit, word, and community that is to be understood, respectively in terms of subjectivity, objectivity, and contextuality. As an imaginative undertaking through which the knowledge of God, self, and the world occurs, theological hermeneutics involves acts of interpretation (Spirit), objects of interpretation (word), and contexts of interpretation (community). Each of the three factors is intrinsically related to each other as the activity of an interpreting subject, the interpreted object or set of objects, and the diverse contexts of the interpreting communities. Although Yong offers these concepts in a heuristic and descriptive manner, he also argues that they are normative in their regulative claim on theological interpretation. In brief, theological interpretation denotes the conjunction and correlation of these three factors.

The trialectic of interpretation begins with the Spirit, a beginning that Yong calls the 'act' or 'activity' of interpretation as a subjective enterprise, though it maintains particular objective and communitarian aspects. It is subjective insofar as it is a 'complex pneumatic activity' that involves persons with their human existence and

---

[41] Yong, *Spirit-Word-Community*, p. 22.
[42] Yong, *Spirit-Word-Community*, p. 220.

experience in relation to others and the world. The idea of subjectivity arises from the fact that human beings are subjects created in the image of God. Thus, theological interpretation involves a subjective reading of an objective fact. In this process of interpretation, the Holy Spirit plays a crucial operational role in inspiring basic human activities of interpretation. This unpredictable interpretive movement or 'break-in-to' of the Spirit takes place through the interpreter's imaginative creativity, responsible freedom, and appropriation of transcendent divine truth beyond self. In this sense, the activity of interpreting Scripture theologically is an activity inspired and guided by the Holy Spirit. The Spirit plays a significant role 'to expand, illuminate, apply, and communicate the truth which is embodied in Jesus'.[43] More than a historical affirmation of its origin, inspiration of Scripture, then, is an ongoing activity of the Spirit in the reading of the biblical texts, which involves the readers' faithful and humble reception of them as God's Word on the one hand and active discernment of what the Spirit has said and done as well as is now saying and doing through them on the other. Thus, 'meaning is finally borne in and by the Spirit through the medium of the Word, and never solely by either on its own apart from the other'.[44]

Yong acknowledges the potential danger of 'unconstrained' subjectivity in treating theological hermeneutics simply as a pneumatological task, or as he phrases it, *sola spiritus*. He simply states, '*Sola spiritus* does not work'.[45] Because of human finitude and fallibility, boundless imagination and creativity can lead to false claims of Spirit-inspired interpretations. In dealing with this danger, Yong outlines the hermeneutics of religious experience, the hermeneutics of the word of God, and the hermeneutics of the ecclesial/theological tradition as the objective principles that constrain theological interpretation. By legitimizing the Christian experience of God, whether it is radical, ritual, or mystical, he posits that experience serves as both medium and object of theological hermeneutics. He asserts, 'Experiences shape – either by confirming, extending, checking, or even sometimes correcting – our reading and interpretation of received

---

[43] Yong, *Spirit-Word-Community*, p. 41.

[44] Yong, *Spirit-Word-Community*, p. 40.

[45] Yong, *Spirit-Word-Community*, p. 312.

scriptural traditions, and that we therefore need to pay attention to the experiential matrices that birth our theological interpretation'.[46]

The significance of the Word of God as spoken, lived, and written functions as an object of theological interpretation by mediating reality, enabling the ongoing experience of reality, and providing possibilities to reconstruct reality. In his discussion of the Word of God, Yong's emphasis lies on the life, death, and resurrection of Jesus Christ as the living Word of God who can be interpreted 'only insofar as he is engaged concretely, interpersonally and intersubjectively'.

> Thus the living Word of God cries out for interpretation, even while, at the same time, enabling mutual encounter, (self-) understanding, and transformation. Whatever other data theological interpretation may work with, it cannot do without, much less ignore, the central given for theological reflection; the living Word of God in Jesus Christ. It is, finally, this person who is the inexhaustible way, truth, and life that serves as the concrete and material norm for all theological interpretation.[47]

With a nod to Barth and Bultmann, Yong notes that the written Scripture is not the Word of God but it makes present the living Word of God in Jesus Christ.[48] Thus, the concrete and materially written word functions as object for theological interpretation in the sense that it represents and points to the living Word of God through reading, preaching, and proclamation. This given objective reality as spoken, living, and written word of God constrains theological understanding against arbitrarily using scriptural proof texts to systematize biblical materials based on philosophical motifs and categories.

Although religious experience coupled with the word of God determines the course of theological interpretation, it is essential to note that reality is always interpreted from various perspectives. The fact that Scripture is given only through historical and theological traditions makes the hermeneutics of ecclesial tradition indispensable to constrain subjectivity and pluralized hermeneutics. 'A hermeneutics of the ecclesial tradition enables us to discern the factors intrinsic to Christian faith that shape our presuppositions, that influence the

---

[46] Yong, *Spirit-Word-Community*, p. 248.

[47] Yong, *Spirit-Word-Community*, p. 258.

[48] Yong, *Spirit-Word-Community*, p. 261.

categories of theological inquiry, and that drive our questions and therefore also our answers.'[49] Yong understands tradition as intertwined with the Spirit's active presence and work in history and human experience as well as the prophetic, living, and written word of God. Christian tradition as historical consciousness of the past events, historical locatedness of an existing practice, and historical activity toward the future signifies the continuous work of the Spirit through biblical and ecclesial identity. Theological hermeneutics needs to take the ecclesial tradition seriously, since it is an objective given to lay claim on the Church because of the inextricable link between tradition and the Church's ecclesial identity and its historical locatedness. Theological interpreters, therefore, need to cultivate essential skills to discern theological traditions as object of the past, present, and anticipated future.

Yong's argument for a trialectic of interpretation establishes the importance of the Spirit as a starting point for theological hermeneutics by mediating, forming, and transforming word and community as much as the word functions as the normative principle to the Spirit that works in the believing community. In a similar way, community has a central function in relation to Spirit and word by providing the contextual possibility for the work of the Spirit and the presence of the word. In describing how community is a place where Spirit and word come together, Yong suggests, 'The Spirit addresses, empowers, quickens or confirms a community of faith with the Word of God, or the Word proclaimed to a docile community of believers creates faith for the reception and experience of the Spirit. Alternatively, the coming together of the activity and the object of interpretation can be seen to occur when theological reflection is contextualized in its various communal arenas.'[50] These various contexts provided by communities shape theological hermeneutics as much as theological reflection informs and transforms them. Obviously, there is always a tension between continuity and discontinuity in the Spirit's activity of transforming the practices, identities, and boundaries of the diverse ecclesial communities. Carefully dealing with this tension, theological interpretation facilitates the communal activities of discerning the Spirit and understanding of the Word toward transformation.

---

[49] Yong, *Spirit-Word-Community*, p. 265.
[50] Yong, *Spirit-Word-Community*, p. 275.

Yong's case for the robust pneumatological component of trinitarian hermeneutics is reflected in his recent work on Pentecostal theological interpretation.[51] As a theologian with a substantial Pentecostal background, the modern Pentecostal movement's sensibilities and
perspectives remarkably influence Yong's views. However, shying
away from a more tradition-specific theological method and evolving
to an all-inclusive approach, his understanding of Pentecostal hermeneutics seems to have a broader spectrum that embraces all Christian
theological interpretation. His trinitarian approach is permeated by
the fundamental traits of modern Pentecostalism, which can well be
perceived in a renewed consideration of the apostolic spirituality and
practice in light of the outpouring of the Spirit on the Day of Pentecost.

Although the growing attention to theological interpretation introduces multiple layers and diverse approaches of reading Scripture
theologically, Yong insists that pneumatology is always an integral aspect of any Christian interpretation of Scripture. The Pentecostal
emphasis on the Spirit of Pentecost as the starting point, therefore,
fulfills the pneumatological and trinitarian vision of theological interpretation. He writes, 'Christian engagement with Scripture proceeds
after Pentecost and hence is not only christological and incarnational
but pneumatological and pentecostal'. He further states, 'Reading
Scripture *after* Pentecost means reading with and through the many
tongues of Pentecost'.[52] Based on the Lukan narrative of the outpouring of the Spirit on all flesh, reading through the many tongues
of Pentecost is a Spirit-imbued reading of Scripture as a body of
Christ that includes not only individuals and wide-ranging ecclesial
traditions, but it also involves intercultural and interreligious hermeneutics.

---

[51] Amos Yong, *The Hermeneutical Spirit: Theological Interpretation and Scriptural* Imagination (Eugene, OR: Cascade, 2017); *idem*, 'Unveiling Interpretation after Pentecost: Revelation, Pentecostal Reading, and Christian Hermeneutics of Scripture',
JTI 11.1 (2017), pp. 139-55.

[52] Yong, *The Hermeneutical Spirit*, p. 258.

Hermeneutical Realism for Theological Hermeneutics: L. William Oliverio

As works in theological method and hermeneutics from the Pentecostal tradition advance in the century, emerging voices arise to intensify the conversation regarding the Spirit's role in theological interpretation of Scripture. L. William Oliverio presents a typological account of the development of the Pentecostal theology and theological hermeneutics in his monograph on Pentecostal theological hermeneutics. By using a typological approach that gives special attention to key figures and historical events, Oliverio accounts for the development of Pentecostal theological hermeneutics. The original Classical Pentecostal hermeneutic, the Evangelical-Pentecostal hermeneutic, the contextual-Pentecostal hermeneutic, and the ecumenical-Pentecostal hermeneutic are four tentative categories that Oliverio uses to identify the progress of modern Pentecostalism and its theological interpretive approaches. For the continual development of Pentecostal theological hermeneutics, he proposes a hermeneutical realism that accommodates the transcendence of reality on the one hand and human constraints of understanding it on the other. In laying out his constructive proposals Oliverio writes:

> My suggestion is that Pentecostal theological hermeneutics be considered in terms of paradigms, and not only descriptively so but also prescriptively for its constructive efforts. Central to this move is my claim that the Pentecostal theological tradition ought to adopt a hermeneutical realism which recognizes that, on the one hand, human understanding is always linguistic and contextual and, on the other, that reality is transcendent to the interpreter's construals of it. I will contend that this basic move to a hermeneutical realism will be essential to the success of Pentecostal theological endeavors in the foreseeable future.[53]

Oliverio uses the framework of theological hermeneutics to approach Pentecostal theology, claiming that doing theology is a hermeneutical act that involves interpreting one's world. Aligning his view with Yong's definition of theological hermeneutics as 'the hermeneutics of the divine', Oliverio identifies the sources of God's

---

[53] Oliverio, *Theological Hermeneutics*, p. 17.

self-revelation as well as the practices and principles exhibited in Pentecostal theological interpretation. He writes, 'Approaching hermeneutics as theological hermeneutics is a different approach to Pentecostal hermeneutics than another common approach that is characterized by its movement back and forth between biblical and general hermeneutics'. He continues:

It is better for Christian theologians to work out a more comprehensive 'hermeneutics of life' that operates from the convictions of Christian faith in order to theologically interpret all of reality. The interpretation of Scripture will thus be one part, albeit a critical one, for this task, and what is sought for in these approaches as general hermeneutics includes much more than a free standing hermeneutical theory informed by a few biblical or theological convictions. Approaching Pentecostal hermeneutics as theological hermeneutics allows for theological convictions to permeate one's general hermeneutics, even while it allows one to learn from the findings and approaches of other disciplines.[54]

Despite the multivalent concepts concerning the tradition both from within and outside the circle, Pentecostal hermeneutics in a general sense involves the interplay between beliefs and experiences in a way that 'experiences shape beliefs while beliefs shape our experiences'.[55] This understanding of hermeneutics itself informs various Pentecostal theological interpretations.

Contrary to the strong assertion among the vast majority of early Pentecostals that their movement circumvented the history of the Church and directly connected to the New Testament Christianity, Oliverio argues that a solid historical root can be traced back to the origins of Pentecostal theology, even though it is appropriate to say that essential elements from the early Church were retrieved and re-appropriated by Pentecostalism. In agreement with key accounts, such as Donald Dayton's *Theological Roots of Pentecostalism* and Archer's *A Pentecostal Hermeneutic*, Oliverio affirms that the Wesleyan Holiness tradition was the primary root for the early Pentecostal movement. He also mentions the Keswick movement, the American revivalists and radical evangelicals, and the nineteenth century coalition that

---

[54] Oliverio, *Theological Hermeneutics*, pp. xv-xvi.
[55] Oliverio, *Theological Hermeneutics*, p. 3.

promoted a premillennial eschatology as fundamental influences on the development of Pentecostalism. The beliefs, practices, and experiences of these four streams of Anglo-American pietism significantly shaped early Pentecostals and their theological hermeneutics.

For Oliverio, the origination of Classical Pentecostalism marks the beginning of early Pentecostal hermeneutic. He claims that the original Classical Pentecostal hermeneutic had four essential characteristics. First, the dialogical interaction between the ultimate authority of Scripture and the general and religious experiences that construct Pentecostal beliefs have a reciprocal strengthening effect in shaping Pentecostal hermeneutics. The emphasis given to Scripture as the authoritative source of theological understanding coupled with contemporary complications in biblical interpretation often generated the primary assumption in Classical Pentecostalism that hermeneutics is all about dealing with Scriptures. With their high view of the sacred texts, early Pentecostals assumed that Scripture provides normative paradigms for Christian experiences and this understanding considerably shapes the way they read Scripture. Oliverio states, 'The human experience of hearing Scripture, in relation to all other human experiences, provided moments of experiencing it as God's word, and these stood out as authoritative and normative for the rest of a Pentecostal Christian's lived experience'.[56]

Second, with Archer, Oliverio claims that the narrative of the Latter Rain provides the primary historical framework for the original Classical Pentecostal hermeneutic. This restorationist motif provided an eschatological prospect for the early Pentecostals to interpret Scripture and their religious experiences with respect to God's plan to restore humankind and revive the Church. With its imminent expectation of the parousia accompanied by the baptism of the Holy Spirit, the Latter Rain theme was at the core of the early Pentecostal hermeneutic. Given the self-understanding that connects the movement directly with New Testament Christianity, bypassing the historical developments of the Church, Classical Pentecostalism perceived the history of the Church simply as tradition obstructing the uninterrupted authentic connection with the 'apostolic faith'.

As the third distinctive feature of Classical Pentecostal hermeneutic, the full gospel, or as Oliverio alternatively writes, 'the four-/five-

---

[56] Oliverio, *Theological Hermeneutics*, p. 31.

fold gospel', shaped Classical Pentecostal hermeneutics. The full gospel framework was employed in early Pentecostalism as a category to interpret Scripture and Christian teaching, as well as the general and spiritual experiences of Pentecostal believers. The early Pentecostal community used spiritual experiences as a means to test their beliefs and essential doctrines against reality. This dynamic correlation between charismatic religious experience, Christian devotion, doctrinal postulations, and Scripture generated a new kind of biblical reading and religious experience. Oliverio states, 'The tenets of the "full gospel" served as these core doctrinal principles in the Pentecostal paradigm, shaping its reading of Scripture even as it emerged from its reading of Scripture'.[57]

Finally, Classical Pentecostalism is characterized by its use of a pragmatic 'naïve realism' that provided the distinct logic within this particular hermeneutical model. Oliverio argues that early Pentecostal common sense rationality was formed by the integration of naïve realism of the words of Scripture, often the King James Version of the Bible, with an understanding of the priority of supernatural experiences.[58] In this dialogical interaction between charismatic experiences and Scripture, Christian theology and doctrines were continuously reinterpreted afresh, although this was not in a consciously theoretical sense. In other words, Oliverio argues that the Classical Pentecostal hermeneutic was 'a radical development of the Protestant belief in the authority and perspicuity of Scripture'. He further writes, 'The original Classical Pentecostal hermeneutic was thus a theological hermeneutic seeking to interpret the Scriptures and the world by reforming Christian beliefs in order to return to the "apostolic faith". But the goal of this theological hermeneutic was living out and experiencing this "apostolic faith", not just forming true beliefs about it.'[59]

The second major type of Pentecostal hermeneutic that Oliverio discusses is the Evangelical-Pentecostal hermeneutic. As the Classical

---

[57] Oliverio, *Theological Hermeneutics*, p. 33.

[58] Oliverio's view that common sense realist tendencies of Pentecostalism already existed in the original Classical Pentecostal hermeneutic is not supported by all Pentecostal theologians. For example, Archer thinks that common sense realism resulted from the Pentecostal encounter with fundamentalism. Archer, *A Pentecostal Hermeneutic*, pp. 48-54.

[59] Oliverio, *Theological Hermeneutics*, p. 34.

Pentecostalism's continual discontinuity began to stabilize and the movement gained the status of an established tradition, the continuous revitalization of its hermeneutics required a more sustainable hermeneutic. American evangelicalism and its systematic approach to doctrinal teaching based on scriptural interpretation, which gave more emphasis to tethering biblical meaning to authorial intention, was appealing to Pentecostals as they turned to develop a more sustainable hermeneutic. The hermeneutic that emerged out of the encounter between early Pentecostalism and Evangelicalism was what Oliverio calls the Evangelical-Pentecostal hermeneutic. As early as the second decade of Pentecostalism (the mid-to-late-1910s), the Evangelical-Pentecostal hermeneutic had become the primary hermeneutic for a majority of Classical Pentecostals, mainly in North America. Oliverio describes the development of Evangelical-Pentecostal hermeneutic in two stages: the early Evangelical-Pentecostal hermeneutic and the contemporary Evangelical-Pentecostal hermeneutic.

Using Stanley Grenz's model of the American evangelicalism's views of Scripture, Oliverio argues that (some) Pentecostals moved from a practical-experiential orientation to a cognitive-doctrinal tendency in their scriptural view, aiming to have a more structural foundation for their beliefs.[60] The primary feature of the early Evangelical-Pentecostal hermeneutic was its use of the authority of Scripture for the purpose of justifying early Pentecostal theological beliefs and experiences. Oliverio states, 'While in the original Classical Pentecostal hermeneutic new doctrines explained Scripture and life anew, in the Evangelical-Pentecostal hermeneutic demonstrating that Pentecostal doctrines were the result of the proper reading of the Bible came to the fore'. Thus, 'doing theology became a matter of discovering what the Bible taught – biblical doctrines – and systematically or topically integrating them'.[61]

In the early Evangelical-Pentecostal hermeneutic many Pentecostals began to appreciate the internal context and history of the biblical texts, although Classical Pentecostal interpreters disregarded their importance. Drawn by the conservative affirmation of the authority

---

[60] See Stanley J. Grenz, *Renewing the Center: Evangelical Theology in a Post-Theological Era* (Grand Rapids: Baker, 2nd edn, 2006).

[61] Oliverio, *Theological Hermeneutics*, p. 84.

of Scripture for life and theology, Pentecostals became accustomed to the philosophical assumptions and theological systems of fundamentalism, particularly dispensationalism, despite their apparent differences. However, as the early Pentecostal theological hermeneutic was more inclined to the evangelical tradition and drew on a theological method not inherent to the core beliefs, doctrines, and practices of Pentecostalism, a reductionism took place that led to the rise of the contemporary version of Evangelical-Pentecostal hermeneutic.

The contemporary Evangelical-Pentecostal hermeneutic began to emerge in the middle of the twentieth century and continues through to the present as the major academic and theoretical hermeneutic of Pentecostalism. This hermeneutic has three major subtypes: hermeneutics of inerrancy, author-centered hermeneutic, and pneumatic interpretation. The Pentecostals' strong affirmation of the authority of the Bible for doctrine and experience played a considerable role in their willingness to embrace key principles of evangelical method, particularly the doctrines of inerrancy and infallibility of Scripture. The author-centered hermeneutic developed with the intention of securing scriptural meaning from ideological or manipulative interpretations by focusing on the intention of the human author as inspired by the Spirit. Although Classical Pentecostalism's common-sense realism contributed to this subtype, Oliverio argues that it was mainly influenced by E.D. Hirsh and Anglo-American author-centered theory. The third subcategory of contemporary Evangelical-Pentecostal hermeneutic focuses on pneumatic interpretation, that is, on dealing with the work of the Holy Spirit in the interpretation of biblical texts. The presence of the Spirit in biblical interpretation is an essential element so the reader can be enlightened and illuminated by the Spirit. Stanley Horton, through his roles as an influential Pentecostal educator and author, has been an important figure in the development of pneumatic interpretation within the contemporary Evangelical-Pentecostal hermeneutic. Oliverio comments, 'The Spirit serves as the mediator of experiential knowledge of Jesus. Thus, beyond operating with a certain restorationist narrative of history and a supernaturalistic presupposition, Horton's theological hermeneutic is pneumatic in that it emphasizes the necessary presence of the

Spirit in the theological interpreter in order to rightly understand the biblical text.[62]

Although the view of scriptural authority as a source of understanding God and human experience remains the same, the contemporary Evangelical-Pentecostal hermeneutic sidetracks from its early version in its use of 'believing criticism', which involves employing historical-critical methods and moving beyond the internal context of the biblical texts to interpret them using external contexts. It is characterized by its turn to 'modernistic propositionalism', in which 'theology is understood to be about merely finding the right propositional statements which correctly state theological truths rather than allowing God to work through stories, song and other genres and forms, or which the biblical revelation is primarily constituted'.[63] The assumption in evangelical theological method that authorial meaning allows access to Scripture, which in turn functions as a basis for biblical theology and then systematic theology, shapes the contemporary Evangelical-Pentecostal hermeneutic. Oliverio discusses Gordon Fee's approach to hermeneutics and theology as an exemplar of this, though it is arguable whether Fee actually represents a Pentecostal hermeneutic. As Oliverio comments, Fee's Evangelical-Pentecostal approach marked him as a 'sympathetic doctrinal outsider' in interpreting the key Pentecostal beliefs, though he continues to be 'an experiential insider'.[64]

Although 'believing criticism' allowed Pentecostals to study the historical contexts of the biblical authors, its inadequacy in dealing with questions concerning the influence of readers and their contexts in understanding Scripture generated a firm criticism from some Pentecostal theologians and biblical scholars. This rejection was a crucial moment for the third category of Pentecostal hermeneutic – Contextual-Pentecostal hermeneutic. Occasioned by these critiques, the Contextual-Pentecostal hermeneutic has developed into constructive philosophical engagement as an interpretive approach involving cultural, social, historical, and linguistic contexts of the readers. Particularly, textual and linguistic concerns in interpretation receive crucial attention, as they are perceived to signify the possibility of human

---

[62] Oliverio, *Theological Hermeneutics*, p. 160. See also Stanley Horton, *What the Bible Says about the Holy Spirit* (Springfield, MO: Gospel Publishing, 1976).

[63] Oliverio, *Theological Hermeneutics*, p. 183.

[64] Oliverio, *Theological Hermeneutics*, p. 176.

understanding. Hans-Georg Gadamer's philosophical hermeneutics play a substantial role in Contextual-Pentecostal hermeneutics by offering an alternative to a hermeneutic influenced by efforts toward objective historical reconstructions of authorial meaning. Although Thomas's and Archer's narrative and communitarian approaches have significantly contributed to this hermeneutic, Oliverio considers James K.A. Smith's creational hermeneutic and Yong's trinitarian-pneumatological approach as its main representatives.

The ecumenical-Pentecostal hermeneutic is Oliverio's fourth type of Pentecostal hermeneutical engagement, which, he claims, has emerged in recent decades. The attempt to interpret God and reality as Pentecostal theologians, yet in relation to other Christian traditions, is the main motivation of this hermeneutic. Despite its marginalized status and irrelevance in the Classical and Evangelical-Pentecostal hermeneutics, tradition, as a prior interpretive commitment, is considered to be a source of theological understanding both as content and as a means of its transmission in the ecumenical-Pentecostal hermeneutic. Oliverio comments, 'The role for tradition that is affirmed in this hermeneutic includes the process of transmission of the faith in its various contexts, and thus the rise of various Christian traditions, as well as the content of the faith itself as it has been passed down'.[65] Ernest Swing Williams and Cecil M. Robeck are pioneering champions of an ecumenical orientation that seeks to overcome the longstanding Pentecostal tendency of disregarding tradition. Participating in formal ecumenical dialogues with other traditions, especially the Roman Catholic, proponents of the ecumenical-Pentecostal hermeneutic attempt to develop systematic theological reflections engaging diverse understandings. Oliverio identifies Frank Macchia's attempt to extend the doctrine of baptism in the Holy Spirit and Veli-Matti Kärkkäinen's attempt at a consensual hermeneutic as key representatives of contemporary ecumenical-Pentecostal dialogues.

These four typological representations allow a paradigmatic understanding of the developments of Pentecostal hermeneutical tradition. On the basis of these categories, Oliverio develops his philosophical and theological proposal for Pentecostal theological hermeneutics. As his portrayal of the Pentecostal hermeneutics suggests,

---

[65] Oliverio, *Theological Hermeneutics*, p. 253.

beyond dealing with scriptural texts, Pentecostal interpretations engage a range of interpretive foci, such as the world, general human experiences, special religious experiences, the human self, rationality, and even tradition. Although conscious reflection on these hermeneutical magnitudes is a recent incident, these assumptions have always been in place, however implicit they may have been within Pentecostal circles. With the aim of forwarding the theological and philosophical reflection by involving current and classical concerns on Pentecostal hermeneutics, Oliverio offers his proposal for hermeneutical realism for Pentecostal theological hermeneutics.

By understanding the Pentecostal theological hermeneutics in terms of comprehensive paradigms, the hermeneutical realism that Oliverio proposes recognizes the linguistic and contextual boundaries of human understanding on the one hand and the transcendence of reality beyond human construals on the other. In other words, he argues for the possibility of the understanding of reality as a 'correct account produced by the engagement of a universally available reason, autonomous from culture, tradition or special revelation that corresponds to reality as it actually and statically is, even if it comes in a "critical" form'. He writes:

> We conceptualize our worlds differently and thus categorize our experiences differently, experiences which we are able to have in the first place because of our ability to relate to that reality through language. So, in the first place, we have different experiences based on our pasts and present agendas. This means that multiple true things can be said. But also, untruths and distortions can still often be distinguished from truths. And almost all of our claims require contextual qualification, though theology is the domain in which the most universal truths are spoken, even as they always come from particular contexts.[66]

'Faith is at the core of a paradigm', claims Oliverio, 'though it is not an indubitable foundation'.[67] In a way similar to Yong's understanding of truth, he contends that his hermeneutical realism allows for the possibility that theories of correspondent, coherent, and pragmatic truth can operate together, recognizing the significance of

---

[66] Oliverio, *Theological Hermeneutics*, pp. 323-24.

[67] Oliverio, *Theological Hermeneutics*, p. 326.

context, tradition, and culture in a manner that experience and belief are not intrinsically disconnected. The interrelation of belief and experience functions as a hermeneutical framework by providing a faithful understanding of reality.[68] In the same manner, beliefs and experiences of the Christian life construct a theological understanding of God and of the world. This understanding of theological hermeneutics is not merely a cognitive reflection; rather, it is an 'embodied and practiced lived experience of Christian *faith*fulness to the Triune God'.[69] The Pentecostal hermeneutical approach and its expression of faith as a response to the actions of God, particularly in its classical form, explain the priority of theological hermeneutics as a practical lived experience.

The paradigmatic approach of theological interpretation in the proposed hermeneutical realism involves the possibility of multiple accounts for varied activities of God in the world. Oliverio suggests that it is a provisional hermeneutical realism given the dynamic nature of reality and finite condition of human understanding. Based on the principal assumption that experience describes conscious human life in its varied forms and allows for theological understanding, doing theology is a human experience as both an event and an act of interpretation by drawing on God-given resources in his self-communication. Although the main resources on which the Pentecostal experience and theological hermeneutics draw are word, creation, culture, and tradition, the interpretive task is carried by the guidance of the presence of the Spirit. The Spirit, as Lord and giver of life, Paraclete, and the Spirit of Truth, makes human theological understanding possible by empowering and indwelling believers. Rather than a prescribed methodological approach, hermeneutical realism, guided by the Spirit, inspires a steady development in the multifaceted and all-inclusive endeavor of theological hermeneutics.

---

[68] Concerning the relationship between beliefs and experiences, Oliverio sees his view in continuity with Vanhoozer's canonical-linguistic approach to Christian theology in that truth cannot be separated from the way of life that is linked with it. See Kevin J. Vanhoozer, *The Drama of Doctrine: A Canonical-Linguistic Approach to Christian Theology* (Louisville: Westminster John Knox, 2005), p. 15.

[69] Oliverio, *Theological Hermeneutics*, pp. 326-27.

Summary

Our study of the approaches taken by Pentecostal theologians indicates a considerable amount of attention given to pneumatology within the Pentecostal hermeneutical tradition of reading Scripture and doing theology. This pneumatological emphasis coalesced with the reader-oriented assumptions in the Pentecostal tradition, thus playing a pivotal role in hermeneutical approaches and theological responsibilities characteristic of Pentecostal theologians and biblical scholars. The explicit sensitivity and commitment to scriptural interpretation as a theological undertaking in the Pentecostal movement confirms the hypothesis that the Spirit has a prominent role in the interpretive practices within the tradition. Consequently, these discussions within Pentecostalism offer a significant contribution to the broader hermeneutical conversations in at least two ways. First, they directly inform and challenge the critical, relative absence of the Spirit's interpretive role in traditional evangelical methodologies of biblical interpretation and theological reflection. Second, these interpretive actions complement promising attempts in the recovery of the practice of theological interpretation of Scripture by stimulating meaningful dialogue concerning the Spirit's interpretive role.

Based on these studies, the main contribution of the Pentecostal interpretive approach in the broader conversation is its emphasis on hermeneutics that involves the Spirit, the believing community, and the biblical texts. Guiding the overall interplay of the three components, the Spirit is the leading constituent in the trialectic or triadic, interdependent relationship. Given the understanding that the presence and work of the Spirit comprise a hermeneutical starting point, these studies underline a pneumatological framework for theological interpretation of the biblical texts. Rather than viewing Scripture as past written documents, the Pentecostals' persistence in locating the inspirational work of the Spirit within the ongoing experience of the Christian community is a significant contribution to advancing the discussion of the Spirit's interpretive role. In many ways, these traditions model and provide a suitable platform for the practical aspects of the Spirit's working in Christian communities in their attempt to understand God, the world, and their mission in the world in light of a better understanding of Scripture.

Contrary to the typical effort in moving from text to context in widely accepted exegetical strategies, the Pentecostal pneumatic hermeneutics takes the importance of community and its special religious experiences into consideration in the interpretive and theological activities. The unsettling difficulty of speaking about how the Spirit mediates scriptural interpretation is given more specific explanation in terms of this interpretive approach that locates the Spirit's active involvement in the ongoing experiences of the community. For the most part, the Spirit's interpretive role is described with reference to its intrinsic relationship with the community and its hermeneutical engagements. Of course, there is a concern attached to this portrayal that leaves the biblical texts, using Archer's expression, 'at the mercy of the community'.[70] However, the sense of interdependence among these three components, articulated by the Pentecostal theologians, is more complementary rather than solitary. In other words, each of these constituents is not self-contained in terms of the interpretive share given to it. As Yong maintains, the *solas*, as in *sola scriptura, sola spiritus,* or *sola communitas*, which assumes control over theological methods and hermeneutics, needs to be strictly rejected since 'community, needs to be transformed by the Spirit and checked by the Word'.[71]

The Pentecostal hermeneutical strategy, permeated by its dynamic, experiential, and existential (in the sense of 'the present') approach, allows the understanding of the ongoing activity of the Spirit in the interpretation of Scripture and its appropriation in the lives of the readers. There is a clear affirmation within Pentecostal theology that the Spirit's correlation with Scripture is not necessarily restricted to the initial role the Spirit had in biblical inspiration. Pentecostal hermeneutics maintains a strong conviction in the ongoing inspirational activity of the Spirit as the Church continues to interpret and proclaim its Bible. This ongoing inspirational activity of the Spirit, which occurs in the Church's continual interpretation and proclamation of the biblical message, is a fundamental hermeneutical assertion in Pentecostal traditions. Of course, the doctrine of divine inspiration in Pentecostal theologies strictly points to the origination of the scriptural texts. However, in a similar way to the Wesleyan tradition that

---

[70] Archer, *A Pentecostal Hermeneutic*, p. 214.

[71] Yong, *Spirit-Word-Community*, p. 314.

prefers the broader sense of inspiration as an ongoing work of the Spirit to illuminate readers, the Pentecostal doctrine of inspiration has an organic extension of the Spirit's inspirational work beyond its historical affirmation of the origin of Scripture. This continuity of the Spirit's inspirational activity is explained in terms of the worshipping community's interpretative engagements and its proclamation of the Scripture.

A theological interpretive approach that involves fresh spiritual experiences and ongoing inspiration of the Spirit allows a meaningful encounter with God through the written Scripture. I have attempted to show the hermeneutical approaches and the correlation between the Spirit and Scripture in the interpretive practices within mainstream ecclesial traditions in the previous chapters. The chapters demonstrate that the doctrinal attitudes, religious experiences, and entire theological culture have a significant bearing on a particular church's practice of theological engagement and biblical interpretation. The pneumatological understanding and pneumatic experiences determine the emphasis each tradition gives on the Spirit in relation to scriptural interpretation and theological activities. In a general sense, each Christian tradition has its own unique center of attention in terms of the Spirit's role in biblical interpretation, although there are some common features in theological perceptions of the churches.

The Pentecostal hermeneutical approach, with its emphasis on the dynamic interplay between the believing community, the scriptural text, and the work of the Holy Spirit is a substantial contribution to the theological and biblical interpretation of the Christian Church. Its openness to hear testimonies of what the Spirit is actively doing and the emphasis on fresh experiences of the Spirit as a primary lens through which Scripture is interpreted offers significant insights to the overall understanding of the Spirit's role in theological interpretation of Scripture.

6

A Way Forward in Understanding the Spirit's Role in theological Interpretation of Scripture

We turn now to the task of constructive theological reflection on the significance and role of the Holy Spirit in a theological reading of Scripture. Pushing beyond relatively well-established views regarding the Holy Spirit in relation to Scripture, discussed in the preceding chapters, Christian theology needs to reflect more on the Spirit's role in theological engagement with Scripture. Theological reflection on the Spirit's role is often considered primarily within the framework of contemporary conversations concerning the practice of theological interpretation, which aims to read the Bible specifically as Scripture, as God's transformative address to the Church in the present. From this vantage point, it is crucial to address how the Spirit works in biblical interpretation and theology for those who want to read the Bible as a Christian Scripture and thus to mitigate the skepticism of modern scholarship that promotes overdependence on humanly devised methods of understanding the biblical texts. A genuine conviction that Scripture is God's way of speaking to us and that we hear his voice through Scripture with the aim of personal and communal Christian formation has as its consequence our recognizing *and* articulating the indispensable role of the Spirit in the Church's interpretive work. That is, the practice of theological interpretation cannot attain its intended objectives without the Spirit's interpretive guidance, which becomes, then, an essential component of reading the Bible as Scripture.

Our study in chapters 3 and 4 dealt with the way the Eastern Orthodox, Roman Catholic, and Protestant traditions perceive the Spirit with regard to theological method and biblical interpretation. Distinct pneumatological perspectives and spiritual experiences within these Christian traditions have shaped diverse approaches to the dynamics among the Spirit, theology, and scriptural interpretation. The hermeneutical approaches within these traditions demonstrate how doctrinal attitudes, religious experiences, and the entire flow of theological currents have significant bearing on biblical interpretive practices. The shared affirmation within these interpretive communities that the Bible is the word of God, given to instruct and edify believers toward generating Christian transformation, as well as their recognition of the considerable need for divine assistance to hear and discern God's voice through Scripture because of prevailing human limitations, is expressed in distinct ways and with distinct emphases. These interpretive traditions have mutual, yet distinctive perspectives and expressions of the Spirit's role in biblical interpretation. The purpose of exploring those approaches within these major Christian traditions was partly to contextualize and, indeed, to open the door to the Pentecostal hermeneutical approaches discussed in chapter 5. Because of the emphasis on *pneumatic hermeneutics* among Pentecostals, examining Pentecostal interpretive perspectives in relation to other, major Christian traditions helps us to deal with the interplay between the Spirit and Scripture within a wider theological landscape.

The previous chapter highlighted important contributions of Pentecostal hermeneutics; particularly that biblical interpretation involves a three-way dialogue between the Spirit, the (Pentecostal) community, and scriptural texts. The interpretive approach that comprises these three components, identified as 'hermeneutical trialectic' or 'tridactic negotiation for meaning', characterizes an important feature in Pentecostal reading of Scripture.[1] It involves a dialogical back-and-forth and interdependence between Scripture and the work of the Spirit as experienced and witnessed by the community of believers, which reinforces a theological interpretation of the biblical texts. Spirit-inspired reading in Pentecostal scholarship is often explained in terms of the communities' pneumatic experiences and their understanding of those experiences.

---

[1] See Yong, *Spirit-Word-Community*; Archer, *A Pentecostal Hermeneutic*.

Leading Pentecostal voices like John Christopher Thomas and Kenneth J. Archer advocate for the role of community in biblical interpretation because it provides a hermeneutical atmosphere for understanding Scripture.[2] Thomas's articulation of the three primary components of interpretation based on the model in Acts 15 provides a biblical precedent for this triadic interpretive approach. The dialogical relationship of the components, as Archer's proposal underlines, is perceived thus: experience of the Spirit shapes the community's understanding of Scripture, while the Spirit's work in the community is interpreted through the scriptural framework. This approach maintains the idea that community functions as a place where the written inspired text and the Spirit's ongoing present activity come to the fore to be assessed, discussed, and discerned. Provided that the community of faith is the contextual playground in which meaning takes place through the reading of Scripture in light of experience and testimony of the work of the Holy Spirit, the faith community plays a key, profound role in this interpretive matrix. It is, therefore, crucial to focus on and extend those Pentecostal hermeneutical approaches that perceive the role of community as an integral aspect of biblical interpretation to address the Spirit's interpretive role in theological reading of Scripture.

Admittedly, there is ambiguity in dealing with the work of the Spirit vis-à-vis the role that community plays in the interpretation of scriptural texts. Amid the growing attention to the Holy Spirit in biblical interpretation, it is difficult to maintain a defensible theological understanding of *pneumatic hermeneutics* without taking the community's interpretive engagement into account. The question is whether we can understand the activity of the Spirit in interpretation in and of itself, without attending to the community's interpretive role. Whether the Spirit's interpretive role is to be seen discretely as one of the three interpretive components or the Spirit's role has to be explained in terms of the community's hermeneutical activities is a significant issue. Some might even ask if we really need a distinctive, pneumatological approach in dealing with biblical interpretation; can we not simply incorporate it into a discussion of the ecclesial communities' interpretive role?

---

[2] Thomas, 'Reading the Bible from within Our Traditions', 108-22; Archer, *A Pentecostal Hermeneutic*, p. 214.

Indeed, one of the criticisms leveled at the triad of Spirit-Scripture-Community is that the community controls the interpretive ground by overshadowing the voices of Scripture and the Spirit. Mark J. Cartledge, for instance, shows concern for the unique emphasis ascribed to the community's hermeneutical role in Pentecostal scholarship.[3] Cartledge asserts that in the trialectic model community mediates both the Word and the Spirit, which he perceives as a risk of conflation where human arbitration housebreaks the divine. He sees in this model that 'the critical capacity of Scripture to challenge the community is simply nullified' and 'the community becomes the *norming norm*, rather than Scripture'.[4] There is always a danger that either a charismatic individual or the community's tradition and experience as opposed to the Holy Spirit will dominate the work of scriptural interpretation. Although the Spirit and Scripture are mediated by the community, Cartledge poses a challenge to the Pentecostal interpretive approach to make a clear distinction between the community's influence and the Spirit's voice in the appropriation of a text.

Keener, in his own way, also questions the emphasis on community in Pentecostal hermeneutics – alarmed as he is by the danger of interpretive circularity.[5] Keener recognizes the significant role that reader-response criticism plays in establishing a wide-range set of questions, interpretive options, and diverse voices for biblical interpretation. However, when reader-response criticism moves beyond a descriptive role and takes up a prescriptive one, he contends, there is a potential risk that interpretation turns out to be a 'political act' of making meaning by misusing or manipulating texts for the community's own goals rather than faithfully hearing the texts of Scripture.[6] He argues that biblical interpretation becomes vulnerable to the improper influence of socio-political power dynamics when the community's interpretive role is overstated. This creates the possibility

---

[3] Mark J. Cartledge, 'Text-Community-Spirit: The Challenges Posed by Pentecostal Theological Method to Evangelical Theology', in Kevin L. Spawn and Archie T. Wright (eds.), *Spirit and Scripture:* Examining *a Pneumatic Hermeneutic* (London: T&T Clark, 2012), pp. 130-42.

[4] Cartledge, 'Text-Community-Spirit', pp. 141-42.

[5] Craig S. Keener, *Spirit Hermeneutics: Reading Scripture in Light of Pentecost* (Grand Rapids: Eerdmans, 2016), pp. 277-85.

[6] Keener, *Spirit Hermeneutics*, pp. 86-87.

that interpretive communities control and silence the voice of the divine author.[7]

Prophecy and discernment are also issues to be mentioned in relation to the emphasis on the role of the Spirit and community in scriptural interpretation. In his response to renewal hermeneutic approaches in *Spirit and Scripture*, James D.G. Dunn sees 'mistaken or misused *charism*' as a fallout of improper stress on the role of the Spirit in prophecy and interpretation.[8] Dunn's concern is that unbalanced emphasis on the Spirit and experience of the community in interpreting Scripture might lead to the problem of false prophecy, a problem well perceived in both the Old and New Testaments, particularly in the Pauline writings. Despite the importance that the Spirit and experience have in interpretation, biblical reading without the community's critical assessment might lead to a mistaken or false interpretation. He recognizes that the community's experience or even tradition are themselves interpretations and need to be critically evaluated lest they go out-of-bounds.

Critiques like these call for careful attention to refine and clarify our understanding of the way people of the Spirit reads Scripture and describe the Holy Spirit's role in the entire process of interpretation. Having this Pentecostal hermeneutical approach and criticisms directed to it in mind, this chapter attempts to suggest a way toward a theological understanding of the Spirit's interpretive role vis-à-vis the role of the Christian community in theological interpretation of Scripture. Dealing with the Spirit's role in forming and shaping the interpretive community may further support the Pentecostal case that maintains the significance of community in interpretation. One way to understand a *pneumatic hermeneutic* is by taking a closer look at how the Spirit works in, through, and by means of the interpretive community, that is, the Church. Thus, recognizing biblical interpretation through the triadic model is warranted and has an important merit and implication on our understanding of reading Scripture as the interplay between the voice of the Spirit and the Church. It helps to affirm that the Spirit's interpretive role is actively perceived through the dynamic engagement of the ecclesial community as it

---

[7] Keener, *Spirit Hermeneutics*, p. 279.

[8] James D.G. Dunn, 'The Role of the Spirit in Biblical Hermeneutics', in Kevin L. Spawn and Archie T. Wright (eds.), *Spirit and Scripture: Examining a Pneumatic* Hermeneutic (London: T&T Clark, 2012), pp. 154-59.

carefully reads and attentively listens to what the Spirit says through the sacred texts.

Making sense of the ongoing active presence of the Holy Spirit in relation to the interpretive community, that is, the Church, is an important hermeneutical and theological task for grasping the Spirit's role in interpretive engagements. In other words, we need a pneumatologically grounded ecclesiology in order to consider the work of the Spirit in theological interpretation of Scripture. The first section of this chapter lays out a theological case for the idea of the Church as the people of the Spirit in order to present an ecclesiology permeated with a pneumatological emphasis. This pneumatological emphasis in ecclesiology helps us to realize the Spirit's interpretive role in light of the grand scheme of the Spirit's integrative work of generating, guiding, and sustaining ecclesial community. In the second section, I discuss the way the Spirit is involved in community formation – its mission, ethical dimension, and hermeneutics – based on a few highlights from the Book of Acts. The final section will point the way forward to establishing a *pneumatic hermeneutic* by maintaining what it means to read Scripture as the people of the Spirit and by providing an appropriate emphasis on the significance of a pneumatological standpoint for interpretive practices.

People of the Spirit: Toward a Pneumatological Ecclesiology

In his article, 'The Closing of the Book: Pentecostals, Evangelicals, and the Sacred Writings', James K.A. Smith raises the question of whether Christianity is a religion of the Book; and whether early Christians were 'a people of the Book' or 'a people of the Spirit'.[9] Although Christianity has always been understood as a religion of the Word, Smith argues that it was not a religion of the Book that centered on textuality, at least in its earliest form, that is, until a later shift occurred; it was rather a charismatic, oral/aural community centered on hearing.[10] Despite the fact that texts and Scripture were present,

---

[9] James K.A. Smith, 'The Closing of the Book: Pentecostals, Evangelicals, and the Sacred Writings', *JPT* 11 (1997), pp. 47-71.

[10] Following Brian Stock, *The Implications of Literacy: Written Language and Models of Interpretation in the Eleventh and Twelfth Centuries* (Princeton, NJ: Princeton University Press, 1983), Smith interprets 'textuality' as something different from literacy.

Smith insists that the prophet and prophecy were given a privileged status in the early charismatic community that defined itself and its vibrant relationship primarily with the risen Lord through the ongoing presence of the Spirit. He claims that contemporary charismatic communities are 'recoveries of the prophetic ministry of the Spirit' in the New Testament Church, although there is a tension within them to maintain textuality on the one hand and the ongoing revelatory ministry of the Spirit on the other.[11]

Smith's characterization of the early Christians as a 'prophetic community' versus a 'textual community' does not necessarily imply allocating lesser value to Scripture, nor does it underestimate the importance of God's written communication in and through the biblical texts. He states, '[T]o assert that the early Christian community was a prophetic/oral/aural community is not to dismiss the presence of texts or even the importance of texts to the first Christians'.[12] Nevertheless, it is an emphasis on the significant identity marker of the community of those who follow Christ as people of the Spirit who are continually shaped and formed by an ongoing experience of the Holy Spirit and their persistence in hearing his voice. The crucial role of the prophets in the early Church only indicates that 'authority does not reside in the texts but in the Lord to whom the texts point'.[13]

Arguably, identifying the Christian community as people of the Spirit has its own merits, at least for our understanding of its hermeneutical engagement and the Spirit's role involved in its interpretive activities. In what follows, I shall seek to explore the Christian community as a group of people who live and worship the Triune God under the empowerment and guidance of the Holy Spirit in order to develop a viable pneumatological ecclesiology that facilitates a way to properly delineate and articulate how the Church as people of the

---

For him a community may possess and use texts without being textual. Being a textual community is not about using texts; rather, it is about the status given to texts. Smith further states, 'A textual community is one that accords primary status to texts as the lens through which all of life is viewed … textuality is that which *transforms* (and perhaps undermines) orality, not a mode which is consonant with an oral/aural way of life. That is not to say, though, that oral communities are without texts; but once again, the presence of texts is not the same as textuality' (p. 57).

[11] Smith, 'The Closing of the Book,' p. 51.

[12] Smith, 'The Closing of the Book,' p. 55.

[13] Smith, 'The Closing of the Book', p. 70.

Spirit interprets its Scripture. In broad terms, an authentic, theological understanding of the Church entails a trinitarian approach that reflects the eternal love and unity of the divine community, that is, the *perichoresis* of the Father, the Son, and the Holy Spirit. The twentieth-century renaissance of the doctrine of Trinity ignited theological and ecumenical discussions across the board, including its interest in the practical significance of trinitarian theology for life of faith.[14] Particularly, the relationship between ecclesiology and trinitarian theology has been one of the issues much discussed in recent decades.[15] The Triune relationship among the persons of the Godhead is fundamental to the Christian community that is called into participation with this eternal intimacy. The communal life of the Church is an invitation of God, who is love, into fellowship in Jesus Christ by the Holy Spirit.

Dealing with trinitarian ecclesiology opens a way to recognize the Holy Spirit in relation to the life and mission of the Church, which in turn helps us identify the Spirit's interpretive role as the Christian Church reads its Scripture. In a discussion of trinitarian ecclesiology, the Eastern Orthodox theologian John Zizioulas offers a helpful perspective on both the nature and relational aspect of the Church in light of the Trinity. Zizioulas seeks to establish the view that knowing the essence of the Triune God is crucial to understanding the Church, its identity, assignment, and operation. He maintains that in the first place the existence and relational ontology of the Church itself is bound to the very being of the Triune God.[16] He states,

> The fact that God reveals to us His existence as one of personal communion is decisive in our understanding of the nature of the Church. It implies when we say that the Church *koinónia*, we mean no other kind of communion but the very personal communion between the Father, the Son and the Spirit.[17]

---

[14] Joy Ann McDougall, 'The Return of Trinitarian Praxis? Moltmann on the Trinity and the Christian Life', *JR* 83.2 (2003), pp. 177-203.

[15] John Behr, 'The Trinitarian Being of the Church', in Khaled Anatolios (ed.), *The Holy Trinity in the Life of the Church* (Grand Rapids: Baker Academic, 2014), pp. 165-82.

[16] John D. Zizioulas, *Being as Communion* (New York: St Vladimir's Seminary Press, 1985), p. 15.

[17] John D. Zizioulas, 'The Church as Communion', *SVTQ* 38.1 (1994), p. 8.

The Church's mode of existence is inextricably linked to the very being of the Triune God and its reflection of the divine community signifies a trinitarian dimension in which the divine *koinonia* is the true nature of what it means to be a Christian community. The Christian community, as *ekklēsia* – called-out ones – is summoned into this trinitarian relationship (*koinonia*) by God through Jesus Christ, his eternal Word, and by the power of the Holy Spirit.

Trinitarian ecclesiology involves a well-defined understanding of the Church in relation to the person and work of Christ and of the Holy Spirit. In other words, Christology and pneumatology are the sources and bases of the doctrine of the Church. There is a sufficient amount of Christological reflection in Christian theology concerning ecclesiology, particularly in Western thought, in which more emphasis is given to the elements of Christology in the doctrine of the Church, perhaps to the detriment of pneumatology. Colin Gunton precisely argues for a 'reconsideration' of this Christological prominence (with the corollary of less attention to pneumatology) in Western theology of the Church and urges that we put a 'greater emphasis on [the Church's] constitution by the Spirit'.[18] Gunton perceives that such a failure to attend to the Spirit in ecclesiology is harmful and he insists on reexamining the relation of Christology and pneumatology in general in Western Christian theologies. At the same time, it is interesting that ecclesiology in Eastern Orthodox theological reflection is predominantly grounded on a pneumatological understanding. This, of course, is associated with the basic difference between the West and the East over issues relative to the *filioque* controversy. Orthodox pneumatology is firmly built on the theological view that the Holy Spirit proceeds eternally from the Father alone in which the visible Church is connected invisibly to the Holy Spirit who proceeded not from the Son. Complex theological controversies aside, the absence of the doctrine of the subordination of the Holy Spirit in the economy of the Trinity in Orthodox Christianity made it easier to safeguard the prominence and significance of the Spirit in the life of the Church as a continuous Pentecost. Eastern Orthodox experience and theology illustrate the possibility of a heightened pneumatological emphasis in the theology of the Church.

---

[18] Colin E. Gunton, 'The Church on Earth: The Roots of Community', in Colin E. Gunton and Daniel W. Hardy (eds.), *On Being the Church* (Edinburgh: T&T Clark, 1989), p. 62.

Given that trinitarian ecclesiology includes both Christology and pneumatology, it is essential to designate the Church as a pneumatological entity as much as it is a Christological one. It makes sense that biblical images depict the Church as the body of Christ and the temple of the Holy Spirit (e.g. Eph. 4.1; 1 Cor. 3.16; 6.19-20; 12.27). As the body of Christ, the Church is also the living community of the Holy Spirit in which the active presence and ongoing work of the Spirit is evident in the world. Since the Spirit is involved in guiding, shaping, and renewing the life of the Church in fellowship with Christ, the identity of the Christian community is firmly tied to the active, empowering presence of the Holy Spirit. The Holy Spirit, as the mutual love of the Father and the Son, takes a significant part in being the relational bond between the Godhead as well as in playing a key role in shaping the distinctive nature of the Christian community to participate in this divine life and love. The Christian community's identity as people of the Spirit derives from this divine relationship accessed by the Holy Spirit (cf. 1 Cor. 12.13; Eph. 2.18). The Church is not defined by its institutional and structural elements or by its cultural and contextual expressions. Rather, the primary way to determine the identity of the Church is its relationship to the Triune God through Jesus Christ as its foundation and source of life by the Holy Spirit.

The Spirit's manifestation in the life and mission of the Church is well portrayed by Jürgen Moltmann's pneumatological ecclesiology.[19] Moltmann perceives the Church within the power and presence of the Holy Spirit. His 'revived interest' in the person and work of the Holy Spirit in relation to the Church underlines the significance of a pneumatological perspective in understanding 'messianic eschatological ecclesiology'.[20] Moltmann highlights the importance of pneumatology in the life of the Christian community by explaining that the Church exists in considerable tension – between history on the one hand and eschatology on the other. The Holy Spirit, in his presence and power, mediates the eschatological hope and the history of Jesus as the Church lives between the past and the expectation of the coming Kingdom. Life in the Holy Spirit represents the Church's divine

---

[19] Jürgen Moltmann, *The Church in the Power of the Spirit: A Contribution to Messianic Ecclesiology* (Minneapolis: Fortress, 1993).

[20] Veli-Matti Kärkkäinen, *An Introduction to Ecclesiology: Ecumenical, Historical and Global Perspectives* (Downers Grove, IL: IVP Academic, 2002), p. 131.

experiences and processes, which it enjoys as the eschatological community in the world and for the world. The Spirit works to form the community of believers through these experiences and processes of worship, prayer, proclamation, and sacraments as well as the *charismata*, the gifts and offices for its own communal edification and for the services that flow from the fellowship toward the society at large. Experiencing the mediation and power of the Holy Spirit, the Church recognizes itself as a messianic and charismatic fellowship that exists for the service of God's Kingdom in the world.[21]

Pneumatology is important in Moltmann's ecclesiology for the reason that its being an ecclesiological community is the same as its being a pneumatological or Spirit-renewed community. In fact, he specifically identifies the Church as a charismatic community that experiences the energies (*charismata*) of new life in the Spirit. It is the community of God's presence where the Spirit's encounter takes place as he continually creates and shapes a new brand of people with a messianic eschatological vision and mission. Moltmann writes:

> The new people of God see themselves in their existence and form as being 'the creation of the Spirit', and therefore as the initial fulfillment of the new creation of all things and the glorification of God. The Spirit calls them into life; the Spirit gives the community the authority for its mission; the Spirit makes its living powers and the ministries that spring from them effective; the Spirit unites, orders and preserves it. It therefore sees itself and its powers and tasks as deriving from and existing in the eschatological history of the Spirit. In this it experiences not only what it itself is, but also where it belongs. It discovers the redeeming future of the world in the overriding span of the Spirit's history.[22]

If the Church is founded Christologically and directed eschatologically, it is the pneumatological feature that makes a connection between the foundation and the direction of the Christian community. People believe in Jesus as the Christ and hope for God's future not by their own strength, reason, and will. Rather, it is the power of the Holy Spirit that creates a living remembrance of Christ and directs their hope towards the parousia. The Spirit shapes the character

---

[21] Moltmann, *The Church in the Power of the Spirit*, p. 198.

[22] Moltmann, *The Church in the Power of the Spirit*, pp. 294-95.

of the individual and the culture of the community by making it possible to live the present reality of Christ in light of history and the
forthcoming Kingdom. The Church's faith in Christ and hope for the
future is achievable only through the vigorous power and presence
of the Spirit. Recognizing the Church as a pneumatically oriented
community guided and shaped by the Spirit helps to identify its authentic identity, characteristics, and mission.

These views on pneumatological ecclesiology resonate with contemporary Pentecostal approaches that perceive the Church as a charismatic missionary community with a remarkable emphasis on the
Spirit's presence as well as a relentless passion for the eschatological
Kingdom. Experiences of Spirit baptism and the eschatological ur-
gency to spread the gospel to the unreached were primary characteristics of early Pentecostal ecclesiology as it was an attempt to recover
the New Testament Church experiences of the Spirit.[23] This was triggered by a renewed appreciation of the book of Acts and of passages
like Mt. 24.14 and Rev. 14.6-7 that shaped the early Pentecostals'
pneumatic experiences and their earnest anticipation of the coming
Kingdom.[24]

For instance, Steven J. Land's account of Pentecostal spirituality,
as an apostolic faith that attempts to recover the apocalyptic/escha-
tological vision, demonstrates an ecclesiology that is future-oriented
and decisively reliant on the witness of the Spirit's presence.[25] Land's
theological understanding of spirituality centers on a Pentecostal experience of the Spirit that implants passion for the Kingdom and
imparts spiritual practices in which the Spirit shapes all things. This
future-directed passion and longing for the Kingdom is experienced
now through justification, sanctification, and the experience of Spirit
baptism. Pentecostal beliefs and practices both express and confirm
that the corporate life of the Christian community is permeated by
apocalyptic reality and the ongoing active presence of the Holy
Spirit.[26]

---

[23] Andy Lord, *Network Church: A Pentecostal Ecclesiology Shaped by Mission* (Leiden:
Brill, 2012).

[24] Lord, *Network Church*, p. 64.

[25] Steven J. Land, *Pentecostal Spirituality: A Passion for the Kingdom* (JPTSup 1; Sheffield: Sheffield Academic Press, 1993), pp. 58-121.

[26] Land, *Pentecostal Spirituality*, p. 59.

Approaches like this, pertaining to Christian community in relation to the active presence of God through the person and works of
the Holy Spirit, carve the identity of Church in a way that it is recognized by its experience of the Spirit's manifestation. Identifying the
Christian community as people of the Spirit is a way of affirming the
active engagement of the Holy Spirit in the Church to inform, form,
and transform individuals as well as the whole community to a life
that is characterized by Christlikeness. Indeed, establishing a pneumatological ecclesiology not only allows an understanding of the
Spirit's involvement in the entire being of the Church, but also helps
maintain the real identity of ecclesial community shaped by the Spirit
to impact the present in light of its historical reality as well as the
future eschatological orientation. Moreover, it facilitates a way to describe the Spirit's role in relation to the Christian community's life
and worship, mission, and interpretive engagements.

A candid outlook toward pneumatological ecclesiology mitigates
challenges pertaining to understanding the interrelation between the
Spirit and the community's role in the interpretation of Scripture.
Precisely, the unique emphasis on the nature of the Church as a community of believers invigorated by the power and presence of the
Spirit prompts a fresh consideration of the Spirit-inspired Scripture,
on the one hand, and the community's interpretive engagements with
it, on the other. An ecclesiology that is substantiated pneumatologically deems the Spirit responsible for generating and sustaining both
the community and the Scriptures. Therefore, the entire discussion
of the Spirit's interpretive role lies on the Spirit's intrinsic impetus to
the Church as well as the Scripture. Indeed, pneumatological ecclesiology provides a distinctive insight concerning the Spirit's interpretive role in and through the community – its faithful practices and
testimonies of the ongoing experience of the Spirit.

The Spirit's Community-forming Presence in Acts

The efforts to understand broadly the Spirit's role of constituting,
guiding, and shaping the Christian Church in its entirety is assisted by
attending to a biblical model from the New Testament Church's experience of the Holy Spirit. It is thus helpful to explore a few passages from the book of Acts to develop in conversation with the Bible an understanding of ways in which the Spirit was involved in

forming the early Christian community. Luke's account of the Acts of the Apostles is a sequel to his writing about the life and works of Jesus in his first volume, the Gospel of Luke. In writing a two-volume book, Luke provides a historical-theological narrative of the story of Christian beginnings from the birth, baptism, ministry, death, and resurrection of Jesus, to how the early Church was born and began to expand throughout the first century Roman Empire. While scholars agree that soteriology is the primary subject matter of Lukan writings,[27] the presence and activity of the Spirit of God is a crucial theme in the entire narrative of both volumes.[28] The Spirit is evident in the Third Gospel not only with reference to the life and ministry of Jesus (Lk. 3.22; 4.1, 14, 18; 10.21), but also as one who inspires others to bear witness to the Messiah and God's eschatological redemption (Lk. 1.15, 17, 35, 41, 67; 2.25-27; 11.13; 12.12). One could say that the Spirit's work in relation to individuals other than Jesus in the Gospel account may be a preview to the things to come in the book of Acts, where the presence and power of the Holy Spirit is substantively active to empower and guide the early witnesses of the Christian message.[29]

The working presence of the Spirit of God and his part in the messianic mission of the early Church is eminent throughout Luke's narrative in Acts. The ongoing activity of the Spirit, commenced by the Pentecost event, is a dominant theme in Acts.[30] In fact, because

---

[27] See, for instance, Robert F. O'Toole, *The Unity of Luke's Theology: An Analysis of Luke-Acts* (Willington, DE: Michael Glazier, 1984); H.C. Kim, *Luke's Soteriology: A Dynamic Event in Motion* (PhD thesis, Durham University, 2008); I. Howard Marshall, *Luke: Historian and Theologian* (Downers Grove, IL: IVP Academic, 1970), pp. 116-56; Joel B. Green, 'The Message of Salvation in Luke-Acts', *ExAud* 5 (1989), pp. 21-34; Robert Maddox, *The Purpose of Luke-Acts* (Studies of the New Testament and its World; Edinburgh: T&T Clark, 1982). Luke 19.10; Acts 4.12; and 28.28 are some of the key verses that express the theme of salvation in the Lukan writings.

[28] See, for instance, Charles B. Puskas and David Crump, *An Introduction to the Gospels and Acts* (Grand Rapids: Eerdmans, 2008); Robert P. Menzies, *The Development of Early Christian Pneumatology: With Special Reference to Luke-Acts* (JSNTSup 54; Sheffield: JSOT Press, 1991).

[29] Perhaps this assessment is supported by the fact that references to the Spirit in Matthew and Mark primarily relate to Jesus and his ministry, whereas Luke mentions the Spirit more in relation to others than to Jesus. See Puskas and Crump, *An Introduction to the Gospels and Acts*, pp. 135-37.

[30] James D.G. Dunn, *Baptism in the Holy Spirit: A Re-examination of the New Testament Teaching on the Gift of the Spirit in Relation to Pentecostalism Today* (London: SCM, 2nd edn, 2010), p. 45.

of the predominant manifestation of the Spirit in Acts, some scholars have suggested renaming it as 'Acts of the Holy Spirit' rather than 'Acts of the Apostles'.[31] Although such a conclusion seems unwarranted, given the extraordinary significance of the Holy Spirit in Acts it is utterly reasonable to recognize it as a book of the Spirit. Even before the outpouring event on the day of Pentecost, the Holy Spirit is seen as an important agent at the beginning of the first chapter where Luke mentions that Jesus was giving instructions to the apostles through the Holy Spirit until the day he was taken up to heaven (Acts 1.2).[32] The Spirit's agency in Jesus' instruction and the promise to the disciples to wait for empowerment in Acts 1.4-5, 8 demonstrate the vital role that the Holy Spirit would have in fulfilling the purpose of God as recounted in the book of Acts.

Discussing the mission and message of Acts, I. Howard Marshall sums up the blessings associated with salvation as forgiveness of sins and the gift of the Holy Spirit, in which this gift is manifested in experiences of joy and spiritual power.[33] According to Acts 2.33-47, Peter claimed that the exalted Jesus poured out the gift of the Spirit on the day of Pentecost as the promise from the Father and this resulted in intensifying and outspreading his works on earth through the apostles' proclamation, teaching, prayers, and performing of signs and wonders, as well as sharing life together (v. 42). Luke portrays the Holy Spirit as creating and sustaining the community of Jesus by directly shaping the missional identity, purpose, and character

---

[31] O'Toole, *The Unity of Luke's Theology*, pp. 28-30; J.H.E. Hull, *The Holy Spirit in the Acts of the Apostles* (London: Lutterworth, 1967), pp. 11-13. Hull insists that it would be fair for the purpose and contents of Acts that the Holy Spirit be mentioned in the title, and he proposed 'The Gospel of all that the Spirit achieved through the Apostles' or 'The Gospel of all that Jesus continued to do and teach through the Holy Spirit' (p. 12).

[32] Because of the ambiguity in the Greek text's syntax for διὰ πνεύματος ἁγίου in Acts 1.2, where it may qualify either ἐντειλάμενος τοῖς or οὓς ἐξελέξατο, there are two possible interpretations of the reference to the Holy Spirit in this verse: in relation to Jesus' giving instructions through the Holy Spirit to the apostles and in relation to Jesus' choosing the apostles through the guidance of the Holy Spirit. I. Howard Marshall opts for the latter option in *The Acts of the Apostles: An Introduction and Commentary* (Leicester: Inter-Varsity, 1994), p. 57. But Menzies takes the first option, drawing attention to 'Luke's emphasis on the Spirit as the source of inspired speech' (*The Development of Early Christian Pneumatology*, p. 200). It is possible that both interpretations are correct, indicating that the Spirit is behind the selection of the apostles and the instructions given to them.

[33] Marshall, *The Acts of the Apostles*, p. 25.

of the early believers. 'The gift of the Spirit', as Luke Timothy Johnson indicates, 'brought about a community which realized the highest aspirations of human longing: unity, peace, joy, and the praise of God'.[34]

The early Church's pneumatic experience is a vital part of God's redemptive program in which the Spirit evidently directs earthly events through the Christian community on behalf of the Trinity. The Spirit's basic roles in Acts are empowering and shaping the Church to bear witness to the risen Lord Jesus Christ and guiding the eschatological restoration of God's people through him (1.8). When the Spirit was given to the early believers, they received an extraordinary, transformative experience of God's presence and an invigorating power that enabled them effectively to communicate the gospel of Christ to all nations, which is the hallmark of the Church's mission. Through this power and presence of the Spirit, a new community was born from both Jews and gentiles who came to be united with Christ and with each other. The coming of the Spirit on the day of Pentecost inaugurated a new eschatological era in which whoever received the Spirit will have participation. This is the reason that Jesus instructed the apostles to wait for the power of the Holy Spirit before they embarked on their mission of witnessing about him.

The Spirit's primary functions in Acts can be summarized in terms of major aspects of the new community's life and mission, that is, 1) his providing them with divine power and guidance to proclaim boldly the good news to the Jews and gentiles; 2) his enabling them to embody the message in their communal living through defining their new identity as the eschatological people of God and followers of Christ; and 3) his helping them understand the message of the gospel in light of the scriptural testimonies and their present experiences. In other words, the Spirit was profoundly involved in equipping the community for its missional assignments, ethical responsibilities, and hermeneutical engagements. The presence of the Spirit among the believers was pivotal to their attempt to make sense of what was going on around them in view of scriptural texts as they were engaged in presenting the gospel message both in words (through proclamation and teaching) and deeds (through faith,

---

[34] Luke Timothy Johnson, *The Acts of the Apostles* (Collegeville, MN: Liturgical, 1992), p. 62.

6

practical living, and service). Although our primary concern is to understand the Spirit's hermeneutical role within the Christian community in Acts, dealing with all three of these aspects provides a broader setting for recognizing the Spirit's involvement in the early Church.

The Spirit's Guiding and Empowering Role

The Spirit in the Book of Acts is primarily associated with the power given to the community of Jesus' followers for their mission of witnessing about him. Because of the outpouring on the day of Pentecost and subsequent pneumatic experiences, the disciples were able to undertake God's mission beyond their natural abilities. Jesus' promise of the power in Acts 1.8 for the disciples is determinative of the entire narrative of Luke's second volume in a similar way that Lk. 4.14-30 is central for the Third Gospel. As the power of the Holy Spirit played a key role in Jesus' ministry, Luke links the same power to the entire mission of the disciples in Acts (e.g. 2.4; 4.8, 31; 6.8, 10). The Spirit's presence within the corporate life of the believers enabled prophetic utterances, signs and wonders, and courage to witness, even in the midst of persecution and trial.

The majority of scholarship on the pneumatology of Luke-Acts concentrates on the Spirit's role to empower and endow prophetic and inspiring speech for the Church's mission.[35] For some, the Spirit's empowerment is limited to prophetic speech that produces special insight and inspired communication for witness,[36] whereas others include signs and wonders as a direct consequence of the Spirit's

---

[35] For a helpful survey of contemporary scholarship on Lukan pneumatology see Max Turner, *Power from on High: The Spirit in Israel's Restoration and Witness in Luke-Acts* (JPTSup 9; Sheffield: Sheffield Academic Press, 2000), pp. 20-79; Matthias Wenk, *Community-Forming Power: The Socio-Ethical Role of the Spirit in Luke-Acts* (JPTSup 19; Sheffield: Sheffield Academic Press, 2000), pp. 13-44. See also Menzies, *The Development of Early Christian Pneumatology*, pp. 51-112, where he argues that the majority of literature in Intertestamental Judaism consistently identifies experience of the Spirit with esoteric wisdom and prophetic inspiration, which, he thinks, is a dominant influence in Luke's pneumatology. The works of Max Turner and John Levison disprove this argument, showing that the Spirit in Jewish writings is also identified with the ethical dimension – beyond ecstasy and inspired knowledge. See Turner, *Power from on High*, pp. 119-37; John R. Levison, *Filled with the Spirit* (Grand Rapids: Eerdmans, 2009).

[36] Menzies, *The Development of Early Christian Pneumatology*, pp. 139-45; Roger Stronstad, *The Charismatic Theology of St. Luke: Trajectories from the Old Testament to Luke-Acts* (Grand Rapids: Baker Academic, 2012).

empowerment.[37] Either way, based on Jesus' instruction in Lk. 24.49 and Acts 1.8 as the fulfillment of John's prophecy in Lk. 3.16, Luke gives emphasis to the Spirit's empowerment as a precondition for the Church's life and ministry. His narrative characterizes the life of the early believers in terms of their experiences of the powerful presence of the Spirit. The dynamic quality of their daily life and the extraordinary phenomena that occur among them were visible evidences to this power.[38]

Several instances in Acts illustrate the power of the Spirit working within the community to provide divine enablement for prophetic utterances and courage to witness. The glossolalia at Pentecost and the following events demonstrate the working of the Spirit's mighty power inspiring them to speak God's words boldly and to perform signs and wonders before the people who were listening to their words (2.4, 17-18, 33; 3.1-10; 4.8; 5.12). Stephen was full of the Spirit's power and wisdom to serve the widows' tables (6.3, 5), for his wonder-working ministry (6.8), and for his vision of the heavens as he was becoming the first martyr of the Christian faith (7.55). The power of the Spirit was directing Philip to preach the gospel to the Ethiopian eunuch (8.29-40) or Peter to the household of Cornelius in different ways to extend the gospel's reach to gentiles, leading to their reception of the Holy Spirit (10.44-46; 11.12). Luke narrates the Spirit's empowering work in Paul's ministry, beginning from his dramatic conversion in Damascus (9.17); his being commissioned by the Spirit along with Barnabas (13.2, 4); and his preaching, teaching, and performing of miracles in his missionary journeys throughout Asia Minor and Greece (13.8-11; 16.6-10; 20.22-23). In light of Acts 10.38 and Lk. 4.18, it is central to Luke's narrative that the supernatural qualities of grace, authority, and power originate from the Holy Spirit in the ministries of the early believers as it was true of Jesus' earthly life and ministry.

---

[37] See, for instance, James B. Shelton, *Mighty in Word and Deed: The Role of the Holy Spirit in Luke-Acts* (Peabody, MA: Hendrickson, 1991), pp. 74-84.

[38] For more discussion, see Gordon Fee, *Gospel and Spirit: Issues in New Testament Hermeneutics* (Peabody, MA: Hendrickson, 1991), pp. 105-19.

The Spirit's Socio-Ethical Role

The early believers' self-understanding of their identity as people of God is one of Luke's major concerns in Acts.[39] In Luke's perspective, the Church has its origin in the ministry of Jesus and was recreated by the risen Christ to be the renewed people of God even before the coming of the Spirit (Acts 1.24). The life and ministry of the Church is firmly identified with Jesus as it was called into existence by him to be an ongoing expression of him as the risen Lord and his ministry on earth (9.4-6, 15-16). By connecting what he wrote in the Gospel with the beginning of Acts, Luke implies his narrative is a continuation of what 'Jesus began to do and teach' through the life and ministry of the new community (1.1). As much as the Spirit is important in his narrative, Luke understands the Church to be Christocentric in its foundation and purpose. This is an important marker for the new community of believers as they continue to learn who they were and live in harmony with their new identity. The coming of the Spirit at Pentecost inaugurates the embryonic Church as a community who shares this identity with Jesus Christ.

We mentioned that there is an overriding soteriological theme in both Lukan writings that regulates the flow of the storytelling. The notion of salvation, as the coming of Jesus Christ, which is an entryway for the Kingdom of God and its saving benefits, runs throughout Luke's narrative. For Luke, Jesus is the embodiment of God's Kingdom as he makes a link between his presence and his activities of preaching, healing, and deliverance with the coming of the Kingdom (Lk. 8.1; 11.20; 17.20). According to Luke, salvation is the realization of the good news of the gospel of Jesus Christ, the liberation and restoration of God's people, Jews and Gentiles. The restoration of God's people as a community with a new religious identity that is neither Jew nor Gentile involves a fresh set of practical and ethical implications. Whether the Spirit had anything to do with the practical and ethical aspects of the early Christian community in Acts is a significant issue that needs to be explored.

As we have noted, for some scholars, the Spirit's role in Acts is narrowly associated with inspired speech and empowerment for mission. Scholarship in Lukan pneumatology has given less emphasis on

---

[39] Graham H. Twelftree, *People of the Spirit: Exploring Luke's View of the Church* (Grand Rapids: Baker Academic, 2009), pp. 52-64.

the Spirit in relation to community formation.[40] Despite the widely held thesis that considers the Spirit only as a prophetic power for mission, approaches that link the quality of the early Christian community's life as a direct consequence of pneumatic experience broaden our understanding of the Lukan doctrine of the Holy Spirit. For instance, Max Turner's approach emphasizes the soteriological and ethical role of the Spirit in Luke-Acts, based on his extensive study on the 'Spirit of prophecy' in Judaism, which he thinks is a substantial background and source for pneumatology in Luke.[41] Turner argues that the Spirit is an ethical influence in Lukan writings, particularly in Acts, where the Spirit is perceived as an important figure regarding the spiritual and ethical renewal in the sense of traditional Jewish understanding. As the Spirit is the power of Israel's restoration that purges and cleanses her as the messianic people of God, the charismatic dimension for mission as well as the transformative aspect of the Spirit's role in the Church is at the heart of Lukan pneumatology.[42]

Luke's portrayal of the Spirit as a leading character and key ethical inspiration to the community suggests his intention of demonstrating that the Church is the community of the Spirit. The story of Ananias and Sapphira in Acts 5.1-11 illustrates not only the Spirit's authority in the community, but also his role in shaping its ethical standard by simulating and reinforcing a certain moral conduct and

---

[40] Wenk, *Community-Forming Power*, pp. 44-45. In fact, according to Wenk, most scholars are either unconcerned or critical of the link between the Holy Spirit experience in Acts and its ethical implications in the life of the early Christian community.

[41] Turner, *Power from on High*, pp. 86-138. Turner understands the term 'Spirit of prophecy' in its broader semantic scope, as in the traditional Jewish understanding in Luke's time to describe the Holy Spirit or the Spirit of God rather than the modern label that limits the Spirit only in relation to gifts of revelation, wisdom, and inspired speech (see p. 89). In a similar way, Wenk asserts that it is fairly common to perceive Lukan pneumatology as an extension of the Jewish concept of 'Spirit of prophecy' (see *Community-Forming Power*, p. 55).

[42] Turner, *Power from on High*, p. 455; See also *idem*, 'The Word of the Holy Spirit in Luke Acts', *Word & World* 23.2 (2003), pp. 146-53. Here Turner shows that for Luke, the Spirit of prophecy is not only a giver of inspired speech and charismatic revelation as a *superadditum* for mission, but a transforming power from on high as promised in Isa. 32.15 and 44.3. '[I]t is precisely through the gift of the Spirit that this "salvation" is poured out: only through the Spirit can the ongoing messianic/transformative reign of Jesus continue to be experienced by his people (and, hence, the Holy Spirit is also now called 'the Spirit of Jesus'; cf. Acts 16.7)' (p. 152).

accountability. The purpose of the story is explicit in that the deception of the couple against the community was a categorical hostility against the Spirit of God, which unequivocally indicates that the Holy Spirit has a direct influence on the ethical values and social norms of the new community of God's people.[43] An intentional contrast can be observed between the community as 'filled with the Spirit' in 4.31 and the heart of Ananias being 'filled by Satan' to lie to the Holy Spirit in 5.3, which provides strong evidence for the moral standard prompted by the Spirit. Peter's reply of astonishment to Sapphira's agreement in this conspiracy to 'test the Spirit of the Lord' in 5.9 signifies the gravity of the disobedience and opposition to the ethical direction that the Spirit is leading the community. Wenk expounds the idea of testing the Spirit as opposing his direction, referring to Acts 5.32; 7.51; 15.10; and 28.25-28 in contexts of disobedience of the Spirit in an ethical sense rather than a 'missionary' one.[44]

The Spirit's role as a transforming power and presence in the early Church can also be observed by carefully analyzing the socio-ethical life of the community. Luke's summary passages in Acts 2.42-47; 4.32-35; 5.12-16; and 9.31 can be used as a helpful literary apparatus to detect the Spirit's influence on the ethical life of the community.[45] Turner underlines the importance of summary passages by stating, 'Perhaps one of the most significant indications of the impact of the Spirit in the life of believers as individuals and as community is afforded by the so called "summary passages"'.[46] On the literary functions of summaries, Wenk argues that 'they contribute to the plot by linking the succeeding story with the events narrated thus far and they generalize individual experiences'.[47] The summaries, as vital segments of Luke's Pentecost narrative, refer to the community's external social expression as caused by the inner dynamics of their life, which is the Spirit. The fact that the first two summaries come immediately after the charismatic experiences of the Church in Jerusalem indicates that the Holy Spirit is the religious and ethical source to the *koinonia* of the community. The community's socio-ethical

---

[43] Turner, *Power from on High*, p. 406.

[44] Wenk, *Community-Forming Power*, p. 306.

[45] Turner, *Power from on High*, pp. 412-18; Wenk, *Community-Forming Power*, pp. 268-70.

[46] Turner, Power *from on High*, p. 412.

[47] Wenk, *Community-Forming Power*, p. 272.

experience, mentioned as their good and mutual care, is a direct result of the Spirit's coming. The third summary follows the incident of Ananias and Sapphira, which is implicitly related to the Spirit's ethical influence in the community. The summary in 9.31 explicitly mentions 'the encouragement by the Holy Spirit' and explains the community's life in terms of the Spirit's presence.

On the basis of this analysis, the Spirit's role in assisting the early believers to understand their new identity as God's community and embody the message of the gospel, incorporating a wide-ranging ethical dimension of God's Kingdom, is a remarkable aspect of pneumatology in Acts. Luke perceives the Spirit to be associated with the religious life of the community, which directly influences the community's ethical praxis. The Spirit is seen as a guiding, transforming, and strengthening power and presence in Acts, who prompts and shapes the socio-ethical aspect of the early Christian community's life. The Church in Acts is more than a prophetic community empowered for a missionary task. Likewise, the Spirit, beyond his role in relation to mission, is involved in the life of the community by shaping their practical living and ethical qualities.

The Spirit's Hermeneutical Role

Another issue that requires fresh attention in conversations on the Spirit's role as a community-forming presence in Acts is the hermeneutical engagement of the early Church. We have maintained that Luke's writing in Acts carefully depicts the Pentecost Spirit as the primary source of guidance and power to the believers as they were grappling with their new identity as the people of God and making persistent efforts to undertake their mission to be witnesses of Christ to the Jews and gentiles. In the process of recognizing the uniqueness of their new fellowship along with the task given to them – proclaiming the gospel message to the world – the testimony of Israel's Scriptures was indispensable in order for them to understand the bigger picture of God's agenda and the meaning of the incidents occurring among them from its vantage point. These incidents of scriptural interpretation in Acts demonstrate the hermeneutical role of the Spirit in Lukan pneumatology. Understanding how the Spirit is involved in the interpretive instances of the early believers according to Acts would provide a model to enrich and deepen contemporary approaches of the Spirit's role in biblical interpretation. Some helpful thoughts on the Spirit, inspired knowledge, and charismatic exegesis in early Judaism furnish proper perspective, before dealing with a few passages from Acts.

There is a reasonable consensus among scholars that early Christian pneumatology, including in Luke-Acts, was strongly influenced by Jewish tradition or understanding of the Spirit.[48] John R. Levison's book, *Filled with the Spirit*, is a pivotal study that offers an in-depth analysis of pneumatology in Israelite literature (the Old Testament), Jewish literature (the literature produced by Jews after the exile and up till the time of Christianity), and Christian literature (the New Testament). Particularly, the robust influence that the Israelite and Jewish writings had on the development of early Christian pneumatology is at the heart of this monograph. Levison's work is an extension of the seminal contribution of Hermann Gunkel, who unlocked the door to the study of Jewish literature by insisting that ancient apostolic doctrine of the Spirit needed to be understood in light of early Judaism.[49] Gunkel's rejection of the popular view in his day with respect to biblical-theological scholarship that ignored the influence of early Judaism in the early Christian texts opened the way to methodical approaches that incorporate Jewish literature along with the Old Testament to understand pneumatic activities in the New Testament writings.[50] Levison reviews and expands Gunkel's groundbreaking approach to show that early Judaism and the Jewish literature during the Greco-Roman era is integral to an understanding of the first century Christian writings on the Spirit.[51]

Walking through several Jewish texts, including the Qumran hymns, Philo, and 4 Ezra, to explore the Spirit and inspired knowledge in the early Jewish tradition, Levison demonstrates that these authors credit 'God's holy spirit' within them for their inspired reading of the scriptures.[52] Despite the underlining differences in

---

[48] Ju Hur, *A Dynamic Reading of the Holy Spirit in Luke-Acts* (The Library of New Testament Studies; London: T&T Clark, 2001), p. 25.

[49] Hermann Gunkel, *The Influence of the Holy Spirit: The Popular View of the Apostolic Age and the Teaching of the Apostle Paul* (trans. R.A. Harrisville and P.A. Quanbeck II; Philadelphia: Fortress, 1979); originally published in German as *Die Wirkungen des heiligen Geistes nach der populären Anschauung der apostolischen Zeit und der Lehre des Apostels Paulus* (Göttingen: Vandenhoeck & Ruprecht, 1888).

[50] Levison, *Filled with the Spirit*, pp. xvii-xviii.

[51] Levison, *Filled with the Spirit*, p. 112.

[52] See particularly chapter 3 of Part II, 'Spirit and Inspired Knowledge', in Levison, *Filled with the Spirit*, pp. 178-201. Levison's thesis is tied to the approach that

their scripts, these authors have a common assumption that 'God can inspire the interpretation of Scripture'.[53] Knowledge, understanding, and wisdom are associated with divine Spirit who is perceived as the source of ecstasy, virtue, and inspired interpretation of scriptures in these writings. Although the process of inspiration is hardly known from the Dead Sea Scrolls, the belief in the inspired interpretation of Scripture flourished during the Greco-Roman era in these Jewish writings.[54] Spiritual dynamism, in which Israel's Scriptures burst into life and 'the holy spirit within' in relation to interpretive practices, was given much more attention during this time. Levison writes, 'This era witnesses to the presence of the spirit from the deepest recesses of individuals to the borders of community, from mind-numbing ecstasy to intellectual acuity'.[55]

This type of inspired interpretation practiced in early Judaism is also known as 'charismatic exegesis' or 'revealed interpretation' in which the interpretation is implicitly or explicitly claimed to be divinely discovered.[56] Charismatic exegesis commonly refers to a wide

---

makes no essential distinction between the Holy Spirit as that of the creator Spirit and the regenerative Spirit. It is fundamental to his proposal that the Spirit is not only the bearer of charismatic endowment, but also the very Spirit that generates life into being and on which human beings are contingent. The 'physical breath' that created life and the 'charismatic spirit' that inspires judges and prophets, for instance, are the same. He explains,

> The two, the so-called life principle and the spirit of God, I am convinced, were understood to be one and the same. The initial endowment of God's spirit at birth must not, therefore, be understood as an inferior presence, a merely physical reality, in comparison with charismatic endowments, but rather in its own right as a vital and powerful presence with its own supernatural effects (p. 12).

Nonetheless, it is important to note that the early Jewish understanding of the 'holy spirit' that works within the individual is not quite the same as the Christian understanding of the Spirit of the Trinity.

[53] Levison, *Filled with the Spirit*, p. 199.

[54] See also John R. Levison, *The Spirit in First-Century Judaism* (Leiden: Brill 1997). Whether the process of inspired exegesis is explained in terms of hearing an unspoken voice or as an experience akin to the ascent of the philosophical mind, Levison argues here also that there is ample evidence in the Israelite and early Jewish literatures to provide precedent for the assertion that divine spirit can inspire the interpretation of sacred texts accurately (p. 210).

[55] Levison, *Filled with the Spirit*, p. 221.

[56] David E. Aune, 'Charismatic Exegesis in Early Judaism and Early Christianity', in James H. Charlesworth and Craig A. Evans (eds.), *The Pseudepigrapha and Early Biblical Interpretation* (JSPSup 14; SSEJC 2; Sheffield: JSOT Press, 1993), pp. 126-50. H.L. Ginsberg and William Brownlee first coined the phrase 'charismatic exegesis' to describe the interpretive practices in the Qumran Community. W.H. Brownlee,

variety of pneumatic interpretive practices in the Qumran community with a shared claim of divine revelation and authority in interpretation of the sacred text. David E. Aune suggests that it is a hermeneutical ideology that legitimizes particular understandings of the Jewish Scriptures.[57] It claims divine interpretation of texts whose meanings are either obscure or require a particular insight not necessarily shared by all who read the same text. The underlining assumption is that proper understanding of the Torah (and the Prophets, particularly in the first and second century CE) can be attained only if God bestows divine insight to his people. Aune points out four characteristics of charismatic exegesis: 1) it is a commentary on Scripture, 2) it is claimed to be divinely inspired, 3) it has an eschatological orientation, and 4) it was a predominant form of prophecy during the Second Temple Judaism.[58] Although the Qumran community unequivocally considered these interpretations to be God-revealed, there is little evidence either to suggest how inspiration takes place or how they thought the Spirit reveals understanding of the truth.

Most scholars would agree that the hermeneutical activities of the early Church might have been deeply influenced by this understanding of inspired or charismatic exegesis, in which the divine Spirit was inexplicably taking part in guiding the interpretation of the Israelite texts.[59] Particularly, the book of Acts reveals a pneumatic hermeneutic as being practiced by the new community of the Spirit in a way similar to Second Temple Jewish biblical interpretation. Luke conspicuously recounts the dramatic event of Pentecost, which involves the extraordinary ability of the early followers of Jesus to speak God's powerful acts in dialects other than their own as a result of Spirit baptism. Yet, the Pentecost experience was not only about ecstasy and glossolalia. It also generated a kind of new and distinctively viable interpretation of Scripture. Without eliminating the ecstatic feature of being filled with the Holy Spirit, Luke extends a few instances of charismatic exegesis in the book of Acts. Three selected

---

'Biblical Interpretation among the Sectaries of the Dead Sea Scrolls', *BA* 14 (1951), p. 61 n. 4.

[57] Aune, 'Charismatic Exegesis', p. 149.

[58] Aune, 'Charismatic Exegesis', pp. 127-29.

[59] Archie T. Wright, 'Second Temple Period Jewish Biblical Interpretation: An Early Pneumatic Hermeneutic', in Kevin L. Spawn and Archie T. Wright (eds.), *Spirit and Scripture: Examining a Pneumatic Hermeneutic* (London: T&T Clark, 2012), pp. 73-98.

cases from Acts (2.14-41; 8.26-39; 15.1-35) demonstrate the significance of Spirit-inspired interpretation of passages from the Old Testament.

Peter's Inspired Speech at Pentecost (Acts 2.14-41)

The Pentecost event in Acts 2 is followed by Peter's sermon – the first of several speeches after the outpouring of the Spirit in Luke's narrative development of his account. The unprecedented ecstatic experience that involved inspired speech to praise God in the languages of people who came for the ceremonial feast 'from every nation under heaven' (2.5) was a strange phenomenon that ignited surprise and confusion among the Jews and the proselytes who heard them 'speaking in [their] native language' (2.8). The bewilderment of the people who witnessed the inexplicable experience of the followers of Jesus led some to ask, 'What does this mean?' (2.12) – and others to conclude mockingly, 'They have had too much wine' (2.13). Peter's speech was a response aimed to address both the perplexity and ill-informed presumption of the bystanders on the event of Pentecost. In his discourse to expound the meaning of this paradigmatic experience of the Spirit Peter was involved in a charismatic exegesis, appealing to Israel's Scriptures and offering inspired interpretations to clarify the misunderstanding and meaningfully describe the outpouring of the Spirit at Pentecost.

The cogent and rhetorically persuasive argument delivered by Peter, who stood up as a spokesman to speak with the support of his fellow apostles in front of the multitude (2.14), disproved the charge against Jesus' followers that they were drunk with too much wine and explained that they were filled with the Holy Spirit. The strange occurrence the people observed that morning was a direct consequence of being filled with the Holy Spirit. It was this pneumatic experience that gave them the ability to make a doxological utterance in tongues other than their own. In fact, speaking with other languages as the Spirit enabled them was actually the primary event that grabbed the crowd's attention to be eyewitnesses of the outpouring of the Spirit. But more than that, their experience with the Spirit enabled them, particularly Peter in this case, to engage in an inspired exegesis of the scriptures at the dawn of the early Church's public testimony about Jesus. Marshall suggests that the term translated as 'addressed' in 2.14 can also be used as 'inspired utterance', which indicates that Luke intends to describe Peter's sermon as 'the work of a man filled with the Spirit'.[60] Through his inspired interpretation Peter clarified the meaning of the Pentecost experience by linking the coming of the promised Spirit and the story of Jesus, the Christ in light of Old Testament prophecy.

The interpretation of Joel 2.28-32 in Peter's speech was inspired by the Spirit to describe the event on the day of Pentecost in terms of the phenomena spoken by the prophet. Larry R. McQueen points out that Luke's use of Joel's prophecy here is programmatic in the sense that it goes beyond mere explanation of the visible and audible phenomena to the soteriological significance that it entails.[61] Peter understands their experience as an initial fulfillment of Joel's prophecy of the Spirit's coming on all people, which is to be demonstrated in participation in prophecy and visions. This not only shows the importance of prophecy for Peter, but also denotes that God is creating a prophetic community inspired by the Spirit to witness the salvation provided through faith in Jesus Christ. There was a natural flow to his description of the outpouring of the Spirit by means of scriptural prophecy, which leads the focus of his sermon to inspired interpretations of other texts about the exalted Jesus Christ (e.g. Pss. 16.8-11; 110.1). Precisely, Peter was explaining who Jesus was and what he had done as the fundamental basis for the coming of the Spirit on the day of Pentecost and, consequentially, the restoration of Israel. His charismatic exegesis articulates how God's agenda to restore his people and the fulfillment of his promise to pour out his Spirit on all people is effected through the person and work of Christ.

Peter's charismatic exegesis of Scripture, as a peculiar interpretive practice, was the palpable effect of the coming of the Spirit. Levison rightly suggests that it is the result of the filling with the Spirit, which 'catalyzes impressive and entirely unexpected abilities of scriptural interpreters'.[62] Inspiration to interpret Scripture is the primary

---

[60] Marshall, *The Acts of the Apostles*, pp. 72-73. Joel B. Green notes that the Greek term ἀποφθέγγομαι used here (also used in Acts 2.4 and 26.25) is mentioned in LXX to refer to a fortune-telling (e.g. Mic. 5.11; Zech. 10.2) and prophetic speech (1 Chron. 25.1; Ezek. 13.9, 19). See 'Spiritual Hermeneutics', in Myk Habets (ed.), *Third Article Theology: A Pneumatological Dogmatics* (Minneapolis: Fortress, 2016), pp. 153-72 (163 n. 17).

[61] Larry R. McQueen, *Joel and the Spirit: The Cry of a Prophetic Hermeneutic* (JPTSup 8; Sheffield: Sheffield Academic Press, 1995), pp. 47-48.

[62] Levison, *Filled with the Spirit*, p. 349.

consequence of being filled with the Holy Spirit in Acts. As Joel B. Green insists, the Pentecost experience 'sparks a hermeneutical exercise, one that demonstrates as a nonnegotiable starting point for faithful interpretation a people who are formed by the Scriptures and whose minds have been opened by their encounter with the risen Lord (cf. Luke 24.45)'.[63] Peter's interpretation, spawned by the Pentecostal Spirit, illustrates the inspiring and guiding role of the Spirit in the hermeneutical activities of the new community. This practice of inspired hermeneutics was the Spirit's way of forming the community as people of God with a clear understanding of their experience as well as God's entire salvific agenda as fulfillment of scriptural prophecies.

Philip's Encounter with the Ethiopian Eunuch (Acts 8.26-39)

Another narrative account that illustrates inspired exegesis at work in Acts is Philip's encounter with the Ethiopian eunuch. Following the experience of the power of the Holy Spirit at Pentecost, when thousands were being added to the initial group of the believers, the new Christian community continued to proclaim the gospel message boldly throughout Jerusalem until their mission thrust began to expand beyond Jerusalem to Judea, Samaria, and the ends of the earth, as Luke sketched the advance of their witness in Acts 1.8. It is fair to say that this is a divine itinerary of the expansion of the gospel message, since it was part of Jesus' instruction to his followers to wait for the coming of the Spirit; this is true even though, evidently, this expansion resulted from the ferocious persecution of the Church in Jerusalem (8.1). Philip was one of those followers of Jesus who had been scattered throughout Judea and Samaria. The Spirit empowered him to proclaim the messiah with signs and wonders in Samaria before he was guided by an angel of the Lord (8.26) for another assignment specifically, to witness the good news about Jesus to an Ethiopian government official.[64]

---

[63] Green, 'Spiritual Hermeneutics', p. 163.

[64] Luke uses the phrase ἀγγελὸς δὲ κυρίου 'the angel of the Lord' in a vivid way to denote the divine guidance in the mission; the phrase is used in his narrative to emphasize the unique presence and activity of God (e.g. Lk. 1.11; 2.9; Acts 12.7, 23) as an alternative to more usual expression 'the Spirit' or 'the Spirit of the Lord' (vv. 29, 39). There seems to be no distinction between 'the angel of the Lord' and 'the Spirit of the Lord' in this passage, as they appear to be closely associated in Jewish thought (23.9). Although it is not known why 'the angel' is used here and

The interesting encounter between Philip and the Ethiopian eunuch was part of the Spirit's plan to expand gradually the Church's witness of Jesus Christ to the gentiles. Luke does not clearly identify the Ethiopian as either a proselyte (a gentile convert to Judaism – e.g. Acts 2.10; 6.5; 13.43) or a God-fearer (a gentile adherent to Jewish monotheism, ethic, and piety – e.g. Acts 10.2; 13.26).[65] However, since we know that he was reading a Jewish scroll of the book of Isaiah and coming back from Jewish worship in Jerusalem at one of the pilgrimage festivals, he could either be a convert or God-fearer. Philip's question to the eunuch, if he was able to understand what he was reading, and the response he gave that he could not understand without an interpretive guide, suggests the need for a distinct interpretive insight to interpret the text. It seems obvious that the interpretation of the servant passage from Isa. 53.7-8 was somehow perplexing him, given his question, 'Who is the prophet talking about, himself or someone else?' (v. 34). The purpose for which Philip was brought to that place by the Spirit was to answer his question about the person in Isaiah's prophecy who was suffering, in pain, shame, and humiliation. Through providing an interpretation of the text's message, Philip would ultimately lead him to faith in Jesus Christ.

A key issue in this passage in relation to inspired exegesis is Philip's identification of the suffering servant of Yahweh with Jesus. Luke does not provide the details of his interpretation, but it is clear that Philip understands the suffering servant as the anticipated messiah (v. 35). Rather than responding to the question directly, Philip's answer was to tell the Ethiopian eunuch the 'good news about Jesus' – or in Charles E. Shepherd's words, it was 'a kerygmatic presentation of the person of Jesus, to which the Scriptures attest'.[66] There is no evidence that in pre-Christian Judaism the messiah was thought of in

---

'the Spirit' in other texts, either way it is clear that the mission was divinely initiated and guided. See F.F. Bruce, *The Book of Acts* (NICNT; Grand Rapids: Eerdmans, 1988), p. 174; Marshall, *The Acts of the Apostles*, p. 161.

[65] For a helpful discussion on the distinctions of gentiles in relation to Judaism, see Irina Levinskaya, *The Book of Acts in Its Diaspora Setting* (Grand Rapids: Eerdmans, 1996).

[66] Charles E. Shepherd, *Theological Interpretation and Isaiah 53: A Critical Comparison of Bernhard Huhm, Brevard Childs, and Alec Motyer* (London: Bloomsbury, 2014), p. 147.

terms of the suffering servant.[67] Philip's interpretation recalls the opening of the minds of Jesus' followers by the risen Lord (Lk. 24.45)[68] as well as the work of the Spirit of Pentecost who gave the interpretive insight in a way similar to what we have seen in Acts 2. As Jesus provided a key to the interpretation of the texts about his crucifixion and death to the disciples (24.25-27, 44-47), so the Spirit was using Philip to unlock the eunuch's understanding of the mystery and significance of the suffering messiah.[69]

Given that the Spirit was guiding the entire progression of this evangelistic encounter and was involved in the Christian community's understanding of the Scriptures, Philip's interpretation of this text in this surprising manner is the result of its being inspired by the Spirit. It was a reading of the text prompted and shaped by the Spirit-empowered mission of the Church in which Philip participated. His Spirit-guided interpretation binds together the scriptural prophecy and its fulfillment in Jesus Christ that eventually resulted in the Ethiopian eunuch's enlightenment and practical response to the gospel message as seen in his request to be baptized. The pneumatic interpretive significance of this narrative needs to be understood in light of the overall purpose, initiative, and guidance of the Spirit who works through Philip as he embodies the remarkable mission of the Church.

The Council at Jerusalem (Acts 15.1-35)

Several scholars consider Luke's narrative of the Jerusalem Council as an important biblical exemplar in conversations concerning the interplay of the Spirit and community in scriptural interpretation.[70] The entire development of the narrative, beginning from Cornelius' conversion in Acts 10 to the hearing and discernment of the Council

---

[67] Joseph Klausner, *The Messianic Idea in Israel: From Its Beginning to the Completion of the Mishnah* (trans. W.F. Stinespring; London: G. Allen and Unwin, 1956), p. 405.

[68] It is interesting to note that there is a parallel between the stories of the road to Emmaus and the Ethiopian eunuch, and some scholars suggest reading the two narratives in light of one another as a plausible direction to understand the texts. See Michael B. Parsons, 'Isaiah 53 in Acts 8', in William H. Bellinger and William R. Farmer (eds.), *Jesus and the Suffering Servant: Isaiah 53 and Christian Origins* (Eugene, OR: Wipf and Stock, 2009), pp. 104-20; Joseph A. Grassi, 'Emmaus Revisited (Lk. 24.13-35 and Acts 8.26-40)', *CBQ* 26 (1964), pp. 463-67.

[69] Marshall, *The Acts of the Apostles*, p. 163.

[70] See my reviews of Fowl, Green, and Thomas in chapter two, above, on the use of Acts 15 as a biblical model for the Spirit's role in interpretation.

in Acts 15 to settle the confusion engendered by the conversion experiences of Gentiles, models apostolic interpretation of Scripture permeated by the Spirit. Luke carefully recounts the gradual development of the new community's understanding of its identity, as people of God comprises of the Jews and gentiles. His accounts of the Ethiopian eunuch and Cornelius seem to be designed deliberately to make the case that gentile inclusion in the promise of salvation is part of God's agenda. The sharp dispute and disagreement that Paul and Barnabas got into with certain Jews who came to Antioch teaching the believing gentiles to be circumcised according to the law of Moses was the primary reason for the convention in Jerusalem (15.1-3). The session eventually came to a consensus by ratifying the gentile mission after hearing testimonies and appealing to Scripture. The apostolic letter sent to the constituents asserts that the final decision of the issue was made 'in agreement with the Spirit' (15.28), which indicates the Spirit's leading role in the whole process.

Taking the prominence of the Spirit in the entire mission of the Church, including the advance to gentile regions, into account, the Spirit's part in the dialogue and consensus of the Council is by no means eccentric. However, the manner in which the Spirit was involved in the decision-making process is open to discussion. Several ways can be suggested as to how this is to be understood as a Spirit-inspired decision. One possibility is that the Spirit through prophecy confirmed the Council's verdict, since there were prophets who at least affirmed the resolution after it was made (15.32; cf. 13.1-4).[71] The fact that everyone was satisfied about the decision could also be recognized as the work of the Spirit. It is also true that Luke's narrative presumes the Spirit had inspired the scriptures (1.16) and testified through them (15.15-17), which associates the witness of the scriptures with the voice of the Spirit. Moreover, the receiving of the Spirit (15.8) and the signs and wonders performed by Barnabas and Paul among them (chs. 13-14; 15.12) marks the acceptance of gentiles by God. All these possibilities, interwoven together, show the Spirit's involvement in this consultation.

Luke's narrative locates the reading of the Scriptures in the Council as part of the final ruling after all the debates and hearings

---

[71] Craig Keener, *Acts: An Exegetical Commentary* (Grand Rapids: Baker Academic, 2014), III, p. 2292.

completed. The assembly began with serious disagreements and there had been much debate, particularly because of the Pharisaic believers who claimed gentiles must undergo circumcision and be required to keep the Law of Moses (15.5). After the debates, Peter stood up to witness about his experience of gentile conversion (15.7), and this is followed by the testimonies of Paul and Barnabas (15.12). James took the platform to summarize the discussion affirming how Peter's testimony and the prophets are in solid agreement (15.13-21).[72] The agreement between the words of the prophets in the Scriptures and the contemporary testimonies of the Spirit's work among the gentiles is a decisive matter in James' conclusive argument. The text he cited from Amos 9.11-12 speaks of two parts of God's promise: 1) God will rebuild the fallen tabernacle of David, which is the restoration of Israel (9.11); and 2) Gentiles 'who are called by my name' (9.12) will gather around to share these blessings. James' interpretation confirms God's intent for gentiles to participate in the messianic blessings of Israel without necessarily becoming Jewish proselytes.

James approaches the text in light of the entire mission of the Church guided and empowered by the Spirit. It is mentioned that the disciples' encounter with the risen Lord and the Pentecostal Spirit has given the new community a key exegetical insight to engage with the testimony of the Scripture in a distinctive manner. This new approach is a way of looking into the things that were revealed and fulfilled through the work of Jesus Christ and the coming of the Spirit. The people of God, inspired by the Spirit, now have a fresh outlook on the reading of the Scriptures – a reading that they believed was inspired by the same Spirit (1.16). As a prominent leader of this community, James' renewed understanding of the text is animated by what God has done in Jesus Christ and continues to do through the Church by the Holy Spirit. The testimonies of Peter, Paul, and Barnabas about what the Spirit was doing in leading the mission to the gentiles confirmed this truth and provided additional insight to the Council. They ultimately claimed to be led by the Holy

---

[72] The fact that James made no reference to Paul and Barnabas' report is probably for political reasons. Although it was the work of Paul and Barnabas that was on trial, it seems that James did not want to create unnecessary offence to the conservative Jewish audience. His reference to Peter by his Jewish name 'Simeon' reinforces this assumption. See Bruce, *The Book of Acts*, p. 293.

Spirit to come to an agreement on their decision of accepting gentile believers without additional burdens, other than asking them to refrain from certain practices considering the mission of the Church and Jewish-gentile fellowship within the Church.[73] As much as the Spirit's ongoing, active presence is confirmed through experiences, signs, and wonders among Jews and gentiles, the Spirit was also guiding the life and mission of the Christian community by inspiring their interpretations of Israel's Scriptures.

Summary

The three passages we have seen from Acts illustrate the early Church's practice of pneumatic hermeneutics and how Spirit-inspired exegesis had a remarkable influence on the Church's understanding of its identity and mission. Although these few instances might not conclusively represent the entire interpretive experiences of the community, these narrative accounts signify the importance of Israel's Scriptures for the followers of Jesus and illustrate the pattern by which the Spirit empowers their hermeneutical practices. In other words, Lukan pneumatology vividly characterizes the triadic hermeneutic by unveiling the work of the Spirit in relation to the Scriptures and the interpretive practices of the community. As part of the role the Spirit had in shaping the believing community into the new people of God, Spirit-renewed interpretation of the Scripture, as they embody its message, had a substantial contribution in the life and mission of the early Church. This interpretive practice serves as a model and provides a fundamental precedent for the Spirit's role in the theological-interpretation practices of the Christian community.

Our analysis of the biblical texts with respect to pneumatic experiences of the early followers of Jesus identifies the Spirit as a community-forming presence uniquely guiding and empowering the believers for Christ-centered life and mission, shaping their fellowship and ethics, and enlightening their minds with insight into God's will through the Scriptures. The early Christian community's relationship with the Spirit is a fundamental aspect of its nature given that the Spirit had a substantial role in its entire existence, worship, and ministry. The biblical models from the book of Acts not only broaden

---

[73] Martin Luther, 'On the Councils and the Church', in Helmut T. Lehmann (ed.), *Luther's Works*, XLI (Philadelphia: Fortress, 1966), pp. 67-80.

our prospect in relation to the Spirit's active presence among the early believers, but they also provide key guidelines to understand how the Spirit works in Christian community's vocation, character, and disposition in regard to theological understanding and scriptural interpretation. The Spirit's interpretive role in Acts is a vital resource to explicate crucial elements in our study of pneumatic hermeneutics. The very notion that the early apostolic Church was a prophetic community with its experience of charismatic and inspired exegesis strengthens the argument that pneumatic hermeneutics is explained in terms of the Spirit working in and through the community in theological reading of Scripture. The Spirit's role in biblical interpretation is to be understood in light of the community's ongoing pneumatic experiences as well as its vigorous engagements with the Scripture.

Pneumatic Hermeneutics and the Community of the Spirit

We have shown that the Church, as the primary interpretive community of the Scriptures, is a pneumatological community animated by the Spirit to embody the divine life and mission in the world. Our theological analysis invigorates a pneumatological ecclesiology that is buttressed by a trinitarian presupposition of the Church in which the community of God's people participates in the divine fellowship through the Spirit. The subsequent biblical exploration from the book of Acts provides an exemplar from the practical experiences of the early Christian community whose mission, ethical life, and hermeneutic is imbued by the Spirit. The theological and biblical assessment bolsters a well-grounded assertion that the Church is a community of the Spirit that has the manifestation of the power and presence of the Spirit as its distinctive nature. With this in mind, we now turn to deal with a pneumatological hermeneutics in theological interpretation of Scripture that involves a faithful reading of the Spirit-inspired text as the community of God's people generated by the Spirit.

The primary concern of theological interpretation is the significance of reading Scripture as an encounter with the Triune God, which is a theological responsibility of attuning to the voice of the Spirit who speaks in and through the Scripture. As a hermeneutical strategy, this interpretive approach characteristically entails the ecclesial community's Christian formation oriented by faith, hope, and love as the ultimate goal of reading Scripture through adjusting dispositions to listening to what the Spirit says here and now. Hearing God's address through the reading of Scripture is an essential theological practice for a community created and cultivated by the Spirit. Recognizing the Spirit's work in generating and sustaining the Christian community is the same as acknowledging the Spirit in every aspect of the practical life of the Church through time and space. Accordingly, the emphasis on the importance of Scripture and the Spirit's interpretive role within the reading community, either implicitly or explicitly, is inherent to Christian practice.

Explaining the work of the Spirit in relation to biblical interpretation is challenging. In fact, a thorough understanding of the Spirit's mysterious involvement in all aspects of the Christian life escapes us on account of both our anthropological limitations and the nature of the Spirit. This difficulty of explaining the mystery of the Spirit in human understanding is well articulated in Jesus' words as he described the work of the Spirit: 'The wind blows where it chooses, and you hear the sound of it, but you do not know where it comes from and where it goes' (Jn 3.8 NRSV). The reality of the wind is recognized by the effect it creates, which is the medium for it to be known and explained. In the same manner, the presence and power of the Holy Spirit in the life of the Christian community is explained by means of the practical effects witnessed from the perspective of a human horizon. In other words, the manifestation of the Holy Spirit is perceived from a human perspective through the mediation of a wide range of practices and experiences of the community. The idea of pneumatological mediation helps to explicate the Spirit's interpretive role expressed through the interpretation practices of the Christian community.[74]

The notion of mediation is not an unfamiliar concept in Christian theology. In its broadest sense, mediation refers to the act of intervening between two different parties with the purpose of reconciliation. It is understood theologically as the means by which God and human beings are reconciled through the person and work of Jesus Christ. One of the biblical expressions of Christ is related to his role

---

[74] See Mark J. Cartledge, *The Mediation of the Spirit: Interventions in Practical Theology* (Grand Rapids: Eerdmans, 2015).

as a mediator between God and humanity (1 Tim. 2.5; Heb. 8.6; 9.15). It is also possible to refer to the Holy Spirit as a mediator between the Godhead and humanity considering his ongoing active role on earth to complement and intensify the reconciliation of the risen Lord.

Mark J. Cartledge's analysis of the mediation of the Spirit is helpful in this discussion. He explains the mediation of the Spirit in connection with the way of salvation that upholds the evident tension between the transcendence and immanence without collapsing one into the other. Engaging with recent Pentecostal scholarship, his argument centers on the significance of pneumatological mediation to practical theology with its considerable implications for ecclesiology and scriptural interpretation. He summarizes the different forms of mediation with five propositions: 1) Christ mediates the Holy Spirit to the Church; 2) the Holy Spirit mediates Christ and the Father to the Church; 3) creation mediates the Holy Spirit to the Church; 4) the Church mediates the Holy Spirit internally (via individuals, groups, worship, and practices); and 5) the Church mediates the Holy Spirit externally (via individuals, groups, public worship, and practices).[75]

Accordingly, the Holy Spirit mediates the Trinity and is mediated by Christ, creation, and the Church. By way of challenging fundamental assumptions of direct and unmediated experience of God through an immediate encounter with the Holy Spirit, the pneumatological mediation proposed by Cartledge entails ecclesiological connotations in understanding the work of the Spirit. It elucidates the vital intermediary role of the Spirit to unite the Triune God and the Church with the purpose of mediating salvation to the world and enabling the Church to participate in the life of the Trinity. It also recognizes that the Spirit is mediated by means of the non-human creation, people, events, and processes. He writes, 'As subject the Holy Spirit mediates the presence of the Trinity. As object, the Holy Spirit is mediated within the created order and especially the church. The intermediary roles of the church and creation are also noted as significant features of pneumatological mediation.'[76]

Cartledge's proposal opens a way to understanding how the Spirit mediates the Triune God and makes his presence recognized through

---

[75] Cartledge, *The Mediation of the Spirit*, p. 109.
[76] Cartledge, *The Mediation of the Spirit*, p. 110.

intermediate features of the created reality. There is a two-way mediation in the sense that the Church, as a community of believers, experiences the intermediary presence of the Spirit in its relationship with Christ on the one hand, and the work of the Spirit as mediated by the community's life and worship on the other. In other words, a different aspect of mediation functions as the community channels the Spirit within itself and to the world. As much as the Spirit is an intermediary agent between the divine and the human, by providing the distinctive eschatological and soteriological presence of God, the Spirit is also mediated by a set of intermediary, created and ordinary ways as he opts to operate and be perceived through them. In this sense, pneumatological mediation is a crucial factor in the Church's participation in the life of the Trinity and God's salvation to the world through Christ.

There is a significant hermeneutical corollary to pneumatological mediation in our discussion of community and the Spirit's interpretive role. The concept of mediation illuminates our understanding of the way in which the Church, as a creature of the Spirit, reveals the work of its creator through practical life and worship. It is a basis for the assertion that the life and religious experience of community mirrors the Spirit's involvement in the hermeneutical exercises of the Church. As the existence of the wind is merely observed through the effects it creates, the work of the Holy Spirit is reflected through the community formed and nurtured by the Spirit. This pneumatological approach intensifies and clarifies our argument that the Spirit's role in theological interpretation is explained in terms of the community's life and practices. A genuine understanding of the Spirit's work in and through the Christian community enables the voice of the Spirit to be heard through the Scriptures and disallows the community's expression overshadow what the Spirit speaks through the Scriptures.

A few important issues can be drawn from our analysis of community and pneumatic hermeneutics. First, understanding pneumatic hermeneutics in this sense requires our recognition of the Spirit's work in the ongoing life of the ecclesial community – the one, holy, and catholic Church through time and space. We are referring to the ecclesial community as the apostolic Church formed by the gospel of Jesus Christ and inaugurated by the coming of the Spirit on the day of Pentecost, which continues to exist through time with its core values and message of salvation. A pneumatic hermeneutic involves dealing with the theological tradition and history of interpretation of the Church in its entirety. Affirmation of the ecumenical Councils and essential theological statements of the heart of the Christian faith continue to serve as means of the Spirit's guidance in the interpretation of Scripture. Pneumatic hermeneutics takes into account the broad recognition within the wider Christian circle that the Spirit is involved in generating, reinforcing, and clarifying the message of the gospel through the activities of writing, editing, and gathering the Scriptures. It also considers the Spirit's part in later developments of theological wisdom marked by the early apologetics, canonization of biblical texts, and the creedal formulation of the Christian Church.

Second, pneumatic hermeneutics recognizes the dynamic nature of the ecclesial community represented in diverse cultural and denominational contexts. One way to understand the contemporary theological and interpretive approaches of ecclesial traditions is to perceive them as part of the dynamic work of the Spirit in building the Church as a community of faith and shaping its theological practices within wide-ranging contextual settings. As Todd Billings observed, 'There is no such thing as a noncontextual reading of Scripture, just as there is no such thing as an untranslated manifestation of Christianity'.[77] Recognizing the Spirit's interpretive role is giving emphasis to the diverse, but unifying role of the Spirit in the expressions of various ecclesial traditions as God's purpose and the larger picture of his plan of redemption unfolds through them. The idea that the Spirit works in different ways within multiple Christian traditions provides a way to understand the fabric of Christian communities and their diverse hermeneutical approaches. Pneumatic hermeneutics involves openness and readiness to realize the Spirit's ongoing work in diversified communities with multiple theological and hermeneutical milieus.

Third, to understand pneumatic hermeneutics is to admit human limitations vis-à-vis interpreting the Spirit-inspired text and to be vulnerable to the guidance of the Spirit through the communal practices that prepare hearts to hear the message of Scripture. It is setting aside the extensive suspicion of modern hermeneutical approaches and exclusive reliance on human interpretive methodologies to read Scripture. It is approaching the Scripture with an underlying conviction

---

[77] Billings, *Word of God*, p. 122.

that the Spirit works in and through the practical experiences of the community in which the inspiring and guiding presence of the Spirit is accessible, as markedly demonstrated in the book of Acts. This kind of approach to Scripture emphasizes, as J.B. Green suggests, 'the Spirit's work in readying us to read Scripture through inculcating in us dispositions and postures of invitation, openness, and availability'. He continues, 'An integrated life of devotion to God and our willing-ness to participate in a repentance-oriented reading of Scripture – these dispositions and concomitant practices are the fruit of the work of the Spirit in our lives'.[78] The community's experience of worship, prayer, preaching, sacrament, service, and mission provides the ap-propriate spiritual context and preparation of heart to hear the voice of the Spirit through faithful reading of Scripture. Therefore, Spirit-inspired interpretation of Scripture is explained by way of the com-munity's ongoing pneumatic experiences and the reading of its Scrip-tures in light of them.

Finally, the emphasis on the community's role in pneumatic her-meneutics needs to be secured by a cautious, vigilant, and critical at-titude to avoid potential misconceptions and misappropriations of the interplay between community and the Spirit in the interpretation of Scripture. By virtue of the fact that community is a mediation of the Spirit, it has a position and a role whereby the Spirit's voice is communicated through its essence and its discernible practices. How-ever, there is always a conceivable challenge as to how the Spirit's voice is mediated through the community. The possibility that com-munity controls and manipulates scriptural interpretation to a direc-tion that misperceives the Spirit's guidance through the Scripture is a significant issue to be carefully approached. Archer helpfully suggests that the Spirit speaks through the Church and Scripture, but his voice does not have to be equated with the community, or even with the biblical text. There has to be a commitment to 'discern the Spirit in the process of negotiating the meaning of the biblical texts as the community faithfully carries on the mission of Jesus'.[79] Without ap-propriate caution, hearing the Spirit's voice through the Scripture re-mains open to fallacy and misuse. Thus, as a community positions itself to approach the Scripture with a faithful and prayerful attitude

---

[78] Green, 'Spiritual Hermeneutics', p. 171.
[79] Archer, *A Pentecostal Hermeneutic*, p. 248.

to hear the voice of the Spirit, there has to be a critical discernment and proper checks and balances in place as well to restrict human abuse of the text and the Spirit.

CONCLUSION

It is clear from contemporary dialogues on theological interpretation that pneumatic hermeneutics has become a growing concern in Christian reading of Scripture. There is an inherent principle at the core of any theological interpretive engagement with Scripture that biblical texts are to be interpreted with the same Spirit that they were originated from. If the hallmark of conversations on theological interpretation is that biblical texts are God's self-revelation and loving address with the ultimate purpose of Christian formation, and if reading them is more than a matter of human exercise, the obvious implication is that the Spirit has a considerable interpretive role in Christian reading of Scripture. The present work began by calling attention to the relative absence of an in-depth theological analysis of the Spirit's role in discussions on theological interpretation of Scripture, although it is a broadly agreed upon issue. The study dealt with pneumatic hermeneutics by providing judicious surveys and analytical treatment of relevant literatures and pointing the way forward to a model for the Spirit's interpretive role in theological interpretation of Scripture.

Recapping the Main Issues

Framing the Spirit's interpretive role within the current conversations on theological interpretation was the task in the first chapter. Despite the recognition that the Holy Spirit had a considerable part in the origination of the sacred Scriptures, it is evident that dealing with the work of the Spirit in reading them has not been given enough attention in Christian theology and biblical interpretation. With heightened sensibilities of reading the Bible as a way of hearing the voice

206 Pneumatic Hermeneutics

of God, recent developments in theological interpretation of Scripture invigorate fresh attention to the Spirit's work in the interpretation of biblical texts. By allowing the voices of its key proponents to be heard, the chapter explored the concerns and interests of theological interpretation and revitalized the importance of the Spirit's work in biblical interpretation. In so doing, we not only indicated that the Spirit's interpretive role is integral to the basic assumptions of theological interpretation, but also called attention to the significant dearth and crucial need for pneumatological interpretive insights in those developments.

The inextricable link between theological reading of Scripture and the Spirit's interpretive role is demonstrated in a few promising efforts to approach the issue from the specific standpoint. The second chapter began dealing with those contributions, prompting the need for more work to be done. Provided that Pentecostal interpretive approaches give emphasis on the Spirit's hermeneutical role, the chapter expanded the conversation, incorporating several contributions from the Pentecostal tradition. This review indicated that examining Pentecostal exemplars with regard to the work of the Spirit in interpretation might broaden the vision and strengthen the efforts in theological interpretation of Scripture. Particularly, the pneumatological and experiential emphasis on interpretation found in Pentecostal hermeneutics reinforces the notion that reading Scripture is a Spirit-inspired Christian practice.

Further background was provided by incorporating diverse voices on the interrelation between the Spirit and Scripture. Thus, chapters three through five attempted to deal with the issue from the perspectives of mainstream Christian traditions. Eastern Orthodox, Roman Catholic, and Protestant approaches provided a way to see the Pentecostal contributions in a broader theological spectrum. In its emphasis on the Spirit, Eastern Orthodoxy is closer to the Pentecostal approaches than the Catholic tradition, although, in comparison, the Orthodox mysticism is more committed to a patristic theological framework than the relatively free spirituality in Pentecostalism. This is true of Catholicism, which is theologically restricted by the early Church fathers like the Eastern tradition. Although Pentecostalism is not directly spawned by these Christian origins, its contributions to the efforts in theological interpretation of Scripture is better off if seen in light of interpretive practices in these churches.

Our study also indicated that Pentecostal hermeneutics goes beyond the Protestant interpretive traditions' emphasis on the doctrines of internal testimony of the Spirit and divine illumination, although the value of the doctrines remains indispensable in Christian biblical interpretation. Particularly, the doctrines' focus on affirming on the nature of Scripture as God's Word and the Spirit's role in enlightening mortal minds to understand its message have a huge contribution in conversations on pneumatic hermeneutics. Considered as the grandfather to the Pentecostal tradition, Wesley's understanding of illumination in terms of the ongoing inspiration of the Holy Spirit provides a basis for the Pentecostals' case that community, as a place where the Spirit is actively working in, is the contextual locus for biblical interpretation.

As a contribution to the contemporary conversations on theological interpretation of Scripture, this study provides direction for theologically understanding the Spirit's role in biblical interpretation. Through a critical examination of Pentecostal triadic interpretive approaches that promote vigorous interaction between the Spirit, Scripture, and community, the study maintained that integrating pneumatic hermeneutics in theological interpretation of Scripture remarkably involves the interpretive community. Understanding the Spirit's interpretive role requires a closer look at the way the Spirit creates and sustains the Church as a Christian community. The study provides an in-depth analysis of the Spirit's work in relation to the life and experience of the community as people of the Spirit. We worked through Pentecostal hermeneutical approaches by urging that the Church simply is the community of the Spirit and showing the hermeneutical importance of the Spirit in Acts. In this sense, I have shown that the best way to understand pneumatic hermeneutics is focusing on the Spirit's ongoing work within the community of believers.

Implications and Contributions

Several implications can be cited for the importance of this study. First, prompted by the ideals of theological interpretation of Scripture as interpretation of the Bible for the Church, the study contributes to efforts at recovering this ancient practice in biblical and theological scholarship. It contributes to the endeavors of retrieving theological interpretation by calling attention to the need for the Spirit's interpretive role and showing ways the Spirit is involved in the practice of reading Scripture as God's word.

Second, the study has an implication for Pentecostal hermeneutics. Recent hermeneutical debates in Pentecostalism trace the development of distinct Pentecostal hermeneutical approaches that emerged out of its captivity to evangelical hermeneutical principles. In its effort to identify distinctive Pentecostal approaches to interpretation, this book provides a theological basis for understanding the role of the Holy Spirit in hermeneutics in light of the pneumatological experiences of Christian/Pentecostal communities.

Third, the study has an ecclesiological implication by extending our understanding of the Church as a pneumatological interpretive community. One of the major emphases in conversations on theological interpretation and Pentecostalism is that the Church, as a community of believers and the context for interpretation, plays a crucial role in biblical hermeneutics. That emphasis demands identifying the Church as a pneumatological fellowship whose origin and sustenance is contingent upon the Holy Spirit. Despite the limitation in addressing the issues comprehensively, this approach points the way forward in the study of pneumatological ecclesiology.

Fourth, the value of this study can extend to the wider Church with regard to its general understanding of biblical interpretation, the Spirit's interpretive role, and the Church's place in the process. Particularly in the majority world, where the Church is growing in its Pentecostal and charismatic forms, such as Ethiopia, my country of origin, this study will have a great deal of impact in addressing issues concerning biblical interpretation and discerning the voice of the Spirit in the interpretive practice.

Although the research undertaken in this monograph has been carefully prepared and achieved its intended aims and objectives, I am aware of the limitations and shortcomings in addressing every issue mentioned. One area that can be recommended for further research would be integrating the Christian interpretive tradition from the Roman Catholic and Eastern Orthodoxy into contemporary conversations on the Spirit's interpretive role in theological interpretation. Especially, excavating the wealth of wisdom from the Orthodox pneumatology and mysticism would be beneficial for both Pentecostal interpretation and wider discussions on theological interpretation of Scripture. Combined with other contributions, the insights in this study not only intensify the current theological and biblical scholarship, but also indicate that we have a lot more to learn about the Spirit's interpretive role in reading Scripture theologically.

BIBLIOGRAPHY

Abraham, William J., *The Divine Inspiration of Holy Scripture* (Oxford: Oxford University Press, 1981).

Achtemeier, Paul J., *Inspiration and Authority: Nature and Function of Christian Scripture* (Grand Rapids: Baker Academic, 1999).

—*The Inspiration of Scripture: Problems and Proposals* (Philadelphia: Westminster, 1980).

Adam, A.K.M., Kevin J. Vanhoozer, Stephen Fowl, and Francis Watson (eds.), *Reading Scripture with the Church: Toward a Hermeneutic for Theological Interpretation* (Grand Rapids: Baker Academic, 2006).

Archer, Kenneth J., *A Pentecostal Hermeneutic: Spirit, Scripture and Community* (Cleveland, TN: CPT Press, 2009).

—'A Theology of the Word ... And That's the Point!' in S.J. Land, R.D. Moore, and J.C. Thomas (eds.), *Passover, Pentecost and Parousia: Studies in Celebration of the Life and Ministry of R. Hollis Gause* (JPTSup 36; Blandford Forum: Deo, 2010), pp. 125-35.

—'Early Pentecostal Biblical Interpretation', *JPT* 18 (2001), pp. 32-70.

—'Pentecostal Hermeneutics: Retrospect and Prospect', *JPT* 8 (1996), pp. 63-81.

—*The Gospel Revisited: Towards a Pentecostal Theology of Worship* (Eugene, OR: Pickwick, 2011).

Archer, Kenneth J., and L. William Oliverio (eds.), *Constructive Pneumatological Hermeneutics in Pentecostal Christianity* (New York: Palgrave Macmillan, 2016).

Arrington, French L., *Christian Doctrine: A Pentecostal Perspective* (3 vols.; Cleveland, TN: Pathway, 1992-94).

—'Hermeneutics', in Stanley M. Burgess and Gary B. McGee (eds.), *Dictionary of Pentecostal and Charismatic Movements* (Grand Rapids: Zondervan, 1988), pp. 376-89.

—'The Use of the Bible by Pentecostals'. *Pneuma* 16.1 (1994), pp. 101-107.

Augustine, *On Christian Teaching* (trans. R.P.H. Green; Oxford: Oxford University Press, 2008).

—*The Confessions of St. Augustine* (trans. John K. Ryan; New York: Doubleday, 1960).

Aune, David E., 'Charismatic Exegesis in Early Judaism and Early Christianity', in James H. Charlesworth and Craig A. Evans (eds.), *The Pseudepigrapha and Early Biblical Interpretation* (JSPSup 14; SSEJC 2; Sheffield: JSOT Press, 1993), pp. 126-50.

Autry, Arden C., 'Dimensions of Hermeneutics in Pentecostal Focus', *JPT* 3 (1993), pp. 29-50.

Baker, Robert O., 'Pentecostal Bible Reading: Toward a Model of Reading for the Formation of Christian Affections', *JPT* 7 (1995), pp. 34-48.

Balthasar, Hans Urs Von, *The Theology of Henri de Lubac: An Overview* (San Francisco: Ignatius Press, 1991).

Barth, Karl, *The Doctrine of the Word of God*; I.2 of Church Dogmatics (ed. G.W. Bromiley and T.F. Torrance; trans. G.W. Bromiley; Edinburgh: T&T Clark, 1958).

—*The Epistle to the Romans* (New York: Oxford University Press, 1968).

—*The Knowledge of God and the Service of God according to the Teaching of the Reformation* (London: Hodder & Stoughton, 1938).

Bartholomew, Craig G., and Heath A. Thomas (eds.), *A Manifesto for Theological Interpretation* (Grand Rapids: Baker Academic, 2016).

Behr, John, 'The Trinitarian Being of the Church' in Khaled Anatolios (ed.), *The Holy Trinity in the Life of the Church* (Grand Rapids: Baker, 2014), pp. 165-82.

Benedict XVI, 'General Audience'. 2 May 2007. Accessed 25 June 2015. http://w2.vatican.va/content/benedict-xvi/en/audiences/2007/documents/hf_ben-xvi_aud_20070502.html.

Bianchi, Enzo, *Lectio Divina: From God's Word to Our Lives* (London: SPCK, 2015).

Billings, J. Todd, *The Word of God for the People of God: An Entryway to the Theological Interpretation of Scripture* (Grand Rapids: Eerdmans, 2010).

Bloesch, Donald G., 'A Christological Hermeneutic: Crisis and Conflict in Hermeneutics', in Robert K. Johnston (ed.), *The Use of the Bible in Theology: Evangelical Options* (Atlanta: John Knox, 1985), pp. 78-102.

—*A Theology of Word and Spirit: Authority and Method in Theology* (Christian Foundations 1; Downers Grove, IL: InterVarsity, 1992).

—*Holy Scripture: Revelation, Inspiration and Interpretation* (Christian Foundations, 2; Downers Grove, IL: InterVarsity, 1994).

—*The Holy Spirit: Works and Gifts* (Christian Foundations; Downers Grove, IL: InterVarsity, 2000).

Bockmuehl, Markus, *Seeing the Word: Refocusing New Testament Study* (Studies in Theological Interpretation; Grand Rapids: Baker Academic, 2006).

Bockmuehl, Markus, and Alan J. Torrance (eds.), *Scripture's Doctrine and Theology's Bible: How the New Testament Shapes Dogmatics* (Grand Rapids: Baker Academic, 2008).

Bowald, Mark Alan, 'The Character of Theological Interpretation of Scripture', *IJST* 12 (2010), pp. 162-83.

Bray, Gerald, *Biblical Interpretation: Past and Present* (Downers Grove, IL: InterVarsity, 1996).

Breck, John, *Scripture in Tradition: The Bible and Its Interpretation in the Orthodox Church* (Crestwood, NY: SVSP, 2001).

Briggs, Richard S., *The Virtuous Reader: Old Testament Narrative and Interpretive Virtue* (Studies in Theological Interpretation; Grand Rapids: Baker Academic, 2010).

Bromiley, G.W., 'Karl Barth's Doctrine of Inspiration', *JTVI* 87 (1955), pp. 66-80.

Brownlee, W.H., 'Biblical Interpretation among the Sectaries of the Dead Sea Scrolls', *BA* 14 (1951), pp. 54-76.

Bruce, F.F., *The Book of Acts* (NICNT; Grand Rapids: Eerdmans, 1988).

Brunner, Emil, *Truth as Encounter* (Philadelphia: Westminster, 1943).

Bulgakov, Sergius, *The Orthodox Church* (Crestwood, NY: SVSP, 1988).

Burgess, Stanley M., *The Holy Spirit: Eastern Christian Traditions* (Peabody, MA: Hendrickson 1989).

Burnett, Richard E., *Karl Barth's Theological Exegesis: The Hermeneutical Principles of the Römerbrief Period* (Grand Rapids: Eerdmans, 2004).

Buschart, W. David, *Exploring Protestant Traditions: An Invitation to Theological Hospitality* (Downers Grove, IL: IVP Academic, 2006).

Calvin, John, *Commentary on a Harmony of the Evangelist, Matthew, Mark, and Luke* (trans. William Pringle; 3 vols.; Grand Rapids: Baker, 1981).

—*Institutes of the Christian Religion* (trans. Henry Beveridge; London: Arnold Hatfield, for Bonham Norton, 1599); accessed 11 November 2013; http://www.ccel.org/ccel/calvin/institutes.pdf.

—*The Catechism of the Church of Geneva* (trans. Elijah Waterman; Harford: Sheldon & Goodwin Printers, 1815); accessed 12 May 2015; https://archive.org/details/catechismofchurc00calv

Campbell, Dennis M., 'Ministry and Itinerancy in Methodism', in William J. Abraham and James E. Kirby (eds.), *The Oxford Handbook of Methodist Studies* (New York: Oxford University Press, 2009), pp. 262-79.

Cargal, Timothy, 'Beyond the Fundamentalist-Modernist Controversy: Pentecostals and Hermeneutics in a Postmodern Age', *Pneuma* 15.2 (1993), pp. 163-87.

Cartledge, Mark J., 'Text-Community-Spirit: The Challenges Posed by Pentecostal Theological Method to Evangelical Theology', in Kevin L. Spawn and Archie T. Wright (eds.), *Spirit and Scripture: Examining a Pneumatic Hermeneutic* (London: T&T Clark, 2012), pp. 130-42.

—*The Mediation of the Spirit: Interventions in Practical Theology* (Grand Rapids: Eerdmans, 2015).

Clark, William Newton, *The Use of Scriptures in Theology* (Edinburgh: T&T Clark, 1907).

Collins, Kenneth J., 'Scripture as a Means of Grace', in Joel B. Green and David F. Watson (eds.), *Wesley, Wesleyans, and Reading Bible as Scripture* (Waco, TX: Baylor University Press, 2012), pp. 19-32.

Congar, Yves, *I Believe in the Holy Spirit* (New York: Crossroad Publication, 1997).

Coniaris, Anthony M., *Introducing the Orthodox Church: Its Faith and Life* (Minneapolis: Light and Life, 2007).

Cummins, S.A., 'The Theological Interpretation of Scripture: Recent Contributions by Stephen E. Fowl, Christopher R. Seitz and Francis Watson', *CurrBiblicRes* 2 (2004), pp. 179-96.

Davis, Ellen F., 'Reading the Bible Confessionally in the Church', *ATR* 84 (2002), pp. 25-35.

Davis, Ellen F., and Richard B. Hays (eds.), *The Art of Reading Scripture* (Grand Rapids: Eerdmans, 2003).

Dayton, Donald W., 'Methodism and Pentecostalism', in William J. Abraham and James E. Kirby (eds.), *The Oxford Handbook of Methodist Studies* (New York: Oxford University Press, 2009), pp. 171-87.

—*Theological Roots of Pentecostalism* (Grand Rapids: Baker, 1987).

De Lubac, Henri, *Medieval Exegesis: The Four Senses of Scripture* (trans. Mark Sebank and E.M. Macierowski; 3 vols.; Grand Rapids: Eerdmans; Edinburgh: T&T Clark, 1998-2009).

—*Scripture in the Tradition* (New York: Crossroad, 2000).

DeYoung, James B., 'The Holy Spirit – The Divine Exegete: How Shall We Be Able to Hear Him?', (Paper Presented at the National Meeting of Evangelical Theological Society; Jackson, MS. November 21, 1996).

Dulles, Avery, 'Vatican II on the Interpretation of Scripture', *Letter and Spirit* 2 (2006), pp. 17-26.

Dunn, J.D.G., *Baptism in the Holy Spirit: A Re-examination of the New Testament Teaching on the Gift of the Spirit in Relation to Pentecostalism Today* (London: SCM, 2nd edn, 2010).

—*Jesus and the Spirit: A Study of the Religious and Charismatic Experience of Jesus and the First Christians as Reflected in the New Testament* (Philadelphia: Westminster, 1975).

— 'The Role of the Spirit in Biblical Hermeneutics', in Kevin L. Spawn and Archie T. Wright (eds.), *Spirit and Scripture: Examining a Pneumatic Hermeneutic* (London: T&T Clark, 2012), pp. 154-59.

Eco, Umberto (ed.), with Richard Rorty, Jonathan Culler, and Christine Brooke-Rose in Stefan Collini, *Interpretation and Overinterpretation* (New York: Cambridge University Press, 1992).

Emmrich, Martin, 'Pneuma in Hebrews: Prophet and Interpreter', *WTJ* 63 (2002), pp. 55-71.

Fee, Gordon D., *Gospel and Spirit: Issues in New Testament Hermeneutics* (Peabody, MA: Hendrickson, 1991).

—*God's Empowering Presence: The Holy Spirit in the Letters of Paul* (Peabody, MA: Hendrickson, 1994).

—*Listening to the Spirit in the Text* (Grand Rapids: Eerdmans, 2000).

Ferguson, Duncan S., 'John Wesley on Scripture: The Hermeneutics of Pietism', *MH* 22 (1984), pp. 234-45.

Forstman, H. Jackson, *Word and Spirit: Calvin's Doctrine of Biblical Authority* (Stanford, CA: Stanford University Press, 1962).

Fountain, Andrew M., 'The Holy Spirit and Hermeneutics', in Michael A. G. Haykin (ed.), *Acorns to Oaks: The Primacy and Practice of Biblical Theology* (Dundas: Joshua, 2003), pp. 77-98.

Fowl, Stephen E., *Engaging Scripture: A Model for Theological Interpretation* (Challenges in Contemporary Theology; Oxford: Blackwell, 1998).

—*Theological Interpretation of Scripture* (Eugene, OR: Cascade, 2009).

—(ed.), *The Theological Interpretation of Scripture: Classic and Contemporary Readings* (Oxford: Blackwell, 1997).

Fowl, Stephen E., and L. Gregory Jones, *Reading in Communion: Scripture and Ethics in Christian Life* (Grand Rapids: Eerdmans, 1991).

Frei, Hans W., *The Eclipse of Biblical Narrative: A Study in Eighteenth and Nineteenth Century Hermeneutics* (New Haven: Yale University Press, 1974).

Gadamer, Hans-George, *Truth and Method* (New York: Crossroad, 2nd edn, 1990).

Goldingay, John, *Models for Scripture* (Grand Rapids: Eerdmans, 1994).

Grassi, Joseph A., 'Emmaus Revisited (Luke 24:13-35 and Acts 8:26-40)', *CBQ* 26 (1964), pp. 463-67.

Green, Chris E.W., *Sanctifying Interpretation: Vocation, Holiness, and Scripture* (Cleveland, TN: CPT Press, 2015).

Green, Garrett, *Theology, Hermeneutics, and Imagination: The Crisis of Interpretation at the End of Modernity* (Cambridge: Cambridge University Press, 2000).

Green, Joel B., 'Modernity, History, and the Theological Interpretation of the Bible', *SJT* 54 (2001), pp. 308-29.

—'Practicing the Gospel in a Post-Critical World: The Promise of Theological Exegesis', *JETS* 47 (2004), pp. 387-97.

—*Practicing Theological Interpretation: Engaging Biblical Texts for Faith and Formation* (Theological Explorations for the Church Catholic; Grand Rapids: Baker Academic, 2011).

—'Scripture and Theology: Failed Experiments, Fresh Perspectives', *Interpretation* 56 (2002), pp. 5-20.

—*Seized by Truth: Reading the Bible as Scripture* (Nashville: Abingdon, 2007).

—'Spiritual Hermeneutics', in Myk Habets (ed.), *Third Article Theology: A Pneumatological Dogmatics* (Minneapolis: Fortress, 2016), pp. 153-72.

—'The Message of Salvation in Luke-Acts', *Ex Auditu* 5 (1989), pp. 21-34.

—'The (Re-)Turn to Theology', *JTI* 1.1 (2007), pp. 1-3.

—'Wesley as Interpreter of Scripture and the Emergence of "History" in Biblical Interpretation', in Joel B. Green and David F. Watson (eds.), *Wesley, Wesleyans, and Reading Bible as Scripture* (Waco, TX: Baylor, 2012), pp. 47-62.

Grenz, Stanley J., *Renewing the Center: Evangelical Theology in a Post-Theological Era* (Grand Rapids: Baker, 2nd edn, 2006).

Grenz, Stanley J. and John R. Franke, *Beyond Foundationalism: Shaping Theology in a Postmodern Context* (Louisville: Westminister John Knox Press, 2001).

Griffiths, Paul J., *Religious Reading: The Place of Reading in the Practice of Religion* (Oxford: Oxford University Press, 1999).

Guigo II the Carthusian, *The Ladder of Monks: A Letter on the Contemplative Life and Twelve Meditations* (trans. Edmund Colledge and James Walsh; Kalamazoo, MI: Cistercian, 1981).

Gunkel, Hermann, *The Influence of the Holy Spirit: The Popular View of the Apostolic Age and the Teaching of the Apostle Paul* (trans. R.A. Harrisville and P.A. Quanbeck II; Philadelphia: Fortress, 1979).

Gunton, Colin E., 'The Church on Earth: The Roots of Community', in Colin E. Gunton and Daniel W. Hardy (eds.), *On Being the Church* (Edinburgh: T&T Clark, 1989), pp. 48-80.

Habets, Myk (ed.), *The Spirit of Truth: Reading Scripture and Constructing Theology with the Holy Spirit* (Eugene, OR: Wipf & Stock, 2010).

Hall, Thelma, *Too Deep for Words: Rediscovering Lectio Divina* (New York: Paulist, 1988).

Hauerwas, Stanley, 'The Moral Authority of Scripture: The Politics and Ethics of Remembering', in *A Community of Character: Toward a Constructive Christian Social Ethic* (Notre Dame, IN: University of Notre Dame Press, 1981), pp. 53-71.

—*Unleashing the Scripture: Freeing the Bible from Captivity to America* (Nashville: Abingdon, 1993).

Hays, Richard B., 'Can Narrative Criticism Recover the Theological Unity of Scripture', *JTI* 2.2 (2008), pp. 193-211.

—'Reading the Bible with Eyes of Faith: The Practice of Theological Exegesis', *JTI* 1.1 (2007), pp. 5-21.

—*The Conversion of the Imagination: Paul as Interpreter of Israel's Scripture* (Grand Rapids: Eerdmans, 2005).

Hirsch, E.D., *Validity in Interpretation* (New Haven: Yale University Press, 1967).

Horton, Stanley, *What the Bible Says about the Holy Spirit* (Springfield, MO: Gospel, 1976).

Hollenweger, W.J., 'Pentecostal and the Charismatic Movement', in Cheslyn Jones, Geoffery Wainwright, and Edward Yarnold (eds.), *The Study of Spirituality* (New York: Oxford University Press, 1986), pp. 549-53.

—*The Pentecostals* (London: SCM, 1972).

Hughson, S.J. Thomas, 'Interpreting Vatican II: "A New Pentecost"', *TS* 69.1 (2008), pp. 3-37.

Hull, J.H.E., *The Holy Spirit in the Acts of the Apostles* (London: Lutterworth, 1967).

Hur, Ju, *A Dynamic Reading of the Holy Spirit in Luke-Acts* (The Library of New Testament Studies; London: T&T Clark, 2001).

Israel, Richard D., Daniel E. Albrecht, and Randal G. McNally, 'Pentecostals and Hermeneutics: Texts, Rituals and Community', *Pneuma* 15 (1993), pp. 137-61.

Jacobsen, Douglas, *The World's Christians: Who They Are, Where They Are and How They Got There* (Chicester: Wiley, 2011).

—*Thinking in the Spirit: Theologies of the Early Pentecostal Movement* (Bloomington: Indiana University Press, 2003).

Jeanrond, Werner, *Theological Hermeneutics: Development and Significance* (New York: Crossroad, 1991).

Jenkins, Philip, *The New Faces of Christianity: Believing the Bible in the Global South* (New York: Oxford University Press, 2006).

—*The Next Christendom: The Coming of Global Christianity* (New York: Oxford University Press, 2002).

Jenson, Robert W., *Canon and Creed* (Interpretation; Louisville: Westminster John Knox, 2010).

—'The Religious Power of Scripture', *SJT* 52.1 (1999), pp. 89-105.

John Paul II, *Dominum et vivificantem* ('On the Holy Spirit in the Life of the Church and the World'). 1986. http://www.vatican.va.

Johns, Cheryl Bridges, 'Grieving, Brooding, and Transforming: The Spirit, the Bible, and Gender', *JPT* 23.2 (2014), pp. 141-53.

Johns, Jackie D., and Cheryl B. Johns, 'Yielding to the Spirit: A Pentecostal Approach to Group Bible Study', *JPT* 1 (1992), pp. 109-34.

Johnson, Luke Timothy, *Scripture and Discernment: Decision Making in the Church* (Nashville: Abingdon, 1996).

—*The Acts of the Apostles* (Collegeville, MN: Liturgical Press, 1992).

Johnson, Paul, *A History of Christianity* (New York: Atheneum, 1976).

Johnston, Robert K., 'Pentecostalism and Theological Hermeneutics: Evangelical Options', *Pneuma* 6.1 (1984), pp. 51-66.

Jones, L. Gregory, and James J. Buckley, (eds.), *Theology and Scriptural Imagination* (Directions in Modern Theology; Oxford: Blackwell, 1998).

Jones, Scott J., *John Wesley's Conception and Use of Scripture* (Nashville: Kingswood, 1995).

Jowett, Benjamin, 'On the Interpretation of Scripture', in Victor Shea and William Whitla (eds.), *Essay and Reviews: The 1860 Text and Its Reading* (Charlottesville: University Press of Virginia, 2000), pp. 477-593.

Kaiser, Walter C., 'A Neglected Text in Bibliology Discussions: 1 Corinthians 2:6-16', *WTJ* 43.2 (1981), p. 301.

Kapic, K.M., 'John Owen (1616-1683)', in Donald K. McKim (ed.), *Dictionary of Major Biblical Interpreters* (Downers Grove, IL: IVP Academic, 2007), pp. 795-799.

Kärkkäinen, Veli-Matti, *An Introduction to Ecclesiology: Ecumenical, Historical and Global Perspectives* (Downers Grove, IL: IVP Academic, 2002).

—'Pentecostal Hermeneutics in the Making: On the Way from Fundamentalism to Postmodernism', *JEPTA* 18 (1998), pp. 76-115.

—*Pneumatology: The Holy Spirit in Ecumenical, International, and Contextual Perspective* (Grand Rapids: Baker Academic, 2002).

—'The Working of the Spirit of God in Creation and in the People of God: The Pneumatology of Wolfhart Pannenberg', *Pneuma* 26.1 (2004), pp. 17-35.

—*Toward Pneumatological Theology: Pentecostal and Ecumenical Perspectives on Ecclesiology, Soteriology, and Theology of Mission* (Lanham, MD: University Press of America, 2002).

Keating, Thomas, *The Better Part: Stages of Contemplative Living* (New York: Continuum, 2000).

Keener, Craig, *Acts: An Exegetical Commentary* vol. 3 (Grand Rapids: Baker Academic, 2014).

—*Spirit Hermeneutics: Reading Scripture in Light of Pentecost* (Grand Rapids: Eerdmans, 2016).

Kelly, Gerard, 'Spirit, Church and the Ecumenical Endeavour', in Steven Pickard and Gordon Preece (eds.), *Starting with the Spirit* (Hindmarsh: ATF, 2001), pp. 153-78.

Kim, H.C., *Luke's Soteriology: A Dynamic Event in Motion* (PhD thesis, Durham University, 2008).

Klausner, Joseph, *The Messianic Idea in Israel: From Its Beginning to the Completion of the Mishnah* (trans. W. F. Stinespring; London: G. Allen and Unwin, 1956).

Klooster, Fred H. 'The Role of the Holy Spirit in the Hermeneutic Process: The Relationship of the Spirit's Illumination to Biblical Interpretation', in Earl D. Radmacher and Robert D. Preus (eds.), *Hermeneutics, Inerrancy, and the Bible* (Grand Rapids: Zondervan, 1984), pp. 451-72.

Knapp, H. M., *Understanding the Mind of God: Owen and Seventeenth-Century Exegetical Methodology* (PhD thesis, Calvin Theological Seminary, 2002).

Kohler, Kaufmann, 'Inspiration', in Cyrus Adler and Isidore Singer (eds.) *The Jewish Encyclopedia* (New York: Funk & Wagnalls, 1904), pp. 607-609.

Koskie, Steven J., *Reading the Way to Heaven: A Wesleyan Theological Hermeneutic of Scripture* (JTISup 8; Winona Lake, IN: Eisenbrauns, 2014).

Land, Steven J., *Pentecostal Spirituality: A Passion for the Kingdom* (JPTSup 1; Sheffield: Sheffield Academic Press, 2001).

Leithart, Peter J., *Deep Exegesis: The Mystery of Reading Scripture* (Waco, TX: Baylor University Press, 2009).

Levering, Matthew, *Participatory Exegesis: A Theology of Biblical Interpretation* (Reading the Scriptures; Notre Dame, IN: University of Notre Dame Press, 2008).

Levinskaya, Irina, *The Book of Acts in Its Diaspora Setting* (Grand Rapids: Eerdmans, 1996).

Levison, John R., *Filled with the Spirit* (Grand Rapids: Eerdmans, 2009).

—*Inspired: The Holy Spirit and the Mind of Faith* (Grand Rapids: Eerdmans, 2013).

—*The Spirit in First Century Judaism* (Leiden: Brill, 1997).

Lindbeck, George A., *The Nature of Doctrine: Religion and Theology in a Postliberal Age* (Philadelphia: Westminster, 1984).

Lord, Andy, *Network Church: A Pentecostal Ecclesiology Shaped by Mission* (Leiden: Brill, 2012).

Lossky, Vladimir, *Orthodox Theology: An Introduction* (Crestwood, NY: SVSP, 1978).

—'Tradition and Traditions', in Leonid Ouspensky and Vladimir Lossky (eds.), *The Meaning of Icons* (Crestwood, NY: SVSP, 1982), pp. 9-22.

—*The Mystical Theology of the Eastern Church* (London: Plymouth, 1957).

Luther, Martin, 'On the Councils and the Church', in Helmut T. Lehmann (ed.), *Luther's Works*, vol. 41 (Philadelphia: Fortress, 1966), pp. 3-178.

MacIntyre, Alasdair, *After Virtue: A Study in Moral Theory* (Notre Dame, IN: University of Notre Dame Press, 1984).

—*Whose Justice? Which Rationality?* (Notre Dame, IN: University of Notre Dame Press, 1988).

Macpherson, John, *Westminster Confession of Faith* (Edinburgh: T&T Clark, 1907).

Maddox, Randy L., 'John Wesley: Practical Theologian?', *WesTJ* 23 (1988), pp.122-47.

—'Reading Wesley as a Theologian', *WesTJ* 30.1 (1995), pp. 7-54.

—*Responsible Grace: John Wesley's Practical Theology* (Nashville: Kingswood, 1994).

Maddox, Robert, *The Purpose of Luke-Acts* (Studies of the New Testament and Its World; Edinburgh: T&T Clark, 1982).

Marshall, I. Howard, *Biblical Inspiration* (Grand Rapids: Eerdmans, 1983).

—*Luke: Historian and Theologian* (Downers Grove, IL: IVP Academic, 1970).

—*The Acts of the Apostles: An Introduction and Commentary* (Leicester: Inter-Varsity, 1994).

—'The Holy Spirit and the Interpretation of Scripture', in Roy B. Zuck (ed.), *Rightly Divided: Readings in Biblical Hermeneutics* (Grand Rapids: Kregel, 1996), pp. 66-74.

Martin, Francis, *Sacred Scripture: The Disclosure of the Word* (Naples, FL: Sapientia, 2006).

—'The Charismatic Renewal and Biblical Hermeneutics' in John C. Haughey, S.J. (ed.), *Theological Reflections on the Charismatic Renewal: Proceedings of the Chicago Conference October 1-2, 1976* (Ann Arbor, MI: Servant, 1978), pp. 1-37.

Martin, George, (ed.), *Scripture and the Charismatic Renewal: Proceedings of the Milwaukee Symposium* (Ann Arbor, MI: Servant, 1979).

Martin, Lee Roy, (ed.), *Pentecostal Hermeneutics: A Reader* (Leiden: Brill, 2003).

McCartney, Dan, and Charles Clayton, *Let the Reader Understand: A Guide to Interpreting and Applying the Bible* (Wheaton, IL: Victor, 1994).

McDougall, Joy Ann, 'The Return of Trinitarian Praxis? Moltmann on the Trinity and the Christian Life', *JR* 83.2 (2003), pp. 177-203.

McGrath, Alister E., *Christian Theology: An Introduction* (Oxford: Blackwell, 4th edn, 2007).

McKinley, David J., 'John Owen's View of Illumination: An Alternative to the Fuller-Erickson Dialogue', *BSac* 154.613 (1997), pp. 103-105.

McQueen, Larry R., *Joel and the Spirit: The Cry of a Prophetic Hermeneutic* (JPTSup 8; Sheffield: Sheffield Academic Press, 1995).

Menzies, Robert P., *The Development of Early Christian Pneumatology: With Special Reference to Luke-Acts* (JSNTSup 54; Sheffield: JSOT Press, 1991).

Menzies, William W., and Robert P. Menzies, *Spirit and Power: Foundations of Pentecostal Experience* (Grand Rapids: Zondervan, 2000).

Mettepenningen, Jürgen, *Nouvelle Théologie – New Theology: Inheritor of Modernism, Precursor of Vatican II* (London: T&T Clark, 2010).

Minto, Andrew, 'The Charismatic Renewal and the Spiritual Sense of Scripture', *Pneuma* 27.2 (2005), pp. 256-72.

Moberly, R.W.L., 'Biblical Criticism and Religious Belief', *JTI* 2 (2008), pp. 71-100.

—'"Interpret the Bible Like Any Other Book?", Requiem for an Axiom', *JTI* 4 (2010), pp. 91-110.

—'Pneumatic Biblical Hermeneutics: A Response', in Kevin L. Spawn and Archie T. Wright (eds.), *Spirit and Scripture: Examining a Pneumatic Hermeneutic* (New York: Bloomsbury, 2012), pp. 160-65.

—*The Bible, Theology, and Faith: A Study of Abraham and Jesus* (Cambridge Studies in Christian Doctrine; Cambridge: Cambridge University Press, 2000).

—'What Is Theological Interpretation of Scripture?', *JTI* 3.2 (2009), pp. 161-78.

Moltmann, Jürgen, *The Church in the Power of the Spirit: A Contribution to Messianic Ecclesiology* (Minneapolis: Fortress, 1993).

—*The Spirit of Life: A Universal Affirmation* (Minneapolis: Fortress, 2001).

Moore, Rickie D., 'A Pentecostal Approach to Scripture', in Lee Roy Martin (ed.), *Pentecostal Hermeneutics: A Reader* (Leiden: Brill, 2013), pp. 11-13.

Muller, Richard A., 'Augustinianism in the Reformation', in Allan Fitzgerald and John C. Cavadini (eds.), *Augustine through the Ages: An Encyclopedia* (Grand Rapids: Eerdmans, 1999), pp. 705-07.

Nash, Ronald H., *The Light of the Mind: St. Augustine's Theory of Knowledge* (Lexington: Kentucky University Press, 1969).

Nassif, Bradley, 'The "Spiritual Exegesis" of Scripture: The School of Antioch Revisited', *ATR* 75.4 (1993), pp. 437-70.

Nebeker, Gary L., 'The Holy Spirit, Hermeneutics, and Transformation: From Present to Future Glory', *ERT* 27.1 (2003), pp. 47-54.

Negrov, Alexander I., *Biblical Interpretation in the Russian Orthodox Church* (Tübingen: Mohr Siebeck, 2008).

Noble, Paul R., 'The Sensus Literalis: Jowett, Child, and Barr', *JTS* 44.1 (1993), pp. 1-23.

O'Connor, Edward D., *The Pentecostal Movement in the Catholic Church* (Notre Dame, IN: Ave Maria, 1971).

O'Keefe, John J., and R.R. Reno, *Sanctified Vision: An Introduction to Early Christian Interpretation of the Bible* (Baltimore: Johns Hopkins University Press, 2005).

Oliverio, L. William, *Theological Hermeneutics in the Classical Pentecostal Tradition: A Typological Account* (Leiden: Brill, 2012).

Osborne, Grant R., *The Hermeneutical Spiral: A Comprehensive Introduction to Biblical Interpretation* (Downers Grove, IL: InterVarsity, 2006).

O'Toole, Robert F., *The Unity of Luke's Theology: An Analysis of Luke-Acts* (Good News Studies, 9; Willington, DE: Michael Glazeir, 1984).

Outler, Albert C., 'Towards a Re-Appraisal of John Wesley as a Theologian', in Thomas C. Oden and Leicester R. Longden (eds.), *The Wesleyan Theological Heritage: Essays of Albert C. Outler* (Grand Rapids: Zondervan, 1991), pp. 39-54.

Owen, John, *Pneumatologia: A Discourse Concerning the Holy Spirit*, in William Goold (ed.), *The Works of John Owen*, vols. 3-4 (Edinburgh: T&T Clark, 1862).

Packer, J.I., *'Fundamentalism' and the Word of God* (London: Inter-Varsity, 1958).

—'Illumination' in *Concise Theology: A Guide to Historic Christian Beliefs* (Wheaton, IL: Tyndale, 1993), pp. 154-56.

Paddison, Angus, *Scripture: A Very Theological Proposal* (London: T&T Clark, 2009).

—'Scriptural Reading and Revelation: A Contribution to Local Hermeneutics', *IJST* 8.4 (2006), pp. 433-48.

Pannenberg, Wolfhart, 'The Doctrine of the Spirit and the Task of a Theology of Nature', *Theol* 75.1 (1972), pp. 8-21.

—'The Working of the Spirit in the Creation and in the People of God', in W. Pannenberg, A. Dulles, and C.E. Braaten (eds.), *Spirit, Faith, and Church* (Philadelphia: Westminster, 1970), pp. 13-31.

Parsons, Michael B., 'Isaiah 53 in Acts 8', in William H. Bellinger and William R. Farmer (eds.), *Jesus and the Suffering Servant: Isaiah 53 and Christian Origins* (Eugene, OR: Wipf and Stock, 2009), pp. 104-20.

Pinnock, Clark H, *Biblical Revelation: The Foundation of Christian Theology* (Chicago: Moody, 1971).

—*Flame of Love: A Theology of the Holy Spirit* (Downers Grove, IL: InterVarsity, 1996).

—'The Role of the Spirit in Interpretation', *JETS* 36.4 (1993), pp. 491-97.

—'The Work of the Spirit in the Interpretation of Holy Scripture from the Perspective of a Charismatic Biblical Theologian', *JPT* 18.2 (2009), pp. 157-71.

Pinnock, Clark H., and Barry L. Callen, *The Scripture Principle: Reclaiming the Full Authority of the Bible* (Grand Rapids: Baker Academic, 2006).

Poloma, Margaret M., *The Assemblies of God at the Crossroads: Charisma and Institutional Dilemmas* (Knoxville: The University of Tennessee Press, 1989).

Powery, Emerson B., 'The Spirit, The Scripture(s), and the Gospel of Mark: Pneumatology and Hermeneutics in Narrative Perspective', *JPT* 11.2 (2003), pp. 184-98.

Puskas, Charles B. and David Crump, *An Introduction to the Gospels and Acts* (Grand Rapids: Eerdmans, 2008).

Rahner, Karl, 'Experiencing the Spirit', in *The Spirit in the Church* (New York: Seabury, 1979), pp. 1-28.

Ramm, Bernard, *Protestant Biblical Interpretation: A Textbook of Hermeneutics for Conservative Protestants* (Grand Rapids: Baker, 1956).

Reno, R.R., 'From Letter to Spirit', *IJST* 13.4 (2011), pp. 463-74.

Ricoeur, Paul, *Essays on Biblical Interpretation* (Philadelphia: Fortress, 1979).

Robertson, Duncan, *Lectio Divina: The Medieval Experience of Reading* (Collegeville, MN: Liturgical Press, 1996).

Sanneh, Lamin, *Whose Religion Is Christianity? The Gospel beyond the West* (Grand Rapids: Eerdmans, 2003).

Sarisky, Darren, *Scriptural Interpretation: A Theological Exploration* (Challenges in Contemporary Theology; Chichester: Wiley-Blackwell, 2013).

—'What Is Theological Interpretation? The Example of Robert W. Jenson', *IJST* 12.2 (2010), pp. 201-16.

Schumacher, Lydia, *Divine Illumination: The History and Future of Augustine's Theory of Knowledge* (Chichester: Wiley-Blackwell, 2011).

Scott, David, 'Speaking to Form: Trinitarian-Performative Scripture Reading', *ATR* 77.2 (1995), pp. 137-59.

Second Vatican Council. *Dei verbum* [Dogmatic Constitution on Divine Revelation]. Vatican Website. November 18, 1965. Accessed July 12, 2013. http://www.vatican.va/archive/hist_councils/ii_vatican_council/documents/vat-ii_const_19651118_dei-verbum_en.html.

Shea, Victor and William Whitla (eds.), *Essay and Reviews: The 1860 Text and Its Reading* (Charlottesville: University Press of Virginia, 2000).

Shelton, James B., *Mighty in Word and Deed: The Role of the Holy Spirit in Luke-Acts* (Peabody, MA: Hendrickson, 1991).

Shelton, R. Larry, 'The Trajectory of Wesleyan Theology', *WesTJ* 21.2 (1986), pp. 159-75.

Shepherd, Charles E. *Theological Interpretation and Isaiah 53: A Critical Comparison of Bernhard Huhm, Brevard Childs, and Alec Motyer* (London: Bloomsbury, 2014).

Siker, Jeffrey S., 'Homosexuals, the Bible and Gentile Inclusion', *ThTo* 51 (1994), pp. 219-34.

Smith, James K.A., 'The Closing of the Book: Pentecostals, Evangelicals, and the Sacred Writings', *JPT* 11 (1997), pp. 47-71.

Snyder, Howard A., with Daniel V. Runyon, *The Divided Flame: Wesleyans and the Charismatic Renewal* (Grand Rapids: Zondervan, 1986).

Spawn, Kevin L., and Archie T. Wright (eds.), *Spirit and Scripture: Exploring a Pneumatic Hermeneutic* (London: T&T Clark, 2012).

Spinks, D. Christopher, *The Bible and the Crisis of Meaning: Debates on the Theological Interpretation of Scripture* (London: T&T Clark, 2007).

Sproul, R. C., 'The Internal Testimony of the Holy Spirit', in Norman L. Geisler (ed.), *Inerrancy* (Grand Rapids: Zondervan, 1980), pp. 337-54.

Staples, Rob L., 'John Wesley's Doctrine of the Holy Spirit', *WesTJ* 21.2 (1986), pp. 91-115.

Starkey, Lycurgus M., *The Work of the Holy Spirit: A Study in Wesleyan Theology* (New York, Abingdon, 1962).

Steinmetz, David., 'The Superiority of Pre-critical Exegesis', *ThTo* 37.1 (1980), pp. 27-38.

Stephens, Randall J., 'The Holiness/Pentecostal/Charismatic Extension of the Wesleyan Tradition', in Randy L. Maddox and Jason E. Vickers (eds.), *The Cambridge Companion to John Wesley* (Cambridge: Cambridge University Press, 2009), pp. 262-81.

Stibbe, M., 'This Is That: Some Thoughts concerning Charismatic Hermeneutics', *Anvil* 15.3 (1998), pp. 181-93.

Stock, Brian, *The Implications of Literacy: Written Language and Models of Interpretation in the Eleventh and Twelfth Centuries* (Princeton, NJ: Princeton University Press, 1983).

Stronstad, Roger, *The Charismatic Theology of St. Luke: Trajectories from the Old Testament to Luke-Acts* (Grand Rapids: Baker Academic, 2012).

—'Trends in Pentecostal Hermeneutics', *Paraclete* 22.3 (1998), pp. 1-12.

Stylianopulos, Theodore, 'Holy Scripture, Interpretation and Spiritual Cognition in St. Symeon the New Theologian', *GOTR* 46.1 and 2 (2001), pp. 3-34.

Tennison, D. Allen, 'Charismatic Biblical Interpretation', pp. 1061-09 in Kevin Vanhoozer (ed.), *Dictionary for Theological Interpretation of the Bible* (Grand Rapids: Baker Academic, 2005).

Thomas, John Christopher, 'Reading the Bible from within Our Traditions: A Pentecostal Hermeneutics as Test Case', in Joel B. Green and Max Turner (eds.), *Between Two Horizons: Spanning New Testament Studies and Systematic Theology* (Grand Rapids: Eerdmans, 2000), pp. 108-22.

—'Women, Pentecostals, and the Bible: An Experiment in Pentecostal Hermeneutics', *JPT* 5 (1994), pp. 41-56.

—'Women in the Church: An Experiment in Pentecostal Hermeneutics', *ERT* 20 (1996), pp. 220-37.

Thorsen, Donald A.D., *The Wesleyan Quadrilateral: Scripture, Tradition, Reason, and Experience as a Model of Evangelical Theology* (Grand Rapids: Zondervan, 1990).

Tillich, Paul, *Systematic Theology* (3 vols,; Chicago: University of Chicago Press, 1963).

—*The Protestant Era* (Chicago: University of Chicago Press, 1948).

Treier, Daniel J., 'Biblical Theology and/or Theological Interpretation of Scripture? Defining the Relationship', *SJT* 61.1 (2008), pp. 16-31.

—*Introducing Theological Interpretation of Scripture: Recovering a Christian Practice* (Grand Rapids: Baker Academic, 2008).

—'Theological Hermeneutics, Contemporary', in Kevin J. Vanhoozer (ed.), *Dictionary for Theological Interpretation of the Bible* (Grand Rapids: Baker Academic, 2005), pp. 787-93.

Trembath, Kern Robert, *Evangelical Theories of Biblical Inspiration* (Oxford: Oxford University Press, 1987).

Trueman, Carl R., *John Owen: Reformed Catholic Renaissance Man* (Aldershot: Ashgate, 2007).

—'Illumination', in Kevin J. Vanhoozer (ed.), *Dictionary for Theological Interpretation of the Bible* (Grand Rapids: Baker Academic, 2005), pp. 316-18.

Tsirpanlis, Constantine N., *Introduction to Eastern Patristic Thought and Orthodox Theology* (Theology and Life, 30; Collegeville, MN: Liturgical Press, 1991).

Turner, Max, *Power from on High: The Spirit in Israel's Restoration and Witness in Luke-Acts* (JPTSup 9; Sheffield: Sheffield Academic Press, 2000).

—*The Holy Spirit and Spiritual Gifts: In the New Testament Church and Today* (Peabody, MA: Hendrickson, 1998).

—'The Word of the Holy Spirit in Luke–Acts', *WW* 23.2 (2003), pp. 146-53.

Twelftree, Graham H., *People of the Spirit: Exploring Luke's View of the Church* (Grand Rapids: Baker Academic, 2009).

Vanhoozer, Kevin J., 'Body-Piercing, the Natural Sense, and the Task of Theological Interpretation: A Hermeneutical Homily on John 19.34', *ExAud* 16 (2000), pp. 1-29.

—*Is There a Meaning in This Text: The Bible, the Reader, and the Morality of Literary Knowledge* (Grand Rapids: Zondervan, 1998).

—*The Drama of Doctrine: A Canonical Linguistic Approach to Christian Theology* (Louisville: Westminster John Knox, 2005).

—'The Reader in New Testament Interpretation', in Joel B. Green (ed.), *Hearing the New Testament: Strategies for Interpretation* (Grand Rapids: Eerdmans, 2010), pp. 259-88.

—'What Is Theological Interpretation of the Bible?', in Kevin J. Vanhoozer (ed.), *Dictionary for Theological Interpretation of the Bible* (Grand Rapids: Baker Academic, 2005), pp. 19-25.

Vawter, Bruce, *Biblical Inspiration* (Philadelphia: Westminster, 1972).

Wallace, Daniel B., 'The Holy Spirit and Hermeneutics', Cited 26 October 2012. Online: http://www.deceptioninthechurch.com/hermHS.htm.

Wall, Robert W, 'Wesley as Biblical Interpreter', in Randy L. Maddox and Jason E. Vickers (eds.), *The Cambridge Companion to John Wesley* (New York: Cambridge University Press, 2010), pp. 113-28.

Waltke, Bruce K., 'Exegesis and the Spiritual Life: Theology as Spiritual Formation', *Crux* 30 (1994), pp. 28-35.

Wariboko, Nimi, *The Pentecostal Principle: Ethical Methodology in New Spirit* (Grand Rapids: Eerdmans, 2012).

Watson, Francis, 'Hermeneutics and the Doctrine of Scripture: Why They Need Each Other', *IJST* 12.2 (2010), pp. 118-43.

—*Text and Truth: Redefining Biblical Theology* (Grand Rapids: Eerdmans, 1997).

—*Text, Church, and World: Biblical Interpretation in Theological Perspective* (Grand Rapids: Eerdmans, 1994).

Webster, John, *Holy Scripture: A Dogmatic Sketch* (Current Issues in Theology; Cambridge: Cambridge University Press, 2003).

—*The Domain of the Word: Scripture and Theological Reason* (London: T&T Clark, 2012).

Welker, Michael, *God the Spirit* (Minneapolis: Fortress, 1994).

Wenk, Matthias, *Community-Forming Power: The Socio-Ethical Role of the Spirit in Luke-Acts* (JPTSup 19; Sheffield: Sheffield Academic Press, 2000).

Wesley, John, *Explanatory Notes upon the New Testament* (2 vols.; repr., Peabody, MA: Hendrickson, 1986; London: Bowyer, 1755).

—*Explanatory Notes upon the Old Testament* (Salem, OH: Schmul, 1975).

—*Journals and Diaries V (1765-75)*, in W. Reginald Ward and Richard P. Heitzenrater (eds.), *The Bicentennial Edition of the Works of John Wesley* vol. 22 (Nashville: Abingdon, 1993).

—*The Letters of Rev. John Wesley*, in John Telford (ed.), *John Wesley's Works* (8 vols.; London: Epworth, 1931).

—*The Works of John Wesley* (ed. Frank Baker and Richard P. Heitzenrater; Nashville: Abingdon, Bicentennial Edition 1984–).

Westphal, Merold, *Whose Community? Which Interpretation? Philosophical Hermeneutics for the Church* (The Church and Postmodern Culture; Grand Rapids: Baker Academic, 2009).

Willimon, William H., *Shaped by the Bible* (Nashville: Abingdon, 1990).

Wood, Charles M., *The Formation of Christian Understanding: An Essay in Theological Hermeneutics* (Philadelphia: Westminster, 1981).

Wood, Susan K., *Spiritual Exegesis and the Church in the Theology of Henri De Lubac* (Grand Rapids: Eerdmans, 1998).

Work, Telford, *Living and Active: Scripture in the Economy of Salvation* (Sacra Doctrina; Grand Rapids: Eerdmans, 2002).

Wright, Archie T., 'Second Temple Period Jewish Biblical Interpretation: An Early Pneumatic Hermeneutic', in Kevin L. Spawn and Archie T. Wright (eds.), *Spirit and Scripture: Examining a Pneumatic Hermeneutic* (London: T&T Clark, 2012), pp. 73-98.

Wright, N.T., *Scripture and the Authority of God: How to Read the Bible Today* (New York: HarperCollins, 2011).

Wyckoff, John W., *Pneuma and Logos: The Role of the Spirit in Biblical Hermeneutics* (Eugene, OR: Wipf & Stock, 2010).

Yeago, David S., 'The Bible: The Spirit, the Church, and the Scriptures: Biblical Inspiration and Interpretation Revisited', in James J. Buckley and David S. Yeago (eds.), *Knowing the Triune God: The Work of the Spirit in the Practices of the Church* (Grand Rapids: Eerdmans, 2001), pp. 49-93.

Yong, Amos, *Spirit-Word-Community: Theological Hermeneutics in Trinitarian Perspective* (Eugene, OR: Wipf & Stock, 2002).

—*The Hermeneutical Spirit: Theological Interpretation and Scriptural Imagination* (Eugene, OR: Cascade Books, 2017).

—'Unveiling Interpretation after Pentecost: Revelation, Pentecostal Reading, and Christian Hermeneutics of Scripture', *JTI* 11.1 (2017), pp. 139-55.

Zizioulas, John D., *Being as Communion* (New York: SVSP, 1985).

—'The Church as Communion', *SVTQ* 38.1 (1994), pp. 3-16.

Zuck, Roy B., 'The Role of the Holy Spirit in Hermeneutics', *BSac* 141.562 (1984), pp. 120-30.

INDEX OF BIBLICAL REFERENCES

INDEX OF AUTHORS

Made in the USA
Coppell, TX
09 August 2024

35789450R00134